GANDHI AND 21st CENTURY

GANDHIAN STUDIES AND PEACE RESEARCH SERIES

1. Gandhian Model of Development and World Peace/**R.P. Misra**
2. Conflict Resolution Through Non-Violence: Role of the Universities, Volume I: Science and Ethics/**K.D. Gangrade** and **R.P. Misra**
3. Conflict Resolution Through Non-Violence: Role of Universities, Volume II: Development without Destruction/**K.D. Gangrade** and **R.P. Misra**
4. The Social Philosophy of Mahatma Gandhi/**K.S. Bharathi**
5. Gandhian Humanism/**Mohit Chakrabarty**
6. Gandhian Holistic Economics/**Shashi Prabha Sharma**
7. Gandhian Spiritualism: A Quest for the Essence of Excellence/ **Mohit Chakrabarty**
8. Gandhian Perspective on Population and Development/ **A.K. Sharma**
9. Thoughts of Gandhi and Vinoba: A Comparative Study/ **K.S. Bharathi**
10. Economic Philosophy of Mahatma Gandhi/**Shanti Swarup Gupta**
11. Political Thoughts of Mahatma Gandhi/**K.S. Bharathi** (Forthcoming)
12. Gandhi and 21st Century/**Janardan Pandey** (Ed.)
13. Gandhian Philosophy of the Spinning Wheel/**Mohit Chakrabarty** (Forthcoming)

About the Editor

Born on 29th September, 1938. Educated at Patna College in Patna University. Got M.A. Degree in Political Science and History, Bachelor of Law, Diploma in Education and Ph.D. Served in the Bhagalpur University for 36 years and specialised in Gandhian Thought. Produced two standard book on "Sarvodaya Ka Rajniti Darshan" and "Swantantrayottar Gandhi Vichar" which are prescribed in the Post-Graduate Syllabus of Gandhian Thought. Worked as Editor of several journals and now Editor of *Gandhi Jyoti*, P.G. Gandhian Thought Deptt., Bhagalpur University. Widely travelled all over the country and abroad. Life member of Indian Political Science Association, Indian Public Administration Association, Indian Society of Gandhian Studies and International Political Science Association. Organised many National Seminars, Symposia and Extra Mural lectures. Presently, University Professor and Head, Department of Gandhian Thought, Bhagalpur University, Bhagalpur.

Gandhian Studies for Peace Research Series - 12

GANDHI AND 21st CENTURY

Edited by

JANARDAN PANDEY

University Professor & Head
University Department of Gandhian Thought
Tilka Maujhi Bhagalpur University,
Bhagalpur - 812007

CONCEPT PUBLISHING COMPANY, NEW DELHI - 110059

ISBN 81-7022-672-4

First Published 1998

Published and Printed by

Ashok Kumar Mittal
Concept Publishing Company
A/15-16, Commercial Block, Mohan Garden,
NEW DELHI - 110059 (India)

Phones: 5648039, 5649024
Fax No. 091-11-5598898

PREFACE

"Gandhi and 21st Century" is a book containing 29 selected articles out of 44 submitted during the National Seminar sponsored and funded by the University Grants Commission, New Delhi.

During 125th Birth Anniversary of Mahatma Gandhi, it was envisaged that Gandhi was born in 19th Century, worked in the 20th Century and his ideas would remain relevant and practical in the 21st century as well. This book is relevant not only for the remaining part of the 20th century, but will be a bacon light in the 21st century as well.

International Monetary Fund (IMF) Director Macdoseus as well as 82 Noble laureautes have unequivocally taken a stand that the future of humanity lies only in Gandhi. Gandhi will stand to the test of time in the 21st century and the global programme of eradication of unemployment, poverty, communal tension, diseases, etc. will be well attended to by the Gandhian Thought in the 21st century.

The essence of Indian Philosophical tradition, which was inherited by Gandhi and practised for the hole of his life, may be stated briefly in terms of doctrine of the *Purusharthas* and the goals are dharma, artha, karma and moksha. Gandhi's ideas were still very much relevant in metaphysical, social, political, economic and ecological spheres. Collected works of Gandhi are spread over oversized 100 volumes which is probably the biggest ever printed collected work on any individual. Gandhism, being the wisdom of sages accumulated over thousands of years, practised and lived by Gandhi, promises to transcend the time barrier provided proper adjustments are made in consonance with the requirements of times.

Gandhi was a philosopher on one hand, a karmayogi on the other. He preached non-violence on the one hand but was not ready to condone cowardice and accepted necessary violence on grounds of comparison on the other. He was conservative on many occasions, a revolutionary on others. The main question, therefore, was to indicate and point out which Gandhi's relevance we are trying to find out. Without ethics, politics was an evil and if we want peace in the world, we should have to restore ethics in politics, which was advocated by Gandhi. Growing atomic weapons, abject poverty, unemployment and consumerist culture required Gandhian remedies because other remedies had already proved ineffective.

Gandhi was probably the most important philosopher whose precepts could guide the crisis ridden world of the 21st century. Gandhi's ideas have withstood the test of time and were potent enough to save the individual from the onslaught of economic imperialism, cultural colonialism, foreign aggression, environmental crisis, capitalism and growing tentacles of market economy. Gandhi's individual centric and human-centric approach can only save the world from getting dehumanized and aggressively individualistic.

The relevance of Gandhi in the 21st century will be on global level. Therefore, his framework cannot be understood in fragments.

In the 21st century, the theory and practice of Gandhian ideology be well understood as there is no alternative to this. Dr. Martin Luther King-II had aptly said "This is an age of guided missiles and misguided men. Hence, man in the 21st century will be guided by wisdom and the sustainable development will be achieved."

Gandhian Economics will solve the problem of distribution, which is a far cry in the 20th century. His economics will be distinguished between economy of needs and economy of wants because without this, sustainable development shall ever remain a far cry.

21st century will adhere to harmonise the economic, political, social, ethical and religious aspects of life and this will lead to Concordantia, which is now the need and desire of the Unipolar world in a holistic way in the 21st century

Gandhi wanted war against prevailing ills but his war was to be non-violent one. For Gandhi, there shall be continuous war without violence to eradicate the total ills from the human society.

Swadeshi will be the cardinal principles for the people in the world and man will keep the machine under thump and machine will not misbehave in the 21st century.

In politics, the cardinal principles will be service to the humanity and Swaraj will replace Ramraj i.e., sovereignty of the people based on pure moral authority.

For achieving Swaraj, dream of constructive programme as envisaged by Gandhi will guide the destiny of human being.

Learned writers through their scholarly articles have tried to prove that humanity is safe in the hands of only those who adhere to the principles of Gandhi, who was most unequivocal in making statement that "My life is my message" and that message is of permanent and emanental values. In the 21st century, men will not have to move from pillar to post for their salvation because Gandhi is like lamp post for all time to come.

New economic policy of globalization was not in tune with Gandhian economics but the defence policy and foreign policy though seemingly in contrast to Gandhi's philosophy of non-violence were in keeping with aggressive nationalism of the initial phase of independence, which has support of Gandhi.

Gandhi provided the best option of the development of the Third World countries of South. His ideas on man-machine equilibrium could change the face of the world by eliminating hunger and poverty from the Globe and help maintain a balance between man and his environment. The inclusion of the Panchayati Raj system in the constitution of the country promises to change the country-side by empowering the people specially the weaker sections.

I express my deep sense of gratitude to the learned paper contributors and to Shri Ashok Mittal of the Concept Publication of Delhi. I owe much to Shri Ganga Prasad Singh, Office Assistant of the University Department of Gandhian Thought, who had helped me in abundance in preparing the manuscripts and get it typed beautifully.

I am sure, the book will receive global ovation and I invite suggestions to improve the book in Second Edition.

Dr. Janardan Pandey
Editor

CONTENTS

LIST OF CONTRIBUTORS

Dr. V.P. Varma
Retd. University Prof. & Head, Deptt. of Political Science,
Patna University.

Dr. N.K. Kumar
Prof. of Political Science, National Defence Academy,
Pune (Maharashtra).

Dr. (Ms.) Ashu Pasricha
Research Scholar, Deptt. of Gandhian Studies,
Panjab University, Chandigarh.

Dr. Joson Joseph
Teekoy, Kerala.

Dr. J. Pandey
University Prof. & Head, Deptt. of Gandhian Thought,
T.M. Bhagalpur University, Bhagalpur-812007

Mrs. S. Seethalakshmi,
President, 'Stri-Sakti', Madras.

Dr. Gopal Prasad Singh
Prof. & Head, Deptt. of Political Science,
Koshi College, Khagaria-851205

Prof. Anil Dutta Mishra
Asstt. Prof., Jain Vishwa Bharti Institute,
Deptt. of Peace and Non-violence, (Deemed University),
Ladnun-341306. (Rajasthan)

Dr. (Mrs.) Kranti Kumar
Lecturer in Political Science, National Defence Academy,
Pune.

Dr. Gopal Krishna Sinha
Head, Deptt. of Philosophy,
Markham College of Commerce. Vinoba Bhave University,
Hazaribagh-825201

Dr. Manoranjan Sarkar
Ex-Joint Secretary, U.G.C. (Retd.)
New Delhi.

Dr. D.M. Diwakar
Reader in Economics, Gandhian Institute of Studies,
Varanasi (U.P.)

Dr. Jai Narain
Senior Lecturer in Economics, Gandhian Studies,
Panjab University, Chandigarh.

Dr. K.B.K. Singh
Prof. of Sociology, P.G. Department of Sociology,
T.M. Bhagalpur University, Bhagalpur.

Dr. Vijay Kumar
Reader, Deptt. of Political Science
T.M. Bhagalpur University, Bhagalpur.

Dr. Baidyanath Labh
Senior Lecturer
Deptt. of Buddhist Studies, Jammu University, Jammu (J&K).

Dr. C.P. Singh
Reader, Deptt. of Political Science
T.M. Bhagalpur University, Bhagalpur.

Dr. (Mrs.) Lakshmi Biswas
Prof. of Philosophy, Deptt. of Philosophy,
T.M. Bhagalpur University, Bhagalpur.

Dr. Ram Binod Singh
Prof. of Economics, C.M. College, Darbhanga,
L.N. Mithila University, Darbhanga.

Dr. R.P. Singh
Reader, Deptt. of Rural Economics & Co-operation,
T.M. Bhagalpur University, Bhagalpur.

Prof. R.R.P. Singh
Professor, Deptt. of Sociology,
T.M. Bhagalpur University, Bhagalpur.

Dr. V.S. Hegde
Reader, Deptt. of Gandhian Studies,
Karnataka University, Dharwad.

Mr. N. Sivaramakrishnan
Hony. Gen. Secretary
Dr. J.C. Kumarappa Memorial Trust, Madras.

Dr. (Mrs.) Sandhya Choudhri
Senior Lecturer, Deptt. of Gandhian Studies,
Panjab University, Chandigarh.

Dr. Chandra B.P. Singh
Reader, Deptt. of Psychology,
T.M. Bhagalpur University, Bhagalpur.

Mr. M. Sreedharan Pillai
Kerala

Dr. Anubha Roy,
Reader, Deptt. of Economics,
S.M. College, Bhagalpur.

Prof. Koshalya Walli
Prof., Deptt. of Sanskrit,
Jammu University, Jammu.

Dr. Sisir K. Dhar
Retd. Prof. of Political Science,
Calcutta University, Calcutta.

1

MAHATMA GANDHI AND HIS MESSAGE AND THEIR RELEVANCE TO MODERN TIMES

—VISHWANATH PRASAD VARMA

Gandhi as a World-Historical Figure

Decidedly, Gandhi was the greatest Indian after Gautam Buddha and was one of the greatest figures in human history of all times. The realm of operation of the great Greek ruler like Pisistratus and Epaminondas was small. The great military leaders like Chinghiz soiled their careers by blood. Louis XIV was steeped in militaristic monarchicalism. Gandhi had the sweetness and saintliness of Ramakrishna Paramhansa and the prophetic spirit of rushing to the cross and the gallows, single and unarmed. He was influenced by Tolstoy. While Tolstoy wrote an epic in prose, the *War and Peace*. Gandhi created his epics in the South African prisons, in the breaking of the Salt Law at the Dandi Seashore and the epic fast unto death in the Yervada prison (1932). The great world-historical heroes do not have a peaceful death by heart-attack in bed in their eighties. Alexander died in Babylon of a malignant fever, incurable even by the blessings of the Babylonan gods. Caesar was killed. Nepolean born exactly one hundred years before Gandhi, died, of cancer in St. Helena at the age of fifty-two. Gandhi was finished by three pistol shots in 1948.

Mahatma Gandhi was a synthetic and comprehensive personality. A man of God and inner divine perceptions believing in a transcendent-cosmic eternal spirit (*sat*), he had been deeply interested in the earthly task of the political liberation of India. He claimed to be always persevering for *moksha*—the emancipation of the spirit but he also delighted in nursing the leper. He regarded the removal of untouchability as a matter of transcendent concern, surpassing in urgency even the political freedom of the country. A devout Hindu, he shocked orthodoxy by getting injected a calf in extremely excruciating pain, facilitating its early death. He was born in Gujarat, the land of Krishna, Hemachandra and Maharshi Dayananda. He received his higher education in London. He experienced the turbulent agressions of racial ethnocentrism in Africa. He came into confrontation with Smuts, Chambelain, Churchill. He had met Churchill on November 27, 1906. (Collected Works of M. Gandhi, Vol. VI. P. 161), Chelmsford, Linlithgow and other spokesmen of imperialism. Mocked and ridiculed by the Indian and external westernizers, he was hailed as the greatest Indian after Gautama Buddha and one of the greatest liberators in human history of all times. The freedom struggle had been begun by the 1857 heroes and was nurtured by eminent Indian Patriarchs like Dadabhai, Pherozeshah, Lokmanya Tilak, Gokhale, Lajpat Rai and Surendranath Banerjee and others. But by organized mass movements beginning with the epoch-making Champaran Satyagraha and culminating in the 1942 Movement. Gandhi brought the liberation struggle to a final successful consummation. A man who wanted to become a *Sthitaprajna*, in the language of the *Gita* and wrote his famous commentary on the *Gita*, he was urgently concerned with fraternizing with the weavers and peasants, the destitute, the despised.

Gandhi's Relevance to the Modern World Politics

Gandhi, in his life and writings, re-asserted the value, efficacy and significance of the moral and spiritual norms and precepts. He believed in the categorical imperatives of truth, non-violence, purity, non-possessiveness, simplicity and Godliness. He was opposed to the cults of the superiority of the right arm, the mailed fist, "blood and iron", and racial imperialism. Force, domination, constraint, coercion, manipulation were ruled out from the Gandhian political philosophy. According to him, even an unarmed man could challenge the whims, caprices, guns, cannons and tanks of an arrogant political sovereign. His protracted struggle (1908-14) for the implementation of the civil and political rights of the small Indian minority in South Africa, revealed to the world outside, the superiority of the technics of Satyagraha which is rooted in the vindication on the inner voice and conscience when in June 1893, a Young Indian barrister with a valid First Class ticket was removed from the railway coach, he was an unhappy man and was meditating over the options open to him to reside there or to return back to Gujarat. Twenty-seven years later, in 1920, Dr. Nolmes declared in the New York Community Church,—Gandhi, is the greatest man in the world proclaiming with Socratic fearlessness and the humility of St. Francis, the superiority of truth as a political technic.

Today, the old colonial imperialism based on the might of the army and the naval fleet, is very much down. But dominant racialism is still going on. The heart of Gandhi would be happy only if the full equality of the Negroid, the Mongolian and the Polynesian races is genuinely recognised as being on par with the White races of Europe and North America. The bipolar world (1945-91) is now an unipolar world. It has to become a world on the full sovereign equality of all nation-states of Asia and Africa. Gandhi would not be content with patronage.

Political violence has been supplemented in modern times by the worst kinds of assassination like those of Indira Gandhi, Rajiv Gandhi, Palme, Saadat, Kannedy brothers and several others. Terrorism, even organised state terrorism is on the ascendant. Sometimes, terrorism is supplemented with fundamentalism. Ethnic violence is also rising. If Algeria, Libya and South Africa are not on the headlines today, the Gulf countries. Bosnia, Chechenya, trans-Caucasia are full of fire. Proxy wars are on the ascendant on the Indian borders.

At such an hour, the message of Gandhi is immensely important. As a man of peace and of endless fortitude, Gandhi would have sanctioned the use of diplomatic and informal negotiations, mediation, conciliation, arbitration and argumentation for conflict-resolutions. He would not be opposed to honest enquiry commissions and judicial remedies. But direct armed confronta-tions, cold-blooded murders of opponents and the liquidation of rivals have no place in the Gandhian system.

Although for the settlement of domestic and foreign disputes, Gandhi accepted the need of discussions and debates and the adoption of a policy of compromise, he would not compromise on justice. He would not like the peace of the grave or peace at any price. Peace with honour and justice with the due maintenance of rights and liberty alone, would be in conformity with the Gandhian formulas.

At a time when violence engineered by terrorists, the secret service agencies of the various governments and hijackers is rising and when threats of biological, chemical and thermonuclear annihilation persist, Gandhism is thoroughly relevant. It is a call to humanity to turn the searchlight within (*Pratyagatmanamaikshat*) and to purge one's hearts of all mental and moral defilements and perversities and make efforts for the advent of a better humanity.

The Social Philosophy of Mahatma Gandhi

Gandhi never sanctioned the doctrine of caste war, class struggle and *rassenkmpb* (fight between races). The very survival of mankind amidst all adverse challenges and antithetical impediments is a testimony to the significance of non-violence and he stated that the Rishis who affirmed the efficacy of *ahimsa* were greater geniuses than Newton, the celebrated founder of the laws of gravitation and motion. Hence Gandhi wanted to solve problems of social tension, social disharmony and social disequilibrium by resorting to the technics of collaboration, sympathetic accommodation and genuine brotherly solidarity. He would never sanction class struggles and caste wars. The violent eruptions in the last three decades in Uttar Pradesh, Bihar, Andhra Pradesh and some other areas would not receive his blessings, no matter howsoever, much some sociologists may interpret them as the counter-attacks of the anti-feudals.

For him, the removal of Untouchability was not a matter of political arithmetic but it was to be the genuine transformation of the heart. Like a devotee of the *Gita*, he was trying to see the Eternal spirit in the suppressed populations and sub-human creatures.

If Gandhi did not concur with the creed of social struggles, he also would not sanction the Max Veberian creed of the rationalization of society brought about by science, formal law and bureaucratic structures. He will like the triumph of the substantial rationality of justice.

Gandhi and Marxism

Gandhi would not be interested in the dialectical concept of the transformation of quantity into quality, the interpenetration of opposites, the negation of the negation and the automatic movement of matter. He would firmly adhere to his own concept of the divine ideology in the universe and history. But he would be sympathetic to the Soviet Marxist concept of the unity of theory and practice. Like the Upanishadic Rishis, he would go even a step further and say that there should be a unity of thinking, willing and acting. More than the Marxists, Gandhi would stress the purification of motives and intentions. The demonstration of the didectical operation of thesis, antithesis and synthesis in the fields of mechanics, physics, chemistry, geology and zoology—a task that intensely delighted Hegal and Engels would not interest Gandhi. He would declare it to be too tedious and even fruitless, because it does not directly contribute to the solution of the problem of the emancipation of the poor, the Dalits and the weaker section of the society.

Both Gandhism and Marxism would like to and the horrors and violence associated with the bourgeois monopolization of power.

Marxism, however, will be far more willing to utilize the methods of high technology for developing the infrastructural and structural foundations of modern methods of agricultural and industrial production. Gandhi would like only limited mechanization. He would not feel enthused even by the concept of appropriate technology because to him, the urgent problem was to reduce rural unemployment. But he would yield to no socialist and communist in his tremendous concern for a better deal to the poor villagers.

Gandhi's Relevance to Modern Economics

Several persons who recognized Gandhi's tremendous role in India's liberation struggle, were sceptical of his economic notions like Swadesi, trusteeship, collaboration between capital and labour; Villagism, de-mechanization etc. In India's Eight Plans some concessions were made to Gandhism in the shape of helping the villages through increased budgetary allotments for rural relief including food subsidies and fertilizer subsidies. But the commanding place had always been assigned to the public sector undertakings. Jawaharlal was fascinated by communism in action because the World Economic Crises (1929-32) did not affect the then U.S.S.R. after World War II, the U.S.S.R. appeared as a vital competitor of the U.S.A. at the economic front. Marx's *Capital*, Vol. 1. appeared in 1867 and the third and the last volume was brought out by F. Engels in 1894. Only five years later Eugene Bohm-Bawerk came out with his *Karl Marx and the Close of His System* in 1899. The Austrian school of economics with its marginal utility theory of value delivered a great challenge to the Marxian labour theory of value. For more than a century, Marx and the Marxists had been criticising the capitalist system of economy for its policies and operative trends like accumulation (concentration and centralization), technological unemployment with vast mass of industrial reserve army, the falling tendency of the rate of profit, decennial cycles, the increasing immiserization of the labouring population, the uneven development of capitalism—all leading towards the inevitable collapse of capitalism and the eventual dawn of a society of free producers. Till the end of the nineteen seventies, the communist economic panaceas seemed to be viable. But Gorbachev with his *Glasnost and Perestroike* not only brought about the political dismemberment of the U.S.S.R., a process considerably hastened by Yeltsin, but also transformed Russia into a willing co-operator with the Group-7 countries, revealing thereby the failures of the communist economic system.

The political dismemberment of the U.S.S.R. and its economic maladies have made people re-think about economic ideologist. India with its vast tradition of Swadeshism cannot swallow the economic reforms under the various names of liberalization, marketization, globalization, GATT agreements and so forth, which have not only the blessing of the International Monetary Fund and the World Bank but also of the U.S. policy-makers. Rajiv Gandhi was possibly initiated into a policy of reforms by the Reagan Government. Gandhi could never tolerate the dominance of external capitalist corporations over the Indian economy. He would also be opposed to the de-culturizing impacts of foreign economic pene-tration. He was not for consumerist gratifications. The question arises—what is the relevance of Gandhian economic ideologies to the present context? Manmohanomics claiming the glory of making possible huge foreign economic reserves, enhanced trade surplus, not-mounting inflation, has, indeed, some plus points. But its economic policy favours the rich and the middle income groups. The really poor and indigent sections of the countryside are not happy. The key concept of the Gandhian economics was the forlorn last man, the *Unto This Last* of the Bible and Ruskin. The question is—have the burdens been taken off from the backs of the poor Scheduled Caste people and the most backward sections, the desperately unhappy widows, and the migrant labourers. With crores of unemployed, uneducated and educated youth in the rural and urban acreas the Gandhian economic *Swaraj* is still far off. But at the economic level, I do not think that the economics of the *Hind Swaraj* and even of the 1944-48 Gandhi's writing can be of total relevance to us. There I favour a revision of Gandhian economic idea.[1]

For strengthening the structure of *swaraj* in a hostile world, India has to strengthen her armed might and even 2400 crores of rupees in the Budget of 1995-96 is not a big figure. To strengthen the armed forces there is the need of advanced multi-sided scientific and technological research as well of enhanced industrialization is also essential for the acceleration of agricultural production.

The main problem is to strengthen India's assets as a modern nation state capable of preserving her hard-won independence and of building a vibrant vital economy oriented to the sustainable growth rate of 8 to 10% of gross domestic production. By agricultural growth alone, India cannot support a viable economic. Industrial growth supplemented with increased investments in agriculture, infrastructure, power and other sectors is essential to put India on a competitive level with economically advanced countries.

Towards the latter part of his life, Gandhi supported the use of electrical power. But he did not have the time or the inclination to discuss complicated financial and economic problems. Hence, the simple economic ideas laid down in Gandhi's *Hind Swaraj* need considerable amendment.

Gandhi and the Beheviouiral Sciences

Gandhi affirmed the essential nobility of human nature and, hence, he was hopeful of converting the most relentless of his opponents. Modern behavioural research Books to strengthen the foundations of democracy by promoting the rational bases of man's psychological functioning. Political democracy has to be buttressed by making education the prolonged process for the release of psychological forces that make rational behaviour possible.

Both Gandhi and the behaviouralists like Dewey, Lasswell and Skinner would try to neutralize psychopathological behaviour by providing to man the basic minimum requirements and by making the children and adults imbibe socially-oriented behaviour-patterns. Some of the categories in Gandhi's Eleven Great Vows (*Ekadasa Mahavrata*) and Lasswell's Eight Basic values like Rectitude and well-being are similar. By stressing the role of conditioning, the Russian psychologist Pavlov has made possible the operativeness of the notion that new modes socially beneficent behaviour can be learned. Definitely, Gandhi would have hoped that even Mir Alam, the Pathan who had hit him in South Africa in February 1908 and Nathuram Godse, could be redeemed. Concepts like conflict resolution, consensus and community growth can be acceptable to the Gandhian political science. But while modern behaviouralists would be content with the growth of rationalism, and the curtailment of emotional disequilibrium, Gandhi would stress, more the need of self-suffering which is a necessary implication of *tapasya*. Of course, the behaviouralists would feel scared by the rigorous austerities, prolonged fastings and the suppression of the senses stressed by Gandhi.

Concluding Reflection: Gandhi, 125 Years after his Birth

Gandhi's life was his message, or in other words the great truths that he propounded, he concretely tried to realize in his own life and in the lives of the people. He was indeed, a prophetic personality and not a pure speculative ontologist like Plato or Kant. He had the scientific spirit. As a student in India, and for his London Matriculation examination, he had studied the elementary physics or heat and light and chemistry. Hence, at least, partly because of his elementary scientific training he was a liberal in matters of religions exegesis and hermeneuties. Scholastic theology was not of much he favoured an idealist, a spiritual and a humanist interpretation of the religious texts.

The permanent part of Gandhi's message is an integral part of the heritage of the perennial philosophy of the world. It is to acknowledge the superiority of the spirit and be a crusader for truth and justice with the full conviction that, ultimately, truth alone conquers. Like Vivekananda, Gandhi was also opposed to bigotry, fanaticism and intolerance. Like the Boddhisativas, Maitreya and Avalokitesvara, he supported the process of the emergization of the old moral and spiritual teaching for the rehabilitation and reconstruction of humanity.

Gandhi stress on simplicity is of epochal significance. In the name of the increase of the standard of living through sophistication, structural bignners and complexity, mechanisation and technological rationality, simplicity is regarded as a guest for primitivism. But with mounting population figures, simplicity is a logical demand of the times, because, the earth, simply, does not have the resources to cater to the material needs of such a mounting population touching the four or more 500 crores (5000 million) figure.

Gandhi championed the notion of heroic but non-coercive resistance to evil. He was a permanent and persistent crusador against untruth and injustice. The sovereign state proclaiming its unhindered, inalienable, imprescriptible, imperialistic omni-competence repelled him. Hence, he had fought Smuts, Reading, Churchill and others. He was opposed to social tyrannies on and to the exploitation of agricultural labourers, marginal farmers, Dalits and other poorer and weaker sections of society. The rampant alienation in the society as a whole drew out his agonising lamentation and he stood up against them even when he was in a minority. Social alienations, economic exploitation and political tyrannies deeply distressed him and he persistently organized his crusading movements against them. Against political economic, social and other types of maladies, Gandhi called for heroic moral protests. This gospel of his is a permanent contribution to the story of the onward march of freedom. His protests were not at the mere academic level. He practised what he preached and he organised protest movements against centres of tyranny. In the zeal of fight, he never lost his patience and would never sanction any compromise with the noble virtues. Hence if his opposition to tyranny and oppression was uncompromising and trenchant, his moral self-scrutiny was also unyielding. Hence, he appeared as a champion of the *sattvika* forces against the *rajasika, tamasika, Rakshasika* and *Asuric* forces, in the language of the *Gita*. Hence, theocratic, oligarchical fascistic and totalitarian oppression could but draw forth his vigorous resistance.

The university is a place where world philosophies and ideologies are discussed and studied. Gandhism has to be objectively analyzed to seek its contemporaneous relevance to India, Asia and the world. The highest merit of Gandhism as a system of thought is that it tries to bring together the gospel of disinterested action of the *Gita*, the simple ethics of the Sermon on Mount, the devotionalism of Tulasidas, the path of holy living of Raichand, the concept of bread labour of Tolstoy, the prophet of the inner kingdom of God in one's heart, and the anti-capitalist economics of Ruskin. It had a profound transforming role to perform in the liberation of India. It has not solved the social conflicts emerging from caste animosities and communal hostilities but, certainly, it has made this matter an issue of topmost priority.

The martyrdom of Gandhi would not be fruitless. Gandhi was a perpetual moral rebel who called for organized movements against imperialistic virulence, social exploitation, economic oppression and slavery to immoral propensities.

At a time when thinkers is the realms of philosophies and social sciences are trying to take stock of the Eastern heritage and western thought. Gandhi stands as symbol of the conjunction of the East and the West. The service of Gandhi in awakening the soul of Asia and Africa is of immense importance. Ho-Chi-Minh and Nelson Mandela have testified to the inspiration the leaders and activists of the two continents—Asia and Africa, received in their work from the trials, sufferings and teachings of the Mahatma. Even the Negro liberationists in North America received inspiration from him.

Romain Rolland had recognised the moral significance of the work of the Mahatma. Both Einstein and Tagore testified to the spiritual eminence of Gandhi. As a time when cultural norms are collapsing and the structure of civilization is imperilled, the deathless spirit of Gandhi stands as a mighty Himalaya—an immense source of strength to those devoted to the emancipation of mankind.

REFERENCE

1. V.P. Varma, *The Political Philosophy of Mahatma Gandhi and Sarvodaya* (Patna, Bharti Bhawan, 1994) pp. 404-18.

2

INDIA'S ARMED FORCES AND GANDHIJI

—N.K. KUMAR

In spite of Soviet collapse, the end of cold war, the emergence of unipolar world and economic globalisation, the peace and security is not breaking out every where in the world, at least in the Indian sub-continent. India is still facing serious threat from a nuclear China, which has embarked on an ambitious modernisation programme with military overtones, a Pakistan on the nuclear threshold involved in subversive activities in India. They magnify threat perceptions.

What should be the strategy of India's defence and security in this post cold war strategic scenario? To what extent Gandhi's view on defence, security and armed forces is relevant in this context? An attempt has been made in this article to analyse Gandhian concept of defence and India's armed forces in terms of present security threats on India.

The first Indian to speak for India's armed forces in the recent history was not Gandhiji but Raja Ram Mohan Roy who advocated the indianisation of army in 1833. The lead given by Ram Mohan Roy was picked up by the Indian National Congress in 1885. It was in Feb-March 1921 that defence was for the first time discussed openly in the Central Legislative Assembly. Towards the end of the same year an important Congress resolution of foreign policy was moved by Gandhiji on November 4, 1921, at Delhi. Indian leaders had till then taken little interest in the Indian Army. Moving the resolution Gandhi said, "The Congress should let it be known to the neighbouring and other non-Indian states that India, as a self-governing country can have nothing to fear from neighbouring states or any states as her people have no designs upon any of them, and hence no intention of establishing any trade relations, hostile to or not desired by the people of such states".[1]

Gandhi did not believe that there was any threat to India from its neighbours. The British had invariably held up the bogey of Russian expansionism and played upon the fears of Russian bearhug. The obsession was manifest in their imperial policy throughout the 19th century. After the Bolshevik revolution in Russia, the anxiety of the British was not lessened, it was heightened all the more. But Gandhiji was convinced that the Soviet Union had no aggressive designs on India. "I have never believed in Bolshevik menace"[2] he said. He was certain that "an India awakened and free" would be friendly with all, with enemity for none. It would have "a message of peace and goodwill" for the groaning world.[3] Gandhiji further said in this context that, "if we do not fear our neighbours, or if, although feeling strong, we have no designs upon them, we must say so".[4] Therefore, Gandhiji was not in favour of Indian troops being sent outside India to achieve imperial goals.

So far as his view about a soldier is concerned, he thought that weaver and a carder were infinitely preferable to a soldier. He said, "I refuse to call the profession of the sepoy honourable when he has no choice as to the time when and the persons or people against whom he is called upon to his sword". He complained bitterly that the services of sepoys had often been utilized, "for enslaving us than for protecting us". In an independent India "the soldiers will not then be hireling, but they will form the national militia for defence and protective purpose alone".[5] He did not have much use for the army which he looked down as mercenary. In free India Gandhi thought of only a national militia and not a regular standing army. The defensive and protective role of the militia was underscored. It was emphasised that the soldiers of the free India would, "never be sent to cut down inoffensive Turks or Arabs in the west or equally inoffensive Chinese or Burmese in the east."[6]

But it must be said to the credit of Gandhi that though he admitted bluntly that, "in my *swaraj* of today there is no room for soldiers, he had the honesty to admit, "I have not the capacity for preaching universal non-violence in the country. I preach, therefore, non-violence restricted strictly to the purpose of our freedom".[7] Gandhi further said, "If India comes to her own demonstrably through non-violence means, India will never want to carry a vast army, an equally grand Navy, and a grander Air Force . . . the paraphernalia of war would be found to useless".[8] Gandhi admitted that "such an India may be a mere day-dream, "but this, he said, would be the implication of India achieving independence through non-violence. What was wanted and what India had learnt was "the spirit of unarmed resistance before which the bayonet runs to rust and gun powder twins to dust".[9]

After some time in 1931 when he was asked whether he envisaged the possibility of doing away with a national army when *swaraj* was obtained, he answered, "as a visionary, yes. But I don't think it is possible for me to see it during my lifetime. It may take ages before the Indian nation can accommodate itself to having no army at all. Again he was asked whether he saw a possibility of non-violence becoming an effective weapon in the international affairs, Gandhi replied, "I consider that non-violence will become such a weapon. First there is a changer in ideas. Nations will rely more and more on consultations and abritration, and progressively less and less on armies. Army may gradually be reduced to spectacular things, just as toys, remnants of something that is past and not as instrument of the nation".[10]

In 1946 when the goal appeared to be within sight, Gandhi wanted to use the army in constructive work as he said, if *Swaraj* is round the bend, we can now look upon the military as ours and need have no hesitation in taking all the constructive work, we can from them. Up till now they have only been employed in indiscriminate firing on us. Today they must plough the land, dig wells, clean latrines and do every other constructive work that they can, and thus turn the people's hatred of them into love".[11] He was asked whether it was possible for modern state to offer non-violence resistance to meet internal disorders and external aggression. Gandhi claimed that a state could be based on non-violence. It could "offer non-violence resistance against a world combination based on armed forces".[12] Again a month before India became independent, Gandhi had been proclaiming that he had never approved of an army for free India. In a non-violent India military forces were not needed. "The defence" he said, lay along the path of non-retaliation". It was incumbent on free India to perfect the instrument of non-violence for dissolving collective conflicts. Gandhi chided Gen. K.M. Cariappa who was reported to have said that "non-violence is of no use under the present circumstances in India and only a strong Army can make India one of the greatest nations in the world. Gandhi made bold to say that "in this age of the atom bomb unadultrated non-violence is the only force that can confound all the tricks of violence put together".[13]

The views of Gandhi on defence was not acceptable to the leaders of an independent India. Gandhi stood alone. He regretted that his colleagues, co-worker and countrymen had not risen to his idealism and hoped that one day they would see reason. Nevertheless, what Gandhi said had a tremendous impact on the minds of the leaders. Gandhi's views on defence and the armed forces left an imprint on the minds of the people and influenced many national leaders who eventually controlled political powers.[14]

About the use of army in democracy, Gandhi said, "Democracy to be true should cease to rely upon the army for anything whatever. . . It will be a poor democracy that depends for its existence on military assistance. Military force interferes with the growth of the mind. It smothers the soul of man".[15] He further remarked "unless India developed her non-violence strength, she had gained nothing either for herself or for the world. Militarization of India would mean her own destruction as of the whole world".[16]

As for military, until 1931, he was willing to retain it.[17] Later, however, he disapproved of the use of military for in training civil liberty and internal peace. He also definitely declared against the Military as the means of defence against foreign aggression.[18] He had always been "against compulsory military training in every case and even under a national government".[19] In a non-violent state he would completely decentralise defence against aggression and injustice. Villages and even individual citizens should be capable of defending their liberties against the whole world.[20]

Gandhi believed that a non-violent state can never be the victim of aggression. Even if it happens, the non-violent defence would be an easy affair. Gandhi said, "a non-violent man or society does not anticipate or provide for attacks from without. On the contrary, such a person or society firmly believes that no body is going to disturb them. If the worst happens, there is no way open to non-violence, to yield possession but non-co-operative with the aggressor. Thus supposing that a modern edition of Nero descended upon India the representatives of the states will let him in but tell him that he will get no assistance from the people. They will prefer death to submission. The second way will be non-violence resistance by people who have been trained in the non-violent way. They would offer themselves unarmed as fodder for the aggressor's cannon. The underlying belief in either case is that even a Nero is not devoid of a heart. The unexpected spectacle of endless rows upon rows of men and women simply dying rather surrender to the will of an aggressor must ultimately melt him and his soldiery."[21] Thus the non-violent state may have a non-violent army. Referring to the training and discipline for a non-violence army Gandhi wrote in 1946 that, "A very small part of the preliminary training received by the military is common to the non-violent army. They are disciplined, drill, singing in chorus, flag hoisting, signalling and the like. Even this is not absolutely necessary and the basic is different the positively necessary training for a non-violent army is an immovable faith in God, willing and perfect obedience to the chief of non-violent army and perfect inward and outward co-operation between the units of the army."[22]

As a war resister, Gandhiji sees neither bravery nor sacrifice in destroying life or property. He said, "there is no bravery in my poisoning my well, or filling it in, so that my brother who is at war with me may not use the water. Nor is there sacrifice in it, for it does not purify me, and sacrifice, at its root meaning implies presupposes purity.[23] According to Gandhiji there is reason, sacrifice and bravery in leaving property intact, if the non-violent resister does so not out of fear but because he refuses to regard anyone as his enemy out of humanitarian motive. Non-destruction involves bravery because the resister deliberately runs risk of the enemy feeding himself at the former's expense and pursuing him, and sacrifice because the sentiment of leaving something for the enemy purifies and ennobles the resister.[24]

In reply to the question about the use of non-violent resistance against the aerial warfare and terrorism in which there is no personal contact face to face. Gandhiji said that, "behind the death-dealing bomb there is the human hand that releases it, and behind that still, is the human heart that sets the hand in motion. And at the back, of the policy of terrorism is the assumption that terrorism if applied in a sufficient measure will produce the desired result, namely, bend the adversary to the tyrant's will. But supposing a people make up their mind that they will never do the tyrant's will, nor retaliate with the tyrant's own methods, the tyrant's will not find it worth his while to go on with his terrorism. If sufficient food is given to the tyrant, a time will come when he will have had more than surfeit."[25] In case of nuclear attack, Gandhiji replied that, "I would meet it by prayerful action. I would come out in the open and let the pilot see that I had not the face of evil against him. The pilot would not see my face at such a height, I know. But the longing in our heart that will not come to harm will reach up to him and his eyes would be opened. Of those thousands who were done to death in Hiroshima by the bombs if they had died with that prayerful action, died openly with prayer in their hearts without uttering a groan, then the war would not have ended as disgraceful as it has."[26]

Regarding a small state in this context Gandhi said, "the weakest state can render itself immune from attack if it learns the art of non-violence. But a small state, no matter how powerfully armed it is, cannot exist in the midst of a powerful combination of well armed states. It has to be absorbed by or be under the protection of one of the members of such a combination."[27] Gandhi prescribes non-violent resistance even to the states which have so far depended on violence as the means of defence. But such a state can use non-violent technique only if it cleanses its hands of all ill-gotten gains, territorial or otherwise. His prescription to the Abyssinians, the Czechs, the Poles, the English and other victim of aggression was to refuse to fight and yet to refuse to yield to the usurper. Refusal to yield means not to bow to the supremacy of the victor and not to help him to attain his object. Thus concerning China he once remarked, "If the Chinese had non-violence of my conception, there would be no use left for the latest machinery of destruction which Japan possesses. The Chinese would say to Japan. "Bring all your machinery, we present half of our population to you. But the remaining two hundred millions would not bend their knees to you." If the Chinese did that, Japan would become China's slave."[28] It was essential to non-violent resistance, he wrote later, that the Chinese must develop love for the Japanese in their hearts, not by remembering their virtues, but in spite of that misdeeds.

In the words of Gopinath Dhawan, "when their country was at war, Gandhi expected pacifists to do nothing to weaken their own government so as to compel defeat."[29] Gandhiji in this context said, "but for fear of so doing they may not miss the only effective chance they have of demonstrating their undying faith in the futility of all wars. This means that they put their conscience and truth before their country's so-called interest. For, regard for one's conscience, if it is really such has never yet injured any legitimate cause or interest."[30] The pacifists should not wish success either to their own country or to the enemy, but pray that the right should prevail. for, "it is very difficult to judge, when both the sides are employing weapons of violence, which side deserves to succeed."[31] While keeping themselves aloof from violence they should not shirk danger but serve friend and foe alike with a reekless disregard of their life.

For a non-aligned country, Gandhiji suggests that it should not allow an army to devastate a neighbouring country. It should refuse passage to the invading army by refusing all supplies. It should also present to the invader a living wall of . . . men and women, and children and invite the invaders to walk over their corpses. The invading army, it may be said, would be brutal enough to walk over the non-violent resisters. But the later shall have done their duty by allowing themselves to be annihilated. Besides, "an army that passes over the corpse of innocent men and women would not be able to repeat the experiment".[32] Gandhiji also favours the economic-boycott of the aggressor nation by neutral states. In answer to a question by some Chinese visitor as to what the prospects of a boycott of Japanese goods by India were, Gandhiji replied, "I wish I could say that there was any great hope. Our sympathies are with you, but they have not stirred us to our depths or else we should have boycotted all Japanese goods, especially Japanese cloth. . . . Japan is not only conquering you but it is trying to conquer us too by its cheap flimsy machine made good . . . we too are a big nation like you. If we told the Japanese we are not going to import a single yard of your Calico nor export any of our cotton to you. Japan would think twice before proceeding with its aggression".[33]

Though in the above passage Gandhiji has also in mind the economic aspect of *Swadeshi*, he obviously stresses, the economic boycott as a form of non-co-operation with the aggressor.[34]

According to Gandhiji, it is the duty of neutral state to extend this moral sympathy and non-violent support to the victim of international aggression, even if latter chooses to put up violent resistance. Gandhiji distinguishes between aggressive and defensive violence and wishes the latter success, though he also wishes that resistance should have been no-violent. If a victim is capable of uttermost bravery and selflessness and fights violently and unequal battle against an aggressor incomparably superior in strength, Gandhiji would consider violence almost as non-violence, for when there is no premeditated violence and when there is no capacity for proportionate violence, violent resistance means "refusal to bend before overwhelming might in the fully knowledge that it means certain death". The Polish resistance of 1939 is an instance of this kind.[35]

If the non-violent states can unitedly offer the moral resistance against the aggressor state, war and aggression would be wiped out, but this can be possible only if the morale level of the average individual in the various states rises considerably. The victim of international aggression would welcome such moral support, but it should be prepared to rely its own non-violent strength to act alone.

Gopinath Dhawan says that war is, infact cultural rather than biological phenomenon and never before was it so costly or so indiscriminate and universal in its destructiveness as it is today. War also necessitates the establishment of dictatorship.[36] Besides being staggeringly destructive and expensive, war only deepens differences instead of settling them. In *Satyagraha*, on the other hand, the loss of men will be much smaller than in war, with absolutely no expenditure in armament and fortifications. The normal force created by genuine non-violent resistance of a state, though it may involve immense suffering, will produce incalculable moral effect and stagger the aggressor, the public opinion of the aggressor country will respond and the government of that country will find it hard to carry their own people with them. Every citizen of a non-violent state may not resort to non-violent resistance for defence as every citizen of a military country is not an expert in the military science. With a handful of experts and with a disciplined non-violent army that may bear the same proportion to the population as does the violent army a country would be able to defy any aggressor. The technique of defence against international aggression, the need of non-violent resistance is more pressing and its efficacy, seems to be certain.

Relevance and Analysis

Gandhian view on different aspects of defence, security and armed forces has been described in the above paragraphs. Gandhi had his own concept of the strategy of all types of warfare—ground, air and naval—relative merits and demerits of non-violent and violent resistance, purity of means and the end of warfare, character of a soldier and his involvement and duties, essential training of army, the use of army in independent democratic India, the size of army, defence expenditure, non-violent resistance against aggression, terrorism and nuclear warfare etc. He had the broad views about all concerned of the armed forces. However, the relevance of his views in his present circumstances in analysed in the following paragraphs:

During the time of Gandhi Indian Army was an imperial force which had to serve the purpose of empire, not the service to the Indian people. Hence Indians were not emotionally attached with the army. They looked at army as a cruel instrument to protect the interest of British against the people of India. British army in India was not allowed to be associated with Indian community. Indians were hating the army. Gandhi was representing Indian people while making statement about the army. Therefore, the situation was different when Gandhi was giving his views about the army. If Gandhi visualised today's role of army in free India he would definitely change his view particularly about the attitudes of soldiers.

Gandhi was ideologically the champion of peace and non-violence. His entire framework of philosophy was basically guided by peace and non-violence. Defence and armed forces was also no exception. However, for Gandhi peace and non-violence was merely a means, though he believed in equality and purity of means and the end. But it does not mean that he wanted to sacrifice the end for the sake of means. No doubt, he preferred non-violent resistance but in case it is not workable he does not hesitate to accept even the violent means to achieve the goal. In any case he does not choose cowardliness against the violence. He never likes to surrender to the aggressor so as to avoid violence. He loved non-violent not for the sake of it, but as a means to transform into a better world. Hence, ideologically Gandhi's thought on defence and armed forces has never been unpractical or outdated.

Gandhi was in favour of a neutral free India. This is why India has been following the policy of non-alignment without being aligned with either of the military blocs. This is the impact of Gandhi on today's defence. Besides, Indian army is basically a defensive force as it has never attacked any one so far. Hence, there is hardly any difference between Gandhian Concept of "peace force" or "non-violent army" and the armed forces of today's India.

India has not yet signed the NPT. It does not mean that India wants to be an aggressive nuclear power. The way nuclear policy is being followed in the region and the world cannot be acceptable to any sensible country like India. Besides, nuclear weapon is not only offensive but also a tool of deferençe as it has been successfully preventing third World War so far. So, India's policy towards NPT is not anti-Gandhian.

Despite India's approval of Chinese action in Tibet, Panchsheel and all that, China attacked India, occupied India's territories and still supporting insurgency inside India and also supplying war materials including nuclear weapon to Pakistan. Pakistan has also launched three rounds of war and constantly involved in subversive activities in India. Inspite of all such humiliations meted out to it India is still unprovoked and tolerant. It is not because India is weak but because of its commitments to the policy of peace, which is the legacy of Gandhi and historical heritage. What more Gandhi would have done for peace and non-violence had he been the policy maker today? Obviously he would have done the same what India has already been following or India would have lost its identity which could have never been the preference of Gandhi, the father of nation.

Some of the Gandhian scholars have accused India for spending a huge amount as defence expenditure for maintaining a too large military force. Their views, it appears, are not based on the hard facts of national security and problems relating to the defence of the country.

The kinds of works assigned to armed forces are not only sensitive, it is also a tough one. The land frontier extends to about 15,200 Km with China, Burma, Bangladesh, Nepal, Bhutan and

Pakistan as neighbours with varied degrees of friendship. India's coastline extends over 7500 Km and the island territories in the Bay of Bengal are more than 1100 Km from the Indian mainland. The territorial sea limit extends to 12 Km and the exclusive Economic zone (EEZ) 200 Km into the sea. The Indian landmass has an area of about 3.2 million sq. Km. and the EEZ has an area of about 2 million sq. Km which includes substantial under-water assets.[37]

The long land and coastal border and the sheer size of India imply that she must be adequately equipped for safeguarding her securities. Its armed forces have to be large enough to reflect the size of country's land borders and littoral interests and facts of its being the seventh largest country in the world.

The size of defence expenditure must have some relevance to the 'size of threat' to India. The sheer size of India forces the economy to devote enough resources for guarding its national frontiers. Keeping in view the threat perception, India needs to incur massive defence expenditure just to keep up with the joneses, her political rivals.

The collapse of Soviet Union and the dissolution of the Warsaw Treaty Organization in 1991 have stimulated the hopes for the worldwide reduction in military expenditure due to improvement in the global security environment. But there has been no such improvement in the south-Asia region. Hence, the external and internal security threat on India continues constantly. In this critical juncture, the reduction in the defence budget for India is not advisable.

It appears that the defence expenditure for India has been increasing but if inflation rate is considered, it has fallen by 20% in the last 15 years. So much so that it has come to the level of defence allocation of 1962.[38] The internal value of 7 Indian rupee, measured as a reciprocal of the all India Consumer price index for industrial workers at 1960 prices, worked out to 8.9 Paise in March 1992, reflecting a decline of 91.1% over the 1960 level.[39]

Even from the GNP point of view, India's defence expenditure has been showing a declining trend in the past few years. As proportion of GNP, it declined from 4.24% in 1987-88 to 3.91% in 1988-89, 3.76% in 1989-90, 3.59% in 1990-91, 3.24% in 1991-92.[40] The percentage of GNP spent on India's defence is the lowest in the world and in any case, much lower than Pakistan and

China,[41] as also the table shows:

Country / Years	ME GNP	ME CGP	ME per Capita (constant 1982)	Armed Forces Per 100 people	Arms imports	Arms exports
India						
1973	2.9	20.3	5	2.7	5.9	0
1983	3.5	17.6	8	1.6	7.1	0
Pakistan						
1973	6.6	33.4	18	6.5	13.3	0
1983	5.4	27.9	20	6.2	7.6	9.7
China mainland						
1973	13.2	42.6	31	3.6	1.5	4.5
1983	8.6	30.8	32	4.0	0	6.3

Source: Y. Lakshmi, "Trends in India's Defence Expenditure", p. 39.

Pakistan's budget increased sevenfolded during 1987-91, from Pakistan Rs. 1,016 crores to Rs. 7100 crores. The revised estimates for the year 1991 placed the Pakistan's defence budget at Rs. 7600 crores while in the current year, it has been placed in the range of Rs. 8500 crores to Rs. 9200 crores accounting for 38% of Pakistan's total budget outlay".[42] A view has been expressed that Pakistan is our main, perhaps only, adversary. This is a dangerously unrealistic assessment. In fact, China remains a potential long term threat to India's security and it would be a strategic blunder to dismiss it as non-existent. Besides, China and Pakistan are still together considering India as the common enemy.

Although China has drastically reduced the number of personnel from 4750,000 in 1981 to 3900,000 in 1985 and to 29,50,000 in 1986 as a part of modernisation, it is still more than double of India's strength about 13,00,000.[43]

Pakistan has one soldier for every 212 citizens for her population. China one for every 450 and India one for every 650. Besides, unlike Pakistan and China, Indian army is badly involved in the internal security assignment which needs additional human and financial support.

Keeping in view the task of the armed forces, inflation-rate, regional security environment and internal-external security threats. India's defence expenditure and the strength of India's armed forces should not be reduced. Gandhi would also have suggested the same.

Conclusion

Gandhi was the apostle of peace and non-violence-peace not of graveyard, and non-violence, not of the weak, with the possibility of a nuclear holocaust as well as low intensive conflict (LIC) threatening to destroy the nation and humanity, the significance of Gandhi's philosophy is even greater today than ever before.

True to the philosophy of the *Geeta*, Gandhiji blessed the despatch of India's armed forces in October 1947 to defend the people of Kashmir against Pakistani invaders.[44]

When Bhagat Singh and B.K. Dutt dropped a bomb in the Central Legislative Assembly in 1929, Gandhi said, "violence is bad but slavery is worse."[45]

Gandhi is not alive today but he lives in the hearts and minds of millions of Indians. His idea always inspires India which can be applied to each concrete situation in context of the changing scene in India and the world. Gandhism is not a doctrinaire or dogmatic creed but a dynamic philosophy that can be applied to complex and concrete problems including national defence, security and warfare.

Gandhi said, "religion of non-violence is not meant merely for *rishies* and saints but is relevant to common people as well." He was not, "pleading for India to practice non-violence because she is weak" but to practice it "being conscious of her strength and power". Nevertheless, he admitted that "I would rather have India resort to arms in order to defend her honour than that she would, in a cowardly manner, become or remain a helpless witness to her dishonour".[46]

REFERENCES

1. Longer V. *The Defence and Foreign Policy of India*, Sterling Pub. p. 6.

2. *Young India*. May 4, 1921.
3. *Young India*. June, 1, 1921.
4. *Young India*. Oct. 20, 1921.
5. *Young India*. Oct. 27, 1921.
6. *Young India*. Oct. 27, 1921.
7. *Young India*. May 07, 1925.
8. *Young India*. May 09, 1929.
9. *Young India*. Dec. 19, 1929.
10. *Young India*. Dec. 19, 1929.
11. Longer V. p. 22.
12. Longer V. p. 22.
13. Longer V. p. 22.
14. Longer V. p. 22.
15. *Harijan*, June 9, 1946.
16. *Harijan*, Dec. 14, 1947.
17. *Young India* (i) & (ii) pp. 641, 924, 1086.
18. *Harijan*, Oct. 23, 1937.
19. *Young India*, Sept. 24, 1925.
20. *Harijan*, May 12, 1946.
21. *Harijan*, April 13, 1940.
22. *Harijan*, May 12, 1946.
23. Dhawan, G. '*The Political Philosophy of Mahatma Gandhi*', Navjivan Publishing House, Ahmedabad, 1962, p. 330.
24. *Harijan*, March 22, 1942.
25. *Harijan*, Dec. 24, 1938.
26. Dhawan G. '*The Political Philosophy of Mahatma Gandhi*', p. 331.
27. *Harijan*, Oct. 07, 1939.
28. *Harijan*, Dec. 24, 1938.
29. Dhawan, G. *The Political .... Gandhi*, p. 332.
30. *Harijan*, April 15, 1939.
31. *Harijan*, Jan. 28, 1939.
32. *Harijan*, Jan. 28, 1939.
33. *Harijan*, Jan. 28, 1939.
34. *Harijan*, Jan. 28, 1939.
35. *Harijan*, Dec. 09, 1939 & Sept. 23, 1939.
36. Dhawan, G. p. 334.
37. Lakshmi, Y. *Trends in India's Defence Expenditure*, ABC Pub., New Delhi, 1988, p. 11.
38. Subramanya, M.K. *The Times of India*, 10-5-92.
39. *The Times of India*, 9-5-92.
40. Rejeev, P.V. *Strategic Analysis*, Nov. 1991, p. 946.
41. Madhok, V.K.M. *Herald*, 11-5-92, p. 6.
42. *The Times of India*, 25-5-92.
43. *International Defence Review*, Vol. 20, Nov. 9, 1987.

44. Kaul, T.N. *Diplomacy in Peace & War*, Vikas Pub. House, New Delhi, 1979, p. 3.
45. Kaul, T.N. *Diplomacy in Peace & War*, Vikas Pub. House, New Delhi, 1979, p. 4.
46. *Young India*, Aug. 11, 1920.

3

DEVELOPMENT MODEL FOR 21st CENTURY IN GANDHIAN PERSPECTIVE

—ASHU PASRICHA

Few people would deny that the world is in a grim state. Although many sparks of light are visible, much of the world appears to be deeply enmeshed in economic crisis. The rattling of nuclear sabres makes many of us wonder whether human civilization will survive for another decade or two. Most observers would agree on many of the symptoms of malaise in the world, and agree that these have not appeared overnight, but rather have been accumulating for decades. Unemployment, alienation from work, cruelty and violence to others, self abuse of many varieties, environmental degradation and a technology that seems to be out of control. These form only the beginning of a possible list of symptoms, symptoms which lead many to argue that a fundamental change in our ways of life is long overdue.

With equal urgency, theoretical assessments of what is wrong with our ways of life have to be accompanied by actions to change or preserve crucial features of our world. And we find here, too, divergences over the implications of the present period of crisis for such action. Many people believe that more economic growth is required as the necessary basis for restoring falling employment levels and satisfactory welfare services. But most of the people argue that economic growth, atleast of the variety we have experienced in recent decades, is itself part of crisis. Simply rejuvenating past patterns of production and consumption is not enough. The economic crisis provides an opportunity for a wider public to be altered to the complex of problems characterising ways of life. With choices posed more starkly than ever, alternative directions for our societies may be seen as not only desirable but realistic and as capable of being realized.

Before selecting an alternative, we can learn from what has already been ventured, from past failures and successes. Most importantly we need to relate our actions to achieve alternative way of life. So that each can inform the other. To put this point another way, we have to grasp both the processes which produce basic features of the present way of life, and those which continually tend to undermine them.

According to one view point, many of the problems currently confronting the world can only be alleviated by the creation and development of more wealth. It is argued that during the prosperity of last three or four decades, people became rather too interested in consumption at the expense of production. The welfare state has likewise grown into an unproductive bureaucratic monster and parasite but interfering short sightedly with economic growth, it has japed enterprise by overtaxation and spawned inflation by printing money. Even the wealth that already exists is used most inefficiently. The necessary change according to this view point, centres around re-establishing efficiency productivity as the motor forces of our economies. The ultimate aim is depicted as being the creation of societies in which the most modern technologies can be rapidly developed. This will enable an ever-increasing variety of social needs to be freely expressed and provided for through consumer sovereignty in the market.

Otherwise also, man has been quick in using to his immediate advantage the technological power he acquired so rapidly. In the last few decades, he had made more material progress than in many centuries before. For our generation, it has indeed been a thrilling experience to see mankind reach pinnacles of knowledge and performance, and then move on, each time to new conquests and ever greater heights. And this has created in many people that urge which is called the revolution of rising expectation.

Mulling over these points time and again, one becomes progressively convinced that the present global crisis, in which every thing in human system seems to be out of balance with particularly everything else is a direct consequence of man's inability to rise to the level of understanding and responsibility demanded by his new power role in world. The problem is within man, not outside him, and so is any possible solution. And this is precisely what Mahatma Gandhi preached. To quote his own words, "The world will live in peace only when the individuals composing it make up their mind to do so". It means that the individual should attain a state when mind and body and speech are in proper co-ordination. It can be summed up in the axiom that the most important factor on which human destiny depends is human quality not only the quality of certain elites but plainly the average quality of the billions of inhabitants of the planet.

Gandhi formulated his economic order in the context of his design of an ideal social order: a non-violent, non-exploitative, humanistic and egalitarian society. His approach to Economics is through the avenue of truth and non-violence . . . Its goal is not pure material benefit but the advancement of humanity on its road to progress by strengthening the character and the individual development of personality or every single person engaged in such activity. No one's gain should be 'anybody's loss—financial, physical, moral or spiritual'. If there is to be a choice, the preference should fall on the eternal constituents of man rather than on the material. It is the first brick upon which the edifice of his entire economic philosophy stands.

The problem, non-violence, gains real urgency, from the strenuous attempt all over the world to develop the under-developed countries. This development is generally conceived along western lines. Yet it is easy to see that the western way of life cannot be permanent and will be incompatible with peace if it spreads to all mankind. It is based on non-renewable resources and rejects any idea of voluntary self-limitation.

Gandhi did not undermine the importance of economic aspect of life rather he gave it, its due importance. All men have material needs. It is neither wrong nor unworthy to devote thought and care to the satisfaction of these needs. In view of the universality of the economic aspect it is not surprising that systematic body of thought, should have grown up, commonly called Economics. But one thing is surprising that the science of Economics is based on one particular outlook on life. The outlook of the materialist. Every concept of Economics is rooted in this outlook. Even there Economics admits that man does not live by bread alone, it counts as cost any activity that fails to cater for material needs.

Economics distinguishes between productive which cater for material wants. Not that Economics had failed to concern itself with welfare. But even welfare is a term completely rooted in materialism.

The concept of 'economic man' is robbing the modern economics of its moral character. Where Mammon is God, no one worships the true God. God lives only in the homes of the poor. Gandhi equated God with "Daridranarayan" meaning God of the poor or God appearing in the hearts of the poor. He emphasized the divinity of man which is epitomised in the great maxim that '*ajiva* is always *ashiva*', a man is by and large divine. And in this respect it is difficult to distinguish between a man and a man. It is on this deep feeling of spirituality and divinity of man that Gandhi based his economic order.

This takes us to the second focal point of his new economic order. The very idea of no-exploitative economy paves the way for decentralisation. A non-violent system such as he wished to see established in India was to him an impossibility, so long as there was a wide gulf between the rich and the poor. As a humanitarian it was the condition of poverty prevailing in the country and the moral and material degradation that they spelt which claimed his attention when, from beyond India's shores, he preached the gospel of self-sufficiency. It was the same humanitarian instinct which first prompted Gandhi, on his setting down in India, to turn to the production of cloth solely with the aid of the hands to provide employment for millions and thus to rid the country of its poverty. That poverty persisted despite the richness of the country's resources in man and material. Gandhi gave a new interpretation to the gospel of *swadeshi* to redress the imbalance between agriculture and industries. The *swadeshi* mentally he averred, should denote a determination to find all the necessaries of life in India. This was possible, he believed. With the aid of labour and intellect of the villagers. He had no doubt that if the proper atmosphere was created all our wants could be supplied from our villages.

Integrated rural development is the next focal point of his economic order. This is closely related with the preceding one. Gandhi had sought to build India from the bottom, that is from the poorest and weakest and have followed the centrality of village. He was deeply pained to see the disintegration and ruin of the villages. "Our cities are not India, India lives in her seven and half lacs of villages. This city people are brokers and commission agents for the big houses of Europe, America and Japan". In the words of reminiscent of Dadabhai Naoroji's concept of drain, the Mahatma referred to the suffering and exploitation of Indian villages as "the bleeding process that has gone on for the past two hundred years'. His heart bled to see the misery of the Indian villagers and he formulated his famous constructive programme a considerable number of whose categories are relevant to them.

Gandhi felt that a strengthened and economically sound rural economy would revitalize Indian economy. He preached, hence the 'gospel of rural mindedness'. A rural economy of self-contained villages alone could be the basis of a non-violent economy. He stated, "You have, therefore, to be rural minded before you can be non-violent and to be rural minded you have to have faith in the spinning wheel". He felt that small communities moulding their lives on the basis of voluntary cooperation would be the best environment for the extinction of exploitation. The regeneration of India he felt to be impossible without village reconstruction. Hence he gave a slogan 'Back to villages'. He gave a call to everybody to go and work in village, develop rural economy, rural industry and rural skill. In small self-sufficient villages producing mostly for their consumption, a peaceful life devoted to the pursuit of democratic values was possible. Big urban concentration, on the other hand, result in the monopolization and accumulation of wealth by a minority. Economic concentration is bound to lead to political centralization. Centralization in its turn, supports violence. He was of the definite view that no-violence could be realized not on the basis of a factory civilization but only on that of self-contained villages.

The goals of Gandhian economic system are quite different from once the country has been pursuing since independence. Therefore, plans for economic development such as one envisaging a seven per cent or eight per cent rate of growth, which are sometimes persented as Gandhian alternatives. I am afraid must be outside the framework of the Gandhian Economic system taken seriously. My submission is that the Gandhian path is not an alternative path of reaching the same goal of economic development which the country is pursuing. It is a path leading to an alternative goal of human life and existence. The Gandhian alternative is *Sarvodaya*, a classless society based on destruction of the class but not on the destruction of the individual who constitute the classes, a system of production that does not fail to make use of science and technology for creating an economy of abundance but does not in the process either kill individual initiative or freedom for development nor create a psychology of ceaseless striving for more and more of material goals, a system of distribution that will ensure a reasonable minimum income for all and, while not aiming at a universal equality of an arithmetical kind will nevertheless ensure that all private property or talent beyond the minimum will be used as a trust for the public good and not for individual, aggrandisement, a social order where all will work but there is no inequality either in status or in opportunity for any individual and a political system where change is the result of persuasion, differences are resolved by discussion, and conflicts by love and recognition of mutuality of interest.

NOTES

Gandhi, M.K., *Constructive Programme: Its Meaning and Place.* (Ahmedabad: Navajivan Publishing House) 1970.

Gandhi, M.K., *Hind Swaraj or Indian Home Rules* (Ahmedabad: Navajivan Publishing House), 1982.

Harijan, 4-11-1939.

Jai Narain, *Economic Thought of Mahatma Gandhi*, (New Delhi: Sehgal Publishers Service), 1991.

Schumacher, E.F., *Future is Manageable.* (New Delhi: Impex India), 1978.

Schumacher, E.F., *Roots of Economic Growth* (Varanasi: Gandhian Institute of Studies) 1962.

Schumacher, E.F., *Small is Beautiful: A Story of Economics if people Mattered* (London: Abacus), 1989.

Sethi, J.D., *Gandhi Today* (New Delhi: Vikas Publishing House Pvt. Ltd.) 1976.

Tendulkar, D.G. (ed.), *Mahatma*, Eight Volumes (Delhi: The Publications Division, Ministry of Information and Broadcasting, Govt. of India), 1962.

Young India, 1-10-1931.

4

NON-VIOLENCE IN THE TEACHINGS OF MAHAVIRA AND MAHATMA AND ITS RELEVANCE IN THE 21st CENTURY

—JOSON JOSEPH

In the literature of world religions, we find that non-violence as a way of life has a very ancient history. Long before the Hindus chanted the hymns of praise to the spiritual oneness of all things. These hymns reflect a deep reverence for life which the Hindu tradition defines as '*Ahimsa*'. '*Ahimsa*' is the ideal for Jainism. As a son of Hindu tradition, Buddha developed his intense sense of reverence for all life into a feeling of compassion for human life. We see the same concept in the Christian teaching—love your enemy.

If we analyse the history of religions, we find that Jainism is the '*Ahimsa*' religion par excellence among all others. Jainism placed strong emphasis on the ethical principle of '*Ahimsa*', not only in discussions of morality but also in epistemology and metaphysics. In fact, '*Ahimsa*' is the central core of Jain Philosophy and religion.

The present great age has known twenty-four Jinas, of whom the first lived millions of years ago. The first Tirthankara or Jina was Rishabha. According to Jain legend, the country of India was named after his eldest son, Bharata. Rishaba is said to have been the first to preach '*Ahimsa*', before achieving his own Kaivalya atop Mount Kailasha in the Himalayas. The last Jina was Vardhamana known as Mahavira (Great man).

The life of Mahavira is sketched in the *Achara-anga Sutra*, the first of the Angas, the sacred book of the Svetambara Jains, in more detail in the later Kalpa Sutra.

Mahavira was born in 599 B.C. as the son of King Siddhartha and Queen Trisila Priyakarini. That was a time when the hold of the true Vedic religion had slackened and a degenerate form of religion, full of sacrificial festivities with macabre manifestations, was in vogue. Material prosperity was accompanied by an indifference to moral values. Vardhamana, though born in a palace, consciously trained himself to be perfect instrument to re-strengthen the moral universe of mankind.

The credit of recognising the historical existence of Mahavira, goes to a German scholar, Prof. Herman Jacabi, who made an English translation of the first Anga, Ahcaranga and published it in the series called the 'Sacred Books of the East' in 1884 A.D. According to us Vardhamana Mahavira was born on Chaitra Shukla Trayodasi, March 30, 599 B.C. Both Digambara as well as Svetambara agree on this date.

The preaching of '*Ahimsa*' is the most important task of Mahavira's life. Feeling of immense respect and responsibility for life inspires his activities.

The doctrine of *Ahimsa* is narrated and analysed in the Agamas as follows:

(a) All violence deserves to be discarded because it leads to sorrow and fear. This is the basic argument of the doctrine of non-violence.
(b) Violence means ending somebody's life or torturing others. Still, the blemishes born on violence depend only on infatuation or attachment and jelousy etc. If there is no infatuation or attachment, mere ending of life cannot come under the category of violence. This constitutes an analysis of non-violence.
(c) The purport of the blemish of violence does not depend upon the relative importance of the size, number and senses of the living beings that are killed. It depends upon the result of the violating person or the intensity or otherwise, his knowing or unknowing action or the use of force. This constitutes the purport of non-violence.

The three matters mentioned above became fruitful in the thought and conduct of Mahavira and are woven in the Agamas.

For the great sage Amritacandra Suri, *Ahimsa* deeper associations pertained to lack of attachment and lack of passion. For Hemachandra, *Ahimsa* was the beneficient mother of all being. As cited in Dr. L.M. Singhvi's essay 'Jain Declaration of Nature', the Jain scriptures read, "All the Arhata (Venerable Ones) of the past, present and future discourse, counsel, proclaim, propound and prescribe thus in unison: 'Do not injure, torture or kill any creature of living being'. For Samantabhadra, *Ahimsa* was the highest bliss".

In the words of Gandhi 'No religion of the world has explained the principle of *Ahimsa* so deeply and scientifically as is discussed with its applicability in every human life in Jainism. As and when the benevolent principle of *Ahimsa* or non-violence will be ascribed for practice by the people of the world to achieve their end of life in this world and beyond. Jainism is sure to have the uppermost status and Lord Mahavira is sure to be respected as the greatest authority on *Ahimsa*.

In Jainism *Himsa* is subdivided into *Bhava-himsa* and *Dravya himsa* or violence in thought and violence in physical action. Jain thinkers have classified violence into 108 varieties so that an aspirant can detect even the minutest form of violence.

The principle of *Ahimsa* has been carried to the extent of avoiding injury even to the feelings of others, and has its application to life in all forms, including human, animal and vegetable kingdoms. It has been laid down that one who has no power of giving life has no right of taking it away on any ground or pretext whatsoever. It goes without saying that strict abstinence from eating meat, eggs, and fish is ordained. All other principles of good conduct leading to formation of character, such as truthfulness, honesty, celebacy, etc. are based upon the principle of *Ahimsa* in its broad application.

It may be noted that in Jainism *Ahimsa-vrata* is binding on all members of Jain society, whether householders or ascetics. In the case of householder, it is applicable with limitation, but in the case of ascetics, it is to be observed absolutely. Both these vows, as applied to householders and ascetics, are called *Anuvratas* and *Mahavratas* respectively.

Jains follow *Ahimsa* in the most severe way and apply non-injury even to sub-human life, that is, even the smallest insect. Some Jain practices became burdensome and Gandhi discarded with the literal interpretation of such teachings. Gandhi did not follow extremist practices, such as speaking through a piece of cloth tied over the mouth to avoid the destruction of life of any organism floating in the air.

Gandhi considers non-violence to be a general rule for human relations. Man does not live by destroying others. Even the violent person is knowingly or unknowingly non-violent as a rule in his behaviour and he is violent as a parasitical exception. This thought becomes clear when Gandhi explains that society, in its mutual intercourse, is founded on non-violent principles. What he suggests is to extend non-violence to include national and international relationships.

In the context of Indian tradition, Gandhi's *Ahimsa* is a midway between the rigid and regorous non-violence of the Jains and a little more elastic non-violence of Manu and other orthodox Hindus. Gandhi's non-violence may be considered an amalgam of Hindu, Jain and Christian moral teachings.

Gandhian *Ahimsa* involves a high degree of morality because to Gandhi, non-violence is not merely abstaining from external and overt injury, it must be from the bottom of our heart, for there is nothing unqualifiedly good but the good-will.

The nature of non-violence was repeatedly made clear by Gandhi by contrasting it with the familiar modes of social action. For instance, non-action was never the meaning of Gandhian non-violence. As Gandhi wrote in *Harijan* of March 14, 1936. In spite of the negative particle 'non' it is no negative force. Non-violence was not a negative concept at all. It is the greatest and the activist force in the world as Gandhi reiterates. If non-violence is not only non-killing or non-injury but an inner feeling of the mind and heart, it means 'the largest love and greatest charity'.

Gandhi was of the opinion that without *Ahimsa* it was not possible to seek and find truth. *Ahimsa* and 'Truth' are so intertwined that it is practically impossible to disentagle and separate them. They are like the two sides of a coin, or rather of a smooth unstamped metallic disc. Who can say, which is the obverse and which is the reverse? Nevertheless, *Ahimsa* is the means; Truth is the end. Means to be means and must always be within our reach, and so *Ahimsa* is our supreme duty.

Non-violence in its dynamic condition means conscious suffering. It does not mean meek submission to the will of the evil doer but it means putting of one's sole against the will of the tyrant.

If we examine the concept of non-violence as advocated by Gandhi we will realize that his was a prescription not of the weak but of the strong. He proved in his life time that even the unorganised and the weak can perform miracles if they got trained in the art of non-violent techniques of change. Non-violence does not mean, passivity or inaction; but a dynamic living force. His non-violence was an instrument in the struggle for justice and freedom. It is a permanent revolution, and therefore, it is dynamic.

Just as one must learn the art of killing in the training for violence, so one must learn the art of dying in the training for non-violence. The votary of non-violence has to cultivate the capacity for sacrifice of the highest type in order to be free from fear. The votary of *Ahimsa* has only one fear, that is God.

Gandhi advocated the practice of non-violence in every walk of life—individual, institutional, political, social and economic. The efficacy of non-violence was demonstrated by Gandhi in many a battle against racial discrimination in South Africa, oppression of peasants in Champaran, Kheda, Bardoli, etc., exploitation of labourers in Ahmedabad, untouchability, Rowlat Bill, Salt Satya-graha and last but not the least against foreign domination of India from the Britishers. Had he been alive during the post-independent era, he might have carried these experiments further.

One can say, if not accused of exaggeration, Gandhi was reborn as Lord Mahavira in the twentieth century—*Sambhvami Yuge Yuge*. Gandhi has now ceased to be a historical person like Mahavira. Gandhi's greatest contribution to the entire humanity is his hunger and thirst for world peace. Nobody in modern times has so sincerely tried for world peace as the Mahatma.

Violent means may bring changes in the society more quickly and more easily. But it is doubtful how long it will last and solve problems. Violence creates more problems than it solves. Therefore non-violence remains the only viable alternative to violence. Today the choice is no longer between violence and non-violence. It is either non-existence or non-violence, between total annihilation or Gandhi.

Albert Schweitzer considers that Gandhi continued what Jainism had begun, and that this can be taken even further in the direction of compassion and reverence for all life.

5

GANDHIAN HUMAN CIVILIZATION IN THE TWENTY-FIRST CENTURY

—J. PANDEY

Gandhi was born in the nineteenth century, lived in the twentieth century but he will be worshipped in the twenty-first century as Einstein had rightly said that "Generations to come will scarcely believe that such a one as this ever in flesh and blood walked upon this earth." He will be remembered as an emancipator of man from the jaws of the imperialism which had reached a stage, where everything good and men would have been devoured by them for all time to come. Gandhi had to fight a battle not for the survival of the human civilization alone but for the mankind itself. During his life time, two fierce battles in the shape of First and Second World War were fought and the horror of Atomic attack on Hiroshima and Nagashaki had totally exposed the misdeeds of the mightest power. But now as we are in the threshold of 21st century, we are sitting on volcano which can destroy "such world of mankind as we have today" atleast for seven times. Gandhi, in the past had to face the visible enemy and he had courage to challenge Franklin D. Roosevelt and Hitler through letters written to them but in the century to come, he will have to fight with invincible enemy because by that time, chemical war would have replaced all other methods of war. Gandhi had deep faith in the Indian civilization. He believes that ancient civilization was not less than the kingdom of God. Gandhi writes:

> "The British Government in India constitutes a struggle between the Modern Civilization, which is the kingdom of Satan and the ancient civilization."[1]

In the next century, materialism will have its say in paramount manner and hence importance of Gandhi will be collosal and ultimately "the key to an understanding of *Hind Swaraj* lies in the idea that worldy persuits should give way to ethical living."[2] This can be clearly viewed that now men have started leading a simple life and their faith in God is increasing and they are trying to lead an ethical life.

Gerale Heard was a firm believer in Gandhi's ideas of human civilization. He opined that *Hind Swaraj* was superior to Rousseau's "*Social Contract*" and Karl Marx's "*Das Capital*".

Though Gandhi calls Parliament as 'prostitute and sterile women" but ultimately he agreed for Parliamentary Swaraj. From the experiences that we have, we have come to understand that the whole world is looking forward for Parliamentary Swaraj as no better substitute has been evolved in its place.

Mahatma had to make a compromise with machinery and the human civilization will have to develop on such compromises, as we find in Gandhi's reply to Dr. R.M. Lohia:

> "I do visualise electricity, ship building, iron works, machine making and the like existing side by side with village handicrafts. But the order of dependence will be reversed. Hitherto the industrialisation has been so planned as to destroy the villages and their crafts. In the state of future, it will subserve the villages and their crafts."[3]

Thus Gandhi wanted removal of poverty and unemployment and in the century that we are entering into these two problems will be confronting each and every nation. He was a firm believer that Western method of large scale industries could not tackle this problem. He wanted the problem to be tackled with less capital outlay and with more labour intensive scheme. It is, therefore, he has made *charkha*, a mere symbol of such technique. Great Economist E.F. Schumacher and T.M.F. Chairman Macdosus lay emphasis, like Gandhi on such techniques which do not displace labour as large scale industry in its very nature tended to displace labour. The twenty-first century will certainly lay emphasis to revive cottage and village industries. Revival of the handicrafts will certainly lead to peace, prosperity and full employment to each and all. This can be substantiated by the writing of Dr. Nageshwar

Prasad in his book—*Hind Swaraj* a fresh look. He states:

> "But it must not be supposed that Gandhi believed in the static, archaic mode of production in the villages prevalent in the past. On the other hand, he welcomed every improvement in the village craft (small unit) if it led to increase in productivity. The only condition attached was that the improvement must not render people unemployed. He was even willing to accept the use of energy (electricity, etc.) if it could be used for village industries, in case the village owned the power plant.[4]

In the years to come, the statement of Gandhi will be fully realised. Gandhi stated:

> "Pandit Nehru wants industrialisation because he thinks that if it is socialised, it would be free from the evils of capitalism. My own view is that evils are inherent in industrialism and no amount of socialisation can eradicate them.[5]

Gandhi again exclaimed:

> "God forbid that India should ever take to industrialism after the manner of the west. The economic imperialism of a single tiny island kingdom (England) is today keeping the world in chains. If an entire nation of 300 millions took to similar exploitation, it would strip the world bare like locusts.[6]

Now we have come to realise the modern technology has reached a stage wherein the very existence of mankind is exposed to danger. Dr. Nageshwar Prasad narrates:

> "Urbanisation, crime, social disorganisation, smoke and dirt, desolation of nature, exploitation of labour and a host of harmful effects were pointed out in the 19th and in the beginning of the 20th century. It was these critics who largely influences the dormation of Gandhi's ideas on machine civilization."[7]

Dr. Nageshwar Prasad further states:

> But more recently, the critics have gone beyond these effects and have suggested that the whole human race is threatened by the unrestrained march of technological innovations. In this discussion, we will allude to two very salient criticisms of technological advancement. The first is the depletion of non-renewable resources which was highlighted by the publication of the Club of Rome thesis, viz., The Limits to Growth. The second is environmental pollution which is supposed to threaten human life with extinction.[8]

An eminent authority on high energy physics, Fritjof Capra says:

> "Even discounting the threat of a nuclear catastrophe, the global ecosystem and the further evolution of life on earth are seriously endangered and may well end in a large-scale ecological disaster. Over-population and industrial technology have contributed in various ways to a severe degradation of the natural environment upon which we are completely dependent for life."[9]
>
> "In effect, therefore, what we are witnessing today is a civilizational crisis. It is crisis because the entire system of machine technology is in crisis, rather threatened with a crash as sensitive minds, scientists and others, are warning us today. Gandhi was perhaps the first in the present century who realized the deeper and long range implications of this technological progress. His whole response to it is one of caution, restraint and limitation. In its broad sweep, the response is not of one civilization to the challenge of another, as Toynbee in his monumental study of history has shown. Undoubtedly, it originated in *Hind Swaraj* as a response of a particular civilization, namely, of the Indian civilization to the Western. But as Gandhi's thinking evolved within the orbit of the world developments (including the two world wars), his response acquired a universal character embracing the whole mankind verging

on a precipice where the large-scale high technology has brought it."[10]

Dr. Prasad further says:

"Gandhi's position is that the so-called under-developed nations suffering from chronic poverty and unemployment will never be able to solve them unless they followed an altogether different pattern, different from the Western industrial technology. And this he found in small-scale technology with less investment of capital and labour-intensive in character. However, once this mode was adopted, Gandhi could easily reconcile it with his basic philosophical position. What emerged from this was a way out of the present civilizational crisis. We may now chart out the basic ingredients of the Gandhian scheme."[11]

From the study of Gandhi's ideals, we come to the following conclusion and we are sure in the 21st century, the whole mankind will have to follow them in letter and spirit to save the human civilization.

1. *Machine and Technology*

   (i) Must cater the basic human needs of food, clothing and housing;
   (ii) Earth or nature should not be exploited beyond its capacity as the Reo Earth Summit has also emphasised;
   (iii) Man should become master and not vice versa as E.F. Schumacher also lays emphasis;
   (iv) End of environmental pollution; and
   (v) Production for Masses and not Mass production.

2. *Labour*

   (i) Importance of physical labour,
   (ii) Emphasis on atleast eight hour labour,
   (iii) No enforcement of labour, and
   (iv) Importance of human labour should be recognised.

3. *Agriculture*

(i) Only tillers should own the land,
(ii) No more mechanical farming,
(iii) Tillers should enjoy production,
(iv) Fertilizer and Insecticides should be fully controlled, and
(v) Cooperative farming should be encouraged.

4. *Wants*

(i) Only basic needs to be fulfilled,
(ii) Practice of less wants.

5. *Political Scenario*

Old Panchayat system should be invoked in new condition. He called it 'Oceanic circle'.[12]

What is darkening the future of human civilization is mentioned below:

1. The modern industrial civilization is over exploiting polluting and exhausting Nature and thus hamming seriously the future of the inhabitants on the earth. Authors of the valuable Report by the Council of the Club of Rome Alexander King and Bertrand Schneider observe, "the human race, in pursuit of material gain by the exploitation of nature, is racing towards the destruction of the planet and itself.[13]
2. The destructive potential of the modern civilization is too high.
3. The industrially advanced countries (IACs) thrive on exploiting ruthlessly the less developed countries (LDCs).
4. The industrial civilization perpetuates a gross unequal distribution of richness and other benefits.
5. The modern industrial civilization causes injury to health (physical and mental) and leads to cultural impoverishment and spiritual degradation.
6. The world is mad and cruel strifes continue—Tagore.
7. Without a global revolution in the sphere of human

> conciousness, nothing will change for the better.... and the catastrophe towards which our world is heading, will be unavoidable.

Like Zarathrushtra, Jesus Christ, Stoic Emperor Marcus Aurelius, poet Wordsworth, Romain Rolland, a great historian of Science George Sarton, Gandhi asserts the concept of 'simple life'. Gandhi asserts: "Civilization in the real sense of the term consists not in the multiplication, but in the deliberate and voluntary reduction of wants. This alone promotes real happiness and contentment, and increase the capacity for service. Actually, a 'simple life'is not only an idealist's yearning it is a 'pragmatic must' not for today only but for all time to come and hence Gandhi's human civilization of 21st century will adhere to this philosophy of life.

Similarly, the elimination of poverty throughout the world is an urgent matter for reducing suffering, animosity and injustice. Gandhi is totally aware that "grinding pauperism" cannot but lead to "moral degradation". Thus the next century will have to replace the predatory economics with "economics of justice".

Gandhian concept of women upliftment will be dominating the future scene as human civilization gets finer and finer with the natural upliftment of women folk. Similarly, racial, communal or secterian hatred will have no place to future world as these harm the proper development of human civilization.

And, as Einstein points out, "His (Gandhi's) work on behalf of India's liberation is a living testimony to the fact that man's will be sustained by indomitable conviction, is more powerful than material forces and that seems insurmountable." And as Gandhi himself says "those who tread the path of virtue should not be disheartened by the thought that virtue is so rare in the world and that they are in a minority." Now the discovery of nuclear weapons and the consequent horrors create a new awareness of the value of non-violence. So also the people may come to learn that acquisitiveness or an urge to dominate can make one rich and powerful but does not give peace and joy, rather destroy them.

Thus, Gandhi's basic thoughts have a universality and they do not appeal only to a handful of romantic idealists. Today forsighted thinkers in the West also feel that material affluence generate greed and selflessness and erode spiritual values, profligate life styles should be curbed, that poverty should be eliminated throughout the world, and the society must be explicit about the importance of values and ethics.

These are the Gandhian thoughts for man's healthy body and healthy mind and will surface more and more with the passage of time. Those who envision a better human civilization are not those who are surviving against currents, rather Truth shall prevail and we shall call *Satyam Jayate* and thus human civilization as envisaged by Gandhi will be a "whole" and not a fragment civilization and will bring forth Vinoba's slogan of *Jai Jagat* on this universe in the twenty-first century.

REFERENCES

1. Preface to Indian Home Rule, C.W.M.G., Vol. 10, p. 188.
2. C.W.M.G., Vol. 12, p. 412.
3. Ahimsa in Practice—C.W.M.G., Vol. 7, p. 130.
4. Dr. Nageshwar Prasad, *Hind Swaraj—A Fresh Look*, p. 19.
5. An American's Question, *Harijan*, 29-9-1940, p. 299.
6. Discussion with a Capitalist, C.W.M.G., Vol. 38, p. 243.
7. Dr. Nageshwar Prasad, *Hind Swaraj—A Fresh Look*, p. 21.
8. *Ibid.*
9. Fritjof Capra, *The Turning Point Science Society and Rising Culture*, London, (1985), p. 3.
10. Dr. Nageshwar Prasad, *Hind Swaraj—A Fresh Look*, p. 22.
11. *Ibid.*, p. 24.
12. *Harijan*, 28-7-1946, p. 236.
13. Alexander King of Bertrand Schnider, The First Global Revolution (A Report by the Council of the Club of Rome), Orient Longman Ltd., 1993.

6

ROLE OF WOMEN IN THE 21st CENTURY ON GANDHIAN LINES

—S. SEETHALAKSHMI

Women—The Mother of Society

The greatest gift that women is endowed with is 'motherhood'. She was termed by Gandhiji as the 'mother, maker and silent leader of man.' Truly she is the mother of society. Her significant contribution to the making and well-being of the society and the preservation of its culture can never be measured or valued. It is the duty of women to preserve the sacredness of this precious gift and hand it down from generation to generation.

Gandhi and Women's Awakening

Perhaps the greatest champion of women's causes in the twentieth century was Mahatma Gandhi. He was known for his forthright views on the status and position of women in society. The credit of bringing women out of their homes into the mainstream of India's social and national life, and entrusting them with great responsibilities of educating and awakening unlettered and hither-to-meek and submissive women to take part in the non-violent struggle either for freedom or for other civil liberties, certainly goes to him. He was uncompromising in the matter of women's rights. 'In my opinion', he said, 'that she should labour under no legal disability, not suffered by man. I should treat daughters and sons on a footing of perfect equality. Great men of India living at that time had great esteem for him, and had no hesitation to do his bidding in the cause of the nation, particularly women's emancipation. His call to women to come out of their homes and take part in the *Satyagraha* against injustice oppression and exploitation was immediately and immeasurably honoured. They came out in their thousands and fulfilled their part. That, perhaps, was the greatest event in this century which significantly contributed to the awakening of women in India.

When women in Europe wanted a message from him in 1932, he quoted to them the part played by women in India in the non-violent struggle for freedom and wrote, 'if only women will forget that they can do infinitely more than men against war'... 'If Europe will drink in the lesson of Non-violence it will surely do so through its women'. This is a clear expression of his view on the place of women in society, for he believed that the woman was most suited to carry on the non-violent movement, for she was its very embodiment. The late Smt. Rajkumari Amrit Kaur, close associate of Mahatma Gandhi writes:

> ". . . Gandhiji never failed to stress that violence was against the fundamental nature of women. But he sorrowed greatly that she had become a slave to manhood simply because she failed to recognise her latent strength and potentialities. He would say that woman is the incarnation of *ahimsa. Ahimsa* means infinite love, which again means infinite capacity for suffering. Who, but woman the mother of man, shows this capacity? Does she not show it when she carries the unborn babe for over nine months end during that period and during lactation changes all her habits for the sake of the welfare of the child, and what is glorious is that she derives joy in the suffering involved. She forgets all the suffering in the joy of creation. Let her transfer that love to the whole of humanity in her capacity as mother, and let her forget, she ever was an object of pleasure. And, she will occupy her proud position by the side of man as his mother, maker and silent leader. It is given to her, and her alone, to occupy that position, and to teach to the warring world, thirsting for that nectar. Gandhiji believed that she could become the leader in *Satyagraha*, which does not require the learning that books give, but does require the stout heart that comes from suffering and faith."[1]

His indignant protest against enforced widowhood, against the crime of child-widows, against the curse of child-marriage, against polygamy, against the cruelty of the *purdah*-system, and against everything that reduced women to a secondary status, are very well-known. He hold the firm view that freedom and liberty to women were not only essential, but expedient to preserve what is precious in Indian culture and Indian womanhood. He was of the view that Indian women have much to give and share with women in the west, and that Indian women would certainly lead the way.

In his various *ashrams*, and other educational and social work organisations carried on Gandhian lines, girls and women were treated on par with boys and men, and were paid equal attention. One could see at once the freedom and self-confidence enjoyed by them, for I was myself one of them during my younger days. Such is rare to be seen in other parts of society. He would discuss matters connected with his institutions with women, as he would with important male co-workers. Dr. J.C. Kumarappa writes:

> ". . . The most sacred and pure form of economy can be seen in the mother-nature of woman, which is worthy of emulation . . . No other form of life is able to express it better than woman, when she cares for the child, not necessarily her own, but all, and the tenderness with which she deals with matters in society. The world shall be richer when left in her hands."[2]

Gandhiji was keen that women should be given, rather should take equal, if not more, responsibilities as men, in anything that he did or in any new undertaking that he ventured to put forth. No doubt, he was not satisfied with the part played by women; he wanted them to take greater responsibilities, not only in the national struggle, but in building up the nation. In all the institutions for which he was directly or indirectly responsible, he gave women a leading part.

Women's Role in Nation-Building

When he included the item 'Uplift of women' in the Constructive Programme, he was said to be sad, for, according to Smt.

Rajkumari Amrit Kaur, he likened it to the blot of untouchability in Hinduism. The launching of the Kasturba Gandhi National Memorial Trust was the culmination and fulfilment of the chosen service he wanted to initiate in the cause of women—which included training of Gram Sevikas, health assistants, teachers in adult education and balwadis—to educate women and children in the rural areas, to teach them the importance of sanitation, health and hygiene, and good manners and be in charge of such activities as village reconstruction, pre-natal and post-natal care of women children, child and women's welfare centres, and generally to awaken women in the rural areas and bring them in the national stream of service. He was keen on entrusting to women such activities that required careful handling and tender care, and the rare quality and ability to reconcile the opposites, and keep peace in the villages. It was privilege to be in such institutions both at Sevagram and elsewhere, and these helped me to understand the problems of women and the ways of their advancement.

In the Constructive Programme, Gandhiji envisaged a great part to be played by women, especially in the following:

(1) Communal Unity,
(2) Prohibition of Intoxicants,
(3) Removal of Untouchability,
(4) Village sanitation, health and hygiene,
(5) Women's Emancipation,
(6) New Education (*Nai Talim*),
(7) Khadi and Village Industries, and
(8) Krishi and *Go-seva*.

He could tell women workers that they could do what men workers would be horrified to do. His assertion was that a woman would be able to fare better in a cause, where rare qualities such as compassion, love, tenderness, ability to reconcile etc. are to be exhibited. Gandhiji would rather prefer women in crisis management. They are better-suited, he would say, for managing the affairs of the society, where precise account-keeping, presence of mind, efficient organisation, capacity to persuade and doing the right thing at the right time and in the right manner are involved.

Women's Role in the 21st Century

I suggest that nothing sudden would happen when we enter the 21st Century, but plenty can happen if we prepare the ground for it even from now. I have been engaged in women's uplift, particularly of the rural areas, and sometimes in the sub-urban areas, for the last four decades and I can share my experience with you, especially in educational, social and development organisations for women.

(1) When we educate a girl or a woman, we educate the whole family. (Some people think that education or training given to women is waste, for they get married and never use it thereafter. My experience is that the opposite is true.)

(2) Girls are definitely brighter and more receptive than boys in educational institutions, we run.

(3) Women perform their duties better and with greater responsibility. They can manage any work given the opportunity and support.

(4) In our Training Institutes for village industries, we found that they are better off even in manual work, especially playing the Ambar Charkha (spinning), weaving, polishing of artificial gem, tailoring and dress-making, dress-designing and in decorative art, and in office-management. They exhibit greater patience, dexterity and skill.

(5) There is practically nothing in which women cannot compete with men of the same calibre.

My intention in putting forth these qualities of women is not to depreciate the ability of my brothers, but to prove the point that the general assumption that women are better suited only in home-management and none other is a fallacy and that it should be done away with.

I am firmly of the opinion that in as much as society comprises of both women and men, there is no justification either to reduce them to an inferior status or for women to feel desolate that they are being denied of their rights and thereby their rightful place in society. I agree most reverently with Gandhiji's view that if women is reduced to a secondary position, it is because she has not understood her latent qualities, and that women are equally to blame for their present position.

Attitude must Change

The present attitude of the society—both men and women—should change. At present the society does not want to grant women the facilities needed for her awakening and emancipation. Men are afraid that if women are educated and given economic independence, they would be on top which may create problems for them. But sane thinking will prove the opposite. If a woman is educated and given economic dependence, she would not only contribute more to the well-being of the family, but will improve the status and performance of the family as a whole. It is doubly beneficial for society. The loss of working hours due to unemployment of women both in the rural areas and in the urban, if taken into account, would run into astronomical figures, granting that all men find enough work to do and prefer women to stay at home. In cities, I have found that unless both of them find work, it would be difficult to eke out a decent living, for the cost of living has gone up considerably now. Many middle class women are not able to balance their budget, and are sinking in debts, or selling away their gold and valuables. The plight of the poor is beyond description. It is a national loss, if women are not educated and provided with facilities to work. I do not mean 'jobs', but opportunities, training and facilities to work and earn. In many industrial enterprises, women can singularly manage and earn good returns.

In the case of marriages, it is a fallacy to think that girls should be married away at the proper age, may be 18 or 21, but the choice should be left to women whether they wish to marry or not. Parents, particularly in the Hindu families, are worried that unmarried women will have no one to care for and will not have protection if they are not married in time. One would like to emulate from Christian families, where to the best of my knowledge, they care more for educating girls to the extent possible and leave the question of marriage to them, when they become economically independent. There are thousands of teachers, nurses and women in other professions, who find it comfortable to be spinsters all their life. I know of several families where this has happened. Hindu families should emulate this example. The attitude of grooms towards dowry will also undergo a change if women are independent in their opinion towards marriage.

Thirdly, I am one of those who strongly believe that the existing facilities for women's education, professional training and employment (including self-employment) should be doubled, if not tribled, for that would solve many national problems at one stroke. Girls' schools should be started in their thousands all over India; there should be professional colleges and training institutes in equal number exclusively for women so that the present stagnation can be eased and women will have better opportunities of participation in national life. In the rural areas, there must be separate organisation for training rural women in various village and cottage industries and handicrafts. The Mahila Mandalis, which are no doubt useful in uniting them and given awareness, but are not efficient instruments for providing economic independence, should be strengthened with wider function and responsibilities. Resources for this should be found.

I have under my charge a few schools for the education of women, and as an experiment, I had conducted an Institute for Rural Adult Women's Continuing Education. We used to admit only drop-out women in the age-group of 15-25, in this institute, we provided them with general education catering to the school-final and higher-secondary examinations and at the same time, train them in one or two crafts, so that they can be fully self-employed after their training. I am glad to say that this project gave us a new experience, that if women are educated and trained in rural areas can easily find employment, also economic independence. It is on the basis of this experience that I suggest that if facilities for education and training are improved rural areas, women can be uplifted, sooner than we expect it to happen.

Conclusion

I have submitted my views on the place and development of women, based on practical experience. In our general educational schools, we insist that every girl in the village comes to the school. We are also improving the quality of education with additional stress on character-formation, fine arts, handicrafts, physical education and general knowledge. All religious prayer is one of the items compulsory for staff and students to participate. I beleive that this is a good beginning, and that after a decade, these children will grow into full-fledged women capable of shouldering greater social responsibilities and translating our ideals into practice.

I genuinely believe that in the 21st Century, the place and status of women, and their participation in the national cause will be much greater than now. I thank the organisers of this National Seminar, particularly Dr. Janardhan Pandey to have given me this opportunity of participation.

REFERENCES

1. *Vishwabharati Quarterly*, Special number dt. 2.10.1949.
2. *Economy of Permanence*, p. 217.

7

RELEVANCE OF GANDHIAN POLITICS IN THE 21st CENTURY

—GOPAL PRASAD SINGH

It is often very difficult to write about a tall silhoutte on whom more than four hundred biographies are already on circulation and who has been acclaimed widely as 'Bapu', 'The Father of the Nation' and Mahatma'. It is also difficult as he has many facts of life as well as myths about him; he is realist as well as utopian; he is human being as well as idealised as the Christ. His ideas has numerous stakes in India's well being which is badly in the vortex of corruption, casteism, communalism, criminalisation of politics and politicisation of crime along with ruthless political opportunism and repression. Not only his ideas have international ramifications from Nelson Mandela to Jr. Martin Luther King, to Cesar Chavez—his ideas have application wherever there are poor and oppressed. His personality is so wide that he has invited both praise as well as blasphemy for his use of word "Harijan" for dalits, and one gentleman at Patna went to the extent of announcing that he refused to recognise him as the father of the Nation, certainly, all these outbrust are for the sake of cheap populism for bringing oneself to the news. His personality and ideas are so contradictory that a rightist political organization or party in India, allegedly, held responsible for his brutal killing embraced 'Gandhian Socialism' as one of its election planks. Even person like Mr. Nehru has acknowledged, "no man can write a real life of Gandhi, unless he is as big as Gandhi". Such was the multi-faceted personality of Mohandas Karamchand Gandhi.[1]

At the same time, it is fascinating and challenging to pen something on Gandhiji and also deliberate about the relevance of his ideas in the coming century as he combines in his personality both the greatness and the goodness.[2] He is the great as he compelled mighty Britishers, on whose empire sun did not set, to quit India and he is the good as he preached the philosophy of truth and non-violence. It is also compelling to write about him as he is credited for leading the Nation to Independence, yet he was murdered by his countryman—a fanatic as well as lunatic.

He was saint and revolutionary; preacher and practitioner; nationalise and cosmopolitan. He was also a philosopher, politician, statesman, diplomat, democrate, socialist, economist, administrator, communicator and, above all, a magician—all rolled into one actually having no flesh on bones, though shining, tight and erect. Thus how much and whatsoever we reflect on this the greatest son and soul of our motherland, it will remain inadequate. However, we would like to dwell upon Gandhijee's views on morality and politics.

We would like to discuss this topic in the context that decent people in politics are a fast-vanishing species in our land. This leads to the question why are more decent people not entering into the fray? This is proving the dictum true that "politics is the last resort of the scoundrel". Today politics has gone a sea-change. Now it stinks. Politics has degenerated to the level of corruption, dishonesty, rank opportunism, expediency, manoeuvrings and manipulations of all kinds and, above all, greed-devoid of moral fabric.[3]

Really today politics is a business, at best an enterprise. The ruling class (both party in power and opposition parties) has completely altered the meaning of politics. Politics today has become a national obsession. It is no longer a calling and mission. It is far from being a noble venture. It has indeed become a business and, of course, a lucrative business. Heredity, family or dynastic connections, rather than ability and character determine success in, politics. Well said by a politician, "I was born in politics; I live in politics; and I will die in politics". So politics is a business and not service. Politics is a greed, often an amoral greed for pelf and power. It is to grab wealth. It has nothing to do with patriotism and service of the people. It is why good people abstain from politics. This is a post-Gandhian phase.

Some eminent people opine that politics has degenerated since the pre-Independence era. The standard of politics is to capture power any how and then to retain it on all costs. No doubt the meaning of politics is to have power. Politics is a search for power (Dahl). So politics is just shaping and sharing political power i.e., in decision-making.[5]

New phenomena added to the dimension of politics is its criminalisation. It is the concerned of all and, at the same time, it is a serious dysfunctionality crept into Indian political system which is still in prismatic stage.

One of the most important element in criminalisation of politics is that a good number of gang leaders and criminals of all hues who were previously helping their mentors in the elections, now managed themselves to enter the legislatures either as an Independent or on party ticket, and usurped social acceptability. So politics remains no more decent as notorious criminals, history-sheeters, smugglers, murderers, mafias, terrorists are swarming in politics, they are prowling in search of prey and plunder. Formerly, they were on the periphery of Indian political life, now they have moved considerably towards the centre to manipulate the gears and levers of political mechines. A criminal of today is a contractor of tomorrow who becomes a politician the day after.[6] It has been reported that 106 known criminals have been elected to the 12th State Assembly in U.P.[7] Hence the day is not far off when politicians would loose control of political process and would be overshadowed by criminals. What is more important is the fact that almost all parties give accommodation to such elements in order to ensure victory at the hustings justifying the saying, "All is fair in election".

So far as politicisation of crime is concerned it means patronage and protection' by political masters to crimes and criminals in lieu of services rendered by the latter to the former in the furtherance of their political ambitions. So it involved the competitive use of anti-social forces for the mobilisation of party funds, for the management and manipulation of elections, for organising meetings and conferences and even for the elimination of political opponents. Further, it means the use and misuse of criminal intelligence and criminals as political tool for blackmailing political adversary as well as maintaining one's political clout and hegemony in his area. So these 'patronage and protection' by political masters anti-social and hoodlum is extended by way of thwarting legal processes and also by way of helping to get licenses, permits, various contracts, etc., to them. It is here we find a thin line of divide in the realm of legal from illegal. 'Value-based politics' and 'clean images' become worst casualty giving place to all types of intrigues, gimmickery, manoeuvring etc., in the game of power. Wrong deeds are justified giving them a cloak of legality. Time tested procedure honoured in letters are to be subverted in spirit so as to produce the clearance to the defendants giving the impression that all have been done properly. What is at stake is legitimacy because legality holds good only when accompanied by legitimacy.[8]

All these have led to the conclusion that politics has deteriorated beyond redemption accelerating the decaying processes. Naturally films, plays or folk arts almost without exception paint politician as a villain and commoners as helpless victims.[9] Commenting on rapid criminalisation of society Rajasthan Governor, B.R. Bhagat as a guest of honour at a function organised by the students and staffs, Patna College Patna, asserted that Gandhi's messages were more relevant in the present context when there had been rapid criminalisation and erosion of moral values.[10]

Let us now take a glimpse of Gandhian concept of politics. We are proud of Gandhian political culture which gives specific importance to the moral aspects of politics; to intellectual and saintly orientation to political action; to purity of means for pure end; to the doctrine of truth and non-violence to the obedience to the dictates of inner conscience; and to the ideal of social justice and freedom. We have a glorious political culture of value-based political behaviour as exhibited by galaxy of Indian leaders. Tagore outlined, 'lofty vision of freedom'; Aurobindo stressed the 'organic totality of social existence'; Gokhale proclaimed the ideal of 'the spiritualisation of politics', Mahatma Gandhi quest was for 'goodness of politics' and Vinoba preached the gospel of self-sacrifice, love and of 'polity without power'.[11]

We have to discuss here the Gandhian premise about the nature of man. For Gandhi man is essentially good in nature. Here he parted company with Hobbes, Machiavelli and Marx who painted man as brutal, selfish and economic, while he kept company with Milton, Jafferson, Mill and Rousseau who saw man as good. Vinoba seeks to drive home this point by comparing man or human nature to the head of a cabbage, whose inner layers always retain their freshness. So Gandhi always instructed

Sarvodaya workers to have faith in man's inward core of goodness.[12] Actually Gandhi holds that man is a abode for *Atman* which is a manifestation of *Parmatma*. It is why Gandhi rejected the Malthusian—Darwinian—Nietzschean emphasis on the biological victory of strong over the weak rather accepted the Vedantic-Buddhist-Stoic-Christian conception of the final victory of truth giving the man moral force.

Naturally Gandhi like Gokhale, wanted a spiritualisation of politics. But Gandhi's attachment to the concept of non-violence was far deeper and more extensive than that of Gokhale.[13]

It is why Gandhi wanted to bring religion into politics. Gandhi is of opinion that "there is no politics devoid of religion. They subserve religion. Politics bereft of religion are a death trap because they kill the soul."[14] Surely, Gandhi believes in Theological determinism as against the economic determinism of Marx. But by this he did not mean in any way the establishment of theocracy. Religion means the assertion of unity with God. It is a dynamic force. So the incorporation of religion in politics means a progressive movement towards justice and truth, because a man of religion will never tolerate any kind of oppression and exploitation.

Let us make it clear here that Gandhi was a firm protagonist of secularism. He was opposed to giving privileges on the basis of religion. He was also opposed to discrimination against any religion or religious groups. In the Harijan dated the 24th August, 1947, he categorically stated that, "the state should undoubtedly be secular". On March 16, 1947 Gandhijee wrote in the *Harijan*, "He did not believe in state religion even though the whole community had one religion. The State interference would probably always be unwelcome. Religion was purely a personal matter". He accepted the spiritual and moral essence of Hinduism which according to him was the essence of all the great religion of mankind as Judaism, Christianity, Islam, Zoroastrian, etc. Hinduism signifies a relentless search after truth. Like Buddha and Ramkrishna he was above the bounds of creeds, cults, rituals and ceremonies.

What we want to stress is that via religion Gandhi added moral connotation to politics and political deeds. Certainly we have presently rejected religion from politics. The recent legislation separating religion and politics is the need of the hour. The model code of conduct imposed by the Chief Election

Commissioner against the exploitation of religious sentiments resorting to religious propaganda has been hailed widely. All these are not in contradiction with the moral postulates of politics preached by Gandhijee. Our motto is to check religious fanaticism and religious fundamentalism. Gandhijee never advocated religious fundamentalism. Of course, he was in favour of the very fundamentals of religion which is morality and goodness. So Gandhijee cannot be criticised for mixing up religion and politics. What actually Gandhijee preached is the spiritualisation of politics and secularisation of religion, not the religious fundamentalism and fanaticism.

It is this ethical connotation of politics and the rigorous ascetic self-denial[15] and abnegation of wants where lies the solution to every problems of world, such as, poverty, illiteracy, environment, Aids, Drugs, terrorism, NPT etc. as all these problems need political solutions and politics requires good men with good intention in Gandhian mould having moral forces behind their thinkings as well as deeds.

Is there a dearth of good people in politics having no morality and more akin to corruption? We have documentary evidence about the corruption of politicians narrated in A.G. Noorani's 'Ministers' Misconduct'. Recently Governor of Tamilnadu has sanctioned Dr. S. Swamy to start prosecution against Ms. Jayalalitha under the Prevention of Corruption Act. In similar situation A.R. Antulay had to relinquish his office of Chief Minister against public outcry for various acts of omissions and commissions.

But there is no dearth of politicians who voluntarily resigned their post on the ground of morality. Former Prime Minister Lal Bahadur Shastri did not wait for a demand for his resignation after a major rail accident. After the Indo-China War in 1962 the then Defence Minister V.K. Krishna Menon also tendered his resignation. Very recently A.K. Anthony, former Union Food & Supplies Minister relinquished the post in the wake of Sugar Scandal. But we know that many Chief Ministers and Central Ministers greedly resisted against their resignation despite being under a cloud. Some politicians continue to rule until they were slapped with an adverse court verdict or a judicial or House inquiry commission report.[16]

So Gandhijee added morality and religion to the politics. To lead a religious life, therefore, is to lead a moral life.[17] So his religion is rooted in morality. And his politics is based on morality.

Thus we find that Gandhi's preaching of morality in politics is relevant today and it will remain relevant for all time to come what to talk of only the 21st Century.

Our polity is heading towards instability. The hung parliament is a definite possibility after the next election. It will be compounded as history-sheeters, criminals and anti-social will most likely to flood the political system. The lowest level of chicanery and opportunism, cut throat factionalism and deceit, and horse-trading will be the order of the day. The morality and ethics in politics will be the worst victim. The worse days are ahead. People in panic are suggesting the change of the system especially switching over to Presidential system of Government.[18] The desperation is so high that one gentleman not less than retired Lieutenant-General S.K. Sinha has suggested limited type of dictatorship for a short span of time to discipline the people and politicians in order to save the system.

But our well considered view is that superstructure hardly matters. What is needed is the role played by the actors in that superstructure. So any political system whether parliamentary or Presidential hardly matters, we need man of character with all morality in politics. For this we have to remember as well as to follow our thoughts and deeds our beloved Bapu whether this century or the next century.

REFERENCES

1. Mehta, Ved, *Mahatma Gandhi and His Apostles*, (Indian Book Company Andre Deutsch, London, 1977), P.O. ix and 3.
2. Varma, V.P., *The Political Philosophy of Mahatma Gandhi and Sarvodaya*. (Lakshmi Narain Agrawal, Agra, 1959).
3. Mathur, A.B., "Mahatma Gandhian's Relevance Today", *The Indian Journal of Political Science*, Vol. L, No. 2, April-June, 1989, p. 156.
4. Rathore, L.S., "Political Culture of India's Ruling Class", *The Indian Journal of Political Science*, Vol. L1, No. 2, April-June, 1990, p. 281.
5. Gandhi, Madan G. *Modern Political Analysis*, (Oxford and IBH Publishing, New Delhi, 1985), p. 42.
6. Gandhi, G.P., "Criminalisation of Politics and Politicisation of

Crime. A Dysfunctionality of 1989 and 1990 Elections in Bihar", *People's Mandate* Edited by Dr. V.M. Bachal, (Usha J. Nagpurkar, Pune, 1992), p. 270.

7. Hafiz, M.A., "106 MLAs in UP with Criminal Record", *The Hindustan Times*, Patna, Dec. 6, 1993, p. 5.
8. Singh, Dr. G.P., *op.cit.*
9. Kumar Ketkar, Radha Rajadhyaksha and Shabnam Minwalla, "Does Politics Stink?", *The Times of India*, Special Report, Patna, April 19, 1995, p. 10.
10. *The Times of India*, Patna, April 24, 95, p. 3.
11. Rathore, L.S., *op.cit.*, p. 278.
12. Doctor, ADI H., "The Man in Gandhian Philosophy", *The Indian Journal of Political Science*, Vol. LIII, No. 2, April-June 1992, p. 153.
13. Varma, U.P., *Modern Indian Political Thought*, (Lakshmi Narain Agarwal, Agra, 1986), p. 350.
14. *Ibid.*
15. Moore, Leroy, "The Relevance of Gandhi in To-day's World", (Bhubneswar, Mayug Publications, 1991), p. 7.
16. "*The Times of India*", Patna, April 18, 1995, p. 12.
17. Upadhyaya, K.N., *Gandhi on Religion, Morality and Politics*, *Gandhi Jyoti*, No. 1, October, 1994, p. 2.
18. Malhotra, Inder, "Political Commentary: Searching for a Panacea", *The Times of India*, Patna, April 28, 1995, p. 6.

8

PREDICAMENT OF TWENTY-FIRST CENTURY AND THE GANDHIAN SOLUTION

—ANIL DUTTA MISHRA

Gandhiji is no more in flesh and blood with us. Even four and half decades after his assasination, his vast corpus of his ideas and the "story" of his "experiment with truth" and non-violence is a part of his legacy. His ideas and actions are still a guiding force to save humanity. A writer of eminence John Haynes Holmes wrote: "when all the kings and princes and great captains of our times, who make so much noise and occupy so central a place upon the stage, when these have long since been forgotten, every one of them, the Mahatma will still be known and referred as the greatest Indian since Gautam the Buddha, and as the greatest man since Jesus Christ."[1]

Gandhism is a living thought for solving the social, economic and political problems of the day. Gandhism is becoming more and more principles in each and every field. Infact, the future generations will recall Gandhi's idea's particularly in two broader specific areas: first, in regard to the use of non-violent methods and for reflecting violence for the resolution of social and political conflicts; and secondly, for trying to come to grips with the problems of the culture of "consumerism" in the past industrial era.[2] Not only that, his ideas will be relevant in 21st century because he combined theory with practice, individual religious outlook with life-affirmation, morality with public activity, non-cooperation with evil with adherence to non-violence, developing a methodology of action with effective force but without malice towards the opponents and rational and experimental attitude together with the fundamental acceptance of an ethical position.[3]

The Predicament

Violence became a cult in contemporary world, whether it is east or west. 20 million people were killed in some 150 wars since 1945, more than the soldiers killed in World War II.[4] Even the domestic violence have increased tremendously. We are living under the shadow of violence and no life is safe.

The developed countries in the name of national security spent twenty times as much on military expenditure as they provided for economic aid. 70% of world military spending is by six major military powers, 15% is by other industrialized countries and remaining 15% by developing countries. The world military expenditure doubled between 1960 and 1983 to reach 800 billion dollars per year[5] and by the beginning of the 21st century it will be doubled again. We will be surprised to know that just one-fifth of annual arms expenditure could abolish world hunger by the year 2000 from the entire world.

For over one lac people in the world there are 556 soldiers but cnly 85 doctors. For every soldier the average world military expenditure is $ 20,000 and for every school-age child the average public education expenditure is $ 380 only.[6] According to the SIPRI report, the nuclear weapons currently in the world's arsenals have total explosive roughly equivalent to that of about a million Hiroshima-type atomic bombs. Near about 424 nuclear reactors are operating world-wide, and more planned for future, which are neither safe nor friendly with environment. The nuclear waste generated from these reactors are dumped into sea is posing a serious environmental threat not only to coastal people but to entire humankind.[7]

Almost all the consumer items that are being promoted to sustain the economic growth have significant impact on society directly or indirectly. Take for example, India. India has 32 million uneducated adults, 36 million unemployed adults and 44 million child labours.[8] There are 2.4 million women forced into prostitution in 1100 red light areas of major and small cities in India.[9] The child prostitution is on the rise. It is interesting to note that the hub of child six industry is in Asia, and that India accounts for 4 lacs children who are sexually abused.[10] Statistics reveal that a woman is molested every 26 minutes, one raped in every 47 minutes, one eve-teasing in every 6 minutes, one kidnapped in every 44 minutes, 7 dowry-death in every 24 hours and every 7 minutes one act of criminal offence against women is committed in this country.[11] The statistics shows that in 1980, the number of reported rape cases was 0.7 per lac in the country. In comparison, the United States witnessed the highest of such cases (36.1 per lac), followed by Sweden (10.7), Canada (0.6), France (3.5), Italy (3.3), Britain (2.5), Japan (2.2) and Bangladesh (0.3).[12] Today 25 per cent of reported rapes are of girls under 16. Infact, there is a rise of 30% rape in major cities in India. If we look carefully all adolescent girls are visually-raped by men.[13]

The progress in areas like health, education and housing is slowed by the diversion of precious human resources for national security, military purposes and in combating terrorism and separatist movement. Most of the major problems facing humanity today like, economic disparities, inflation, over population, unemployment, terrorism, pollution, malnutrition, illiteracy, hunger are due to maldevelopment. We should not forget that there are 870 million adults who cannot read and write, 500 million people who have no jobs or are less than fully employed, 130 million children who are unable to attend primary school, 450 million people who suffer from hunger and malnutrition, 12 million babies who die every year before their first birthday, 42 million people who are blind or nearly so, 200 million people who live in urban slums or shanty towns.[14] By 2,000 about three billion people would be living in urban areas. The 21st century will be still more urban. By 2020, about two-thirds of the human race would be living and working in urban settlements.[15] Not only that the persistence of hunger in a world of plenty, with 750 million men, women and children going hungry everyday in the world's poor countries, is one of the most daunting development challenges facing the global community according to World Bank Report on "Reducing Poverty and Hunger".[16]

The Gandhian Solution

Mahatma's ideas about the dangers of western civilization have assumed significance in the context of several issues concerning the survival of the humanity and evaluation of a just and viable world order. Gandhi saw clearly the moral degradation and cultural decay long back. The *Hind Swaraj* of Mahatma Gandhi published in 1908, long before the negative consequences of industrial civilization were exposed to the common experience, must have appeared to the generation of his times, a book of reaction and retreat from modernity and civilization. The fact is that long before the people in 21st century will be awakened to the perils and limits of unrestrained economic growth and technological innovations, Gandhiji pointed out the pitfalls of industrialism and the damage to nature and man. He strongly criticised the emerging trends of consumer culture in future in all spheres of life and emphasised austerity and the moral principle in development, which is essential for tomorrow's world.

Gandhian concept of Sarvodaya will be very useful for solving the social problems of today and of 21st century. The concept can be interpreted as the "awakening of one and all". In addition to the awakening of everyone, it refers to the awakening of the total human spirit and personality. Sarvodaya is also related to achieving the highest level of self-realization in which one sees one's manifestation in all others.[17] The main theme of the Sarvodaya in the 21st century will be same as exemplified in the following Vedic verse: *Sarve bhavantu sukhinah, Sarve santu niramaya, Sarve Bhadrani pashyantu, Ma Kaschit dukh-bhag bhavet.*

From the above verse, we can see that the Sarvodaya concept stresses duty of individuals to themselves and beyond their immediate families to the entire world. "Sarvodaya believes that by tapping their innermost beliefs and values, one can awaken people to their *swa-shakti* (personal awakening or power) and *Janashakti* (collective awakening of people's power)" in order that their *Dharma* can be realized.[18] Infact, Sarvodaya will be very useful for establishing ideal society i.e., free from evils like 'politics without principles'. 'wealth without work', 'knowledge without character', 'commerce without morals', 'science without mankind' and 'service without sacrifice'.[19] The Sarvodaya ideal, apart from standing for the meaning of the welfare of all, implies the meaning of the universal welfare and integrated development of all. As a universal ideal it aims at not only fulfilling the material needs but also developing the ethico-spiritual aspects of all people.[20]

At the same time *Swadeshi* will be the greatest tool for solving the economic problems of the 21st century. *Swadeshi* means self-reliance in every field. In other words, *Swadeshi* is service, and if we understand it, we shall simultaneously benefit ourselves, our families, our country and the world. Gandhi delineated the *modus operandi* of *Swadeshi* in terms of limited wants and the capacity of local surroundings and resources to meet the need of the people. In his famous sentence he laid down his dictum: "Nature produces enough to meet the needs of all the people, but not enough to satisfy the greed of anyone". A life of simplicity with self-respect is any time better than a life of luxury for the few bought with loss of self-esteem and independence to other nations.[21] Our motto in 21st century should be simple living high thinking so that we can stop the evils of the society.

Infact *Swadeshi* Movement may become a part of renaissance in 21st century. Because it conveys the idea of returning to one's own country—to its culture and heritage, its own genius and tradition and serve the need of the next door neighbour. This is the appropriate time for us to understand the concept of *Swadeshi* and implement it in every possible manner and we will be doing this progress by making ourself self-reliant and self-sufficient in every field and we would be free from moral degradation, economic exploitation, and political subjugation.[22]

Satyagraha will be also an important means by which individuals and groups can have an immediate effect on government policy and programmes. Individuals and groups can organise the people and draw the attention of the Government and masses on issues of, terrorism, exploitation, deteriorating law and order, pollution, poverty, malnutrition etc. to save society. At a personal level also lot of people can work. To operationalize the '*Satyagraha* for better future', it would be desirable to bring like minded people under one umbrella to fight against injustice and wrong governmental policy which is creating social tensions.

In a nutshell, the Gandhian approach to 21st century economic problem will be based on maximum labour-intensive, employment-oriented and minimum capital intensive industry, thus avoiding the unnecessary and excessive use of machine and the everrising spiral of industrial and technological expansion. In social field, it will be based on 'politics with principles', 'wealth with work', 'knowledge with character', 'commerce with morals', 'science with spirituality' and 'service with sacrifice'.

Summing up

If there is anything that can solve the problems in 21st century, is the Gandhian path, alongwith the opportunities which will emerge from modern science and technology. Our approach to development and economic growth must be harmonized with human value. Our aim should be to have worth living place and worth living life which can be achieved through change of our life style and controlling our unlimited needs and greeds. We must follow the Indian tradition of self-sacrifice. We require a proper synthesis of science and spirituality to usher in an era of welfarism in 21st century i.e., *Bahujan Hitaya, Bahujana Sukhaya*. The task is difficult, as the analysis of economic, political and social situation would show, but the Indian tradition has a great resilence and Indian mind a great capacity to overcome hurdles.

We have to start somewhere to come to right path—the Gandhian path. Still it is not too late to make a beginning to save 21st century for future generation.

REFERENCES

1. Anil Dutta Mishra, *Fundamentals of Gandhism*, New Delhi: Mittal Publications, 1995, p. 1.
2. K.P. Karunakaran, *Gandhi-Interpretations*, New Delhi: Gitanjali Publishing House, 1985, p. 1.
3. *Ibid.*
4. N. Radhakrishnan (ed.), *Multiple Streams of Peace Movement*, Dr. G.R. Institute of Non-Violence, 1986, p. vi.
5. *Ibid.*
6. *Ibid.*
7. Anil Dutta Mishra, *Environmental Challenges and the Gandhian Solution*, Paper presented at 16th Annual Conference of ISGS at Kanyakumari, 2-4 Sept. 1944.
8. *The Hindustan Times*, 5th April, 1995.
9. *The Hindustan Times*, 22nd April, 1995.
10. *The Hindustan Times*, 5th April, 1995.
11. *The Hindustan Times*, 27th April, 1995 and *The Hindustan Times*, 4th January, 1995.
12. *The Hindustan Times*, 29th March, 1995.

13. Anil Dutta Mishra, "Status of Women and Girl-child in India", *Teaching Politics*, Vol. XX, Nos. 1-4, 1994, p. 122.
14. N. Radhakrishnan (ed.), *op. cit.*
15. *The Hindustan Times*, 12th April, 1995.
16. *The Hindustan Times*, 27th April, 1995.
17. O.P. Dwivedi, "Global Dharma to the Environment", *IJPA*, July-Sept. 1993, Vol. XXXIX, No. 3, p. 572.
18. *Ibid.*, pp. 572-73.
19. Anil Dutta Mishra, *op. cit.*, pp. 14-15.
20. *Ibid.*, p. 17.
21. Ali Ashraf, "Gandhian View of Sustainable Development, *IJPA*, July-Sept. 1993, Vol. XXXIX, No. 3, p. 274.
22. Anil Dutta Mishra, *op. cit.*, pp. 85-86.

9

INDIA'S FOREIGN POLICY AND GANDHIJI

—KRANTI KUMAR

Mahatma Gandhi was not the foreign policy-maker, but was the maker of the man who made the foreign policy. He did not handle foreign policy; but handled the man who handled the foreign policy. Gandhi was also not an architect of the foreign policy, but the mentor of the 'architect' of the foreign policy of modern India.

Gandhi had the dream of such a foreign policy that could bring all the nations together under one world.[1] The concept of Gandhi's one world has been beautifully painted by Tagore as under:

> "Where the mind is without fear and the head is held high; where knowledge is free;
> Where the world has not been broken into fragments by narrow domestic walls;
> Where words come out of the depth of truth;
> Where tireless striving stretches its arms towards perfection;
> Where the clear stream of reason has not lost its way into the dreary desert sand of dead habit;
> Where the mind is led forward by thee into ever widening thought and action;
> Into that heaven of freedom, my Father, let my country awake."

Describing the idea of One World as a goal of the foreign policy, Gandhi stated that "the only condition on which the world can live is being united under one central governing body composed of representatives of the component parts".[2] Gandhiji further said, "the better mind of the world desires today not absolutely independent states warring one against another but on a federation of friendly inter-dependent state."[3]

In the above statements Gandhi has said about "federation of friendly inter-dependent states" as well as "central governing body." It refers to Gandhi's dream of the world governments, the government of the world which would follow the policy of peace and non-violence as an essential means to settle international differences and disputes. In other words, Gandhi, being an idealist, wanted a non-violent international order composed of non-violent states and the problems among such states should be resolved through pacific means. There is no place of war or violence in any form. This is inspired by the ideal of world unity rooted in the highest truth, the spiritual oneness of mankind and it stands for a country learning to live not by exploiting others but by serving others and dying for others.

The objective of Gandhi's foreign policy aims at following peaceful means and non-violent techniques in maintaining international relations. However, Gandhi also stresses upon non-violent nationalism as an essential precondition of sound internationalism. Gandhi said, "it is impossible for one to be an internationalist without being a nationalist. It is not nationalism that is an evil, it is the narrowness selfishness, exclusiveness which is the bane of modern nations which is evil. Indian nationalism wants to organise itself or to find full self-expression for the benefit and service of humanity at large."[4]

According to Gandhiji, the truth and non-violence as a means of diplomacy should be followed in such a way that other country can also learn from India. It will be the greatest service to the mankind. Gandhi said in this context that, "the adoption of non-violence to the utmost extent possible . . . . will be India's great contribution to the peace of the world and the establishment of a new world order."[5] Gandhi further said, "through the deliverance of India, I seek to deliver the so called weaker race of the earth from the crushing heels of western exploitation. India's coming to her own will mean every nation doing likewise."[6]

Gandhi does not believe that the nation should be self-centred. He rather insisted on self-sacrifice to the cause of mankind. In his words, ". . . . an individual has to die for the village, the village for the district, the district for the province and the province for the country, even so a county has to be free in order that it may die, if necessary, for the benefit of the world."[7]

Gandhi said that the objective of the foreign policy should be decided in such a way which can maintain friendly relationship with neighbours based on self-sacrifice and service to the neighbouring countries. "The neighbours then understand the spirit in which such service was given. They would also know that they would be expected to give their services to their neighbours. The spirit of self-sacrifice also implies that "a true free India is bound to run to the help of its neighbours in distress." By implication the neighbours of India's neighbouring countries are India's neighbours also.[8]

Gandhi has pointed out as why the free India should prefer the policy of self-sacrifice and service to the nearest and immediate neighbours. Because the capacity of service is limited by our knowledge of the world in which we live. So we must, as our first duty, dedicate ourselves to the service of our immediate neighbours the nearest and the best known to us? Pure service of one's neighbour can never result in disservice to those who are remotely situated. On the other hand, if one sets out to serve people in a distant place one is doubly guilty. He is guilty of culpable neglect of his neighbours who have acclaim on its service. His attempt would also be an unintended disservice to the people of distant place, for in his ignorance he would very likely disturb the atmosphere of the new place, besides it is an arrogance to think of serving distant places when one is hardly able to serve even his immediate neighbours.[9] Thus one has "the scientific limitation of human capability for service."[10]

About international organisation, Gandhiji says that a non-violent state should co-operate the world organisation based on non-violence. He says peace will come not merely by changing the institutional forms but by regenerating those attitudes and ideals of which war, imperialism, capitalism and other forms of exploitation are the inevitable expression. The international organisation should be freely established and maintained by non-violence which can solve all the problems of the world.[11] In 1931 speaking at Geneva about the League of Nations he remarked, "It (The League) is expected to replace war, and by its own power, to arbitrate between nations who might have differences amongst themselves. But it has always seemed to me that the League lacks the necessary sanctions. . . . I venture to suggest to you that the means we have adopted in India supply the necessary sanction not only to a body like the League of Nations, but to any voluntary body or association that would take up this great cause of the peace of the world."[12] A non-violent world organisation requires the giving up of armaments and of the use of force to defend even proved right. Proved rights should be capable of being vindicated by right means as against the sanguinary means."[13]

In order to control violent outbreaks between states Gandhiji accepted an international non-violent police force resembling peace brigades or the police force of a non-violent state. It means the present system of peace-force attached to the UNO is an important instrument being used to restore peace and security in the world.

For disarmament Gandhiji said, "some nation will have to dare to disarm herself and take large risks. The level of non-violence in that nation will naturally have risen so high as to command universal respect. Her judgment will be unerring, her decisions will be firm, her capacity for heroic self-sacrifice will be great and she will want to live as much for other nations as for herself. International order and disarmament rule out imperialism. According to Gandhiji, there will be an international league only when all the nations, big or small, composing it are fully independent. In a society based on non-violence the smallest nation will feel as tall as the tallest. The idea of superiority and inferiority will be wholly obliterated."[14]

Non-violence inside the state should also manifest itself in the foreign policy of the state. The non-violent Indian state, when it comes into existence, will endeavour to live on the friendliest terms with its neighbour whether they be great powers or small as nations, and shall covet no foreign territory."[15] As pointed out earlier the non-violent state will share its material and moral resources with people across its neighbours. Neither exploiting, nor being exploited it will be at peace with the rest of the world. It will work, for total disarmament and for establishment of a non-violent international order. Its non-violence will command universal respect and arouse the goodwill of the neighbours. For its defence it will rely on goodwill of the whole world.[16]

Gandhiji, thus, stands for establishment of just political and economic international relations and the ending of the domination of one state over another. For the elimination of imperialism it was necessary for great nations to shed competition and the desire to multiply wants and material possessions.[17] The new world order will take time to evolve. Meanwhile there may be cases of international injustice and aggression. According to Gandhiji aggression against a non-violent state will be unlikely and it will be easy for it to defend itself non-violently. The democratic socio-economic structure of non-violent state being rooted in justice and equality, there will be no internal struggle for economic power which leads to imperialism or revolution.[18]

During the lifetime Gandhi had seen both the world wars, the rise and fall of the League of Nations as well as the formation of the UNO, the use of atom bomb, the beginning of the cold war, the expansion of communism, the explosion of newly independent Asian, African and Latin American States, the end of the old concept of colonialism and the emergence of neo-colonialism.

Pakistan's invasion of Kashmir and also the beginning of India's foreign policy and its relations with neighbours and the world.

At present the political phenomenon of the world has been drastically changed, particularly after the collapse of the erstwhile Soviet Union. Now the entire strategic economic, and political scenario is absolutely different at the global level. There is no cold war today and also the system of bipolar world has been vanished. The ideological competition between capitalism and communism appears to be over. Now the system of economic globalization has been emerged. Communism in the USSR (former) as well as other states of the eastern Europe is out of sight. USSR as a nation has been broken into fifteen pieces.

However, peace may be there at the USA the single super power of the world and also in western Europe which in turn must have changed international security environment but there is no change in Indian sub-continent so far as the security is concerned. The situation between India and Pakistan and India and China and other neighbours is the same as it used to be. There is no improvement at all in any respect. Besides, the collapse of the USSR is definitely the biggest loss for India, and perhaps for the entire third world. Now there is no country which can stand behind

India in the most critical juncture like during Bangladesh liberation. The loss of the USSR means the loss of 70% of India's armed forces requirements as well as atleast seventy-five highly sophisticated industrial projects are in critical condition.

In this situation what should be the foreign policy of India which can protect, and promote India's interest in the critical hours. At this stage people remember Gandhiji. How far did Gandhi's philosophy influence India's foreign policy and her relations with the world? How far is Gandhi relevant today?

Gandhiji, perhaps, foresaw the shape of the things to come and nominated Pt. Nehru as his political heir in preference to others who were more Gandhian than Nehru.[19] Gandhi and Nehru might have differences on other issues but there was hardly any difference in their attitudes to foreign policy. They agreed on the basic policy of peace, equality of individuals as well as nations, the right of all colonial countries and people to independence, opposition to all forms of discrimination against and exploitation of one country or individual by another, on grounds of race, colour, creed, sex or wealth.

Pt. Nehru had formulated the foreign policy of India in consonance with these basic principles. Non-alignment and peaceful co-existence, opposition to racist policies in Africa and elsewhere and anti colonialism the pillars of India's foreign policy in Nehru's time were the application of Gandhi's thought to the concrete conditions prevailing in India and the world. Disarmament, general and total, the non-use of force or threat of force in the resolution of international disputes, were the further development by Nehru of Gandhi's doctrine of foreign policy and the world peace, although Gandhi also wanted disarmament and the non-use of force in international relation as described earlier.

As regards the principles of the foreign policy of independent India is concerned they are based on Gandhi's philosophy as well as such principles are the expression of India's historical and cultural heritage. The pillars of India's foreign policy are considered as one of the best in the world so far as its commitments for world peace and security and other tenets of foreign policy is concerned. But the conduct of foreign policy has raised eyebrows as it has led to controversy at many occasions since the beginning of the independence particularly India's policy towards Kashmir problem and its attitudes towards territorial disputes with China.

However, the situation was also responsible for carrying out the principles of foreign policy in practice without properly protecting national interest. When India became free hers was an almost lone voice in the international forums, but as more and more countries achieved independence these principles of foreign policy and international conduct gained greater strength. This led to a worldwide movement of non-alignment, anti-colonialism, non-racialism etc. which cut across regional, racial, geographical and political barriers. As per the desire of Gandhiji, it brought together developing and newly independent countries throughout the world, inspite of their different social, economic and political system. It softened the impact of the cold war on them and contributed to the lessening of tensions in the world.

Despite bitter and strained feelings between India and Pakistan, owing to large-scale mutual killings and partition of the sub-continent, Gandhi persuaded the government of India to give a sum of Rs. 550 million to the newly formed Government of Pakistan.[20] Gandhi was a very broad minded person. He struggled throughout his life against British imperialism who called it as satanic and yet he had not bitterness against the people of Britain. Under this situation as well as learning the lesson from Gandhi; Pt. Nehru did not take India out of the Commonwealth even after its independence.

T.N. Kaul has rightly said that, "Gandhi's India was economically poor and militarily weak and yet it was able to exercise a healthy, peaceful and sobering influence on the war-like trends developing after the World War II. This was because Nehru insisted, as Gandhi had done, on the use of right means to achieve right ends. The right ends could not justify the use of wrong means. Peace could not be maintained through war and domination. Nehru raised his voice against threats to peace and sovereign equality of nations is consonance with the philosophy of Gandhiji."[21]

Foreign Policy of India could not be separated from the interest of the nation and domestic policies. Nor could it ignore the legitimate interests and aspirations of other countries. The art of deplomacy lies in reconciling idealism with self-interest and the interest of other countries. In course of maintaining foreign policies a country has to deal with sovereign states which have different policies and interests. No country, however powerful economically or strong militarily, can impose its will or policies on others for long but in order to stand up to such pulls and pressures it must not be dependent on others. It appears similar to Gandhi's view of self-reliance in domestic affairs as well as foreign policy which India has been following in practice.

Gandhi had insisted on international co-operation, otherwise country might be forced to live in isolation. In the world of today no country can afford to be isolated. But co-operation must be based on equality of nations rather than domination. The sooner India achieves self reliance, the greater will be her capacity to play her due role in national and international affairs. As long as India goes round with the begging bowl seeking aid from the more developed countries, her voice in the world will not be effective at all. Therefore, Gandhi's message of self-reliance is still significant.

Gandhi was neither a capitalist nor communist. He had his own concrete theory in this concern. He was not influenced by the market economy, nor by planned economy, but he was aware of the positive sides of both of them. On the basis of this concept, the concept of mixed economy was emerged in India. India's foreign policy was guided by national interest based on mixed economy particularly in the economic field.

The legacy left by Gandhi to India was many sided and multidimensional. It embraced the individual and his relationship with his family society, country and the world. It also covered the sort of relation that should develop between various sections of the society and between countries and the world in general. It penetrated the deep layers of thousands of years of tradition, culture and religion and produced an awakening that is still strengthening the roots of India's internal and external policies.[22]

Gandhiji had experimented civil disobedience and non-cooperation, the most effective weapon and unarmed people can use against a mighty empire, in south Africa in the struggle against racism. The same method Gandhiji applied in India also. It symbolised the urge for independence and freedom of all nations suffering under colonial and imperialist rule. Gandhi's emphasis on peace and peaceful struggle are more relevant today. India's emphasis on disarmament in general and nuclear disarmament in particular, is but a natural corollary of Gandhi's concept of peace.

Gandhi was against violence and the use of conventional or nuclear weapons. This has influenced India to a maximum extent.

Taking into account the development of nuclear weapon in most of the powerful countries in the world including China and Pakistan, India in spite of demonstrating her nuclear capability has not made a single nuclear weapon. She has unilaterally declared that she would not use nuclear technology except for peaceful purpose. Despite a lot of pressure on India it has not signed the NPT. Why should India give up her sovereign right in this concern particularly when they themselves are not prepared to accept the same. In view of the strategic scenario in the region and the world, India's decision not to accept NPT is absolutely justified. This is according to Gandhi's thought of national prestige and dynamic approach towards security.

India's policy of non-alignment is also based on Gandhian philosophy of peace which gained greater relevance for the newly independent developing countries during the period of cold war. This policy has encouraged India to take part in the world politics actively without being involved itself in any of the military and the power blocks in the world so that it can fearlessly and with confidence fight for world peace and security and organise the third world against imperialism and racism.

As stated earlier, Gandhi was not directly involved in making or formulating India's foreign policy. Gandhi, infact, was the source of thoughts and ideas on the basis of which a policy can be shaped and enforced. He was the champion of non-violent policies to be followed by a non-violent state so as to establish One world based on his concept of *Ramrajya* in the interest of the mankind as a whole. However, he was not orthodox and conservative in approach. He was rather dynamic in outlook and emphasis. Therefore, his thought is perhaps more significant and relevant in today's India and the world.

REFERENCES

1. Kaul, T.N., *Diplomacy in Peace and War*, Vikas Pub. House, New Delhi - 1979, p. 4.
2. Dhawan, G. *The Political Philosophy of Mahatma Gandhi*, Navajivan Pub. House, Ahmedabad, 1962, p. 327.
3. Dhawan, G. *The Political Philosophy of Mahatma Gandhi*, p. 327.
4. *Young India*, March 26, 1937.
5. *Harijan*, June 21, 1942.

6. *Young India*, March 26, 1931.
7. *Young India*, March 26, 1937.
8. *Harijan*, March 23, 1947.
9. *Harijan*, March 22, 1936.
10. *Harijan*, March 23, 1947.
11. G. Dhawan, *The Political Philosophy of Mahatma Gandhi*, p. 341.
12. *Harijan*, June 8, 1947.
13. *Harijan*, Oct. 14, 1939.
14. *Harijan*, Feb. 11, 1939.
15. *Harijan*, April 20, 1940.
16. *Harijan*, Feb. 19, 1940.
17. *Harijan*, May 16, 1936.
18. Dhawan, G. p. 328.
19. Kaul, T.N. *Diplomacy in Peace and War*, p. 1.
20. Kaul, T.N. *Diplomacy in Peace and War*, p. 2.
21. *Ibid.*, p. 2.
22. *Ibid.*, p. 4.

10

GANDHIAN THOUGHT IN THE 21st CENTURY

—GOPAL KRISHNA SINHA

The Twentieth Century has been the time of rapid progress of science and technology. Science and technology has given unlimited power to man. They seem to be responsible for production in man the conviction that man can be made happy by adopting materialistic attitude. They have also produced in man the conviction that he can succeed in bringing heaven on earth by muscles powers. On this account man finds himself in the midst of deep and pervasive crisis such as intellectual confusions, the feeling of insecurity, environmental pollution, mass unemployment, poverty etc. If these multidimensional crisis continue by the turn of the century man seems to be ceased to exist; and no one can think of happy and golden twenty-first century. So the world has been facing challenge of unprecedented one. It is rightly remarked, "the world as a whole has never been so challenged as it is today".[1]

Here a question arises: Will unprecedented global challenge become to an end even in the twenty-first century? The reply is, Gandhian thought is the only system that provides to salvage the world from challenges in the twenty-first century. In other words Gandhian thought becomes more relevant even to the twenty-first century. In this chapter I would attempt to give account of significance of Gandhian thought in the twenty-first century in brief.

Man has two aspects: Physical and Spiritual. Man today wants to remain sound physically; and spiritual nature is over-looked today, but man cannot be considered to be perfect being apart from his spiritual nature. So both physical and spiritual nature of man should be explained jointly. If this status stands till the twenty-first century, he seems to become animal alike even inspite of having the quality of rationality. In that circumstances Gandhian thought would relevant to the twenty-first century. Gandhi's ideology provides a sense of awakening of spirituality in man, which is today absent from human mind.

We see today that science and technology have much more developed. Man, having advance knowledge of science and technology today, might be able to produce the plenty of food or clothing in the twenty-first century by means of sophisticated computer technology. Man may also be able to see and talk with the other persons belonging to other continents while at home or even while travelling. Similarly, twenty-first century may enable modern man and women to produce children of same nature as they have in required number in factories. Again, it may be possible that man would manufacture such sophisticated tools that help him in doing all his works—whether those are intellectual or physical or artistic works.

All these developments of science and technology explain physical nature of human beings only and do not satisfy the goal of entire mankind. The main goal of entire mankind consists in spiritual perfection which can be realized only in end through the life of moral action. There are places and occasions when Gandhiji identifies religion and morality. This is clarified when Gandhiji says "there is no such thing as religion, oversiding morality"; and "There is no religion higher than Truth and Righteousness".[2] He is also a rationalist as well as moralist in his religious outlook. He says, "I reject any religious doctrine that does not appeal to reason and is in conflict with morality".[3] Philosopher and religious men of both India and West are hardly inclined to attach importance to reason, they lay emphasis on exclusively faith for religion. This religious view of Gandhi has a significant position in the twentieth century and people will think of religious and moral action on reason basis, not only on faith basis tomorrow, the twenty-first century.

Apart from the extensive progress of science and technology, three events in the history of West seem also to be responsible for reducing the vitality of man's belief in God as 'pseudo-concept or belief'. First event is Darwin theory of evolution and its principle that man has survived in his struggle for existence. This creates in us the idea that by the proper type of struggle man can go higher and higher. The second event is 'dialectical Marxism' put forwarded by Karl Marx which encourages faith within human heart that through change of circumstances, i.e., social, economical and political changes man can solve all his problems. The third event which latest one is 'philosophical movement' known as 'logical positivism' or 'Scientific empiricism'. This doctrine condemns religion and morality on the basis of verifiability. All three events provide materialistic interpretation that made setback in social, economic and political balance. The whole trend of human life, therefore, is towards the external circumstances and not towards man, a teaching of Christ "will all your worries add a single movement to your life"? has been completely forgotten, the environmental and material comforts come uner external circumstances that creates tension frustration, violence and ecological crisis.

Gandhian thought is a way of life, it suggests that man should be free his mind from tension, hatred, violence, frustration and from ecological crisis so that ill-will, destructive passions and bad tendencies what we can also said mental pollution may not be emerged. Gandhiji believes that unless put a brake on our desire we can make neither ourselves happy, nor can allow others to remain happy. This message of Gandhi would be fruitful even for the twenty-first century and then we can hope for the betterment of the world against the present position of the world.

It seems to be that the twenty-first century will be age of terrorists' and separatists' movements because groupism, communalism, linguistic conflicts and regionalism are being dominated everywhere in the society. If so, no one can save the world from the further division in abundant number. So these wrong values must be eradicated. But how will these values be eradicated? This question has remained unsolved. Gandhian concept of non-violence conceived as science and religious creed as well serves the need of brotherhood and harmony in the society. Gandhi has formally confident that non-violence can be practiced universally.

Today we being lost faith in non-violence are also losing faith in ourselves and depend on others for their works. Dependence is more or less violence or war. Therefore, people should be imparted such discipline that will assist to develop faith in them, and that will evolve the rational nature of man. Gandhi exercised *Satyagraha* conceived as a technique of non-violence to be the most effective discipline for the promotion of self-dependent and self-confident as well as. Gandhi develops an ethico-religious system based on the principles of *Karmayoga*. Gandhian thought that give us an exalted and ascending structure of society has an eternal social significance as it gives probably the only antidote to the root cause of all social problems.

Gandhian thought is not altogether new. But his application of *Satyagraha* into practical life is his most original contribution to the world. Gandhi's philosophy revolutioned the contemporary political social thinking. One who obeys the codes (love or non-violence of Gandhi is called *Satyagrahi*. *Satyagrahi* is likely a kind to *sthitpragya* of *Gita*. It is *Satyagraha* methods through which Gandhiji occupied a unique position in 20th century. Diwakar rightly remarks "It is not Gandhiji who made *Satyagraha* but *Satyagraha* which has made Gandhiji. If it is a matter of obligation between the two, it is *Satyagraha* which has obliged Gandhiji rather than its reverse".[4]

Gandhiji is widely credited with having brought about political awakening and consciousness among the Indian masses. The secret of Gandhi's appeal to those masses was his strict adherence to belief that 'Truth is God and God is Truth'. It seems to me that Gandhi tends to identify God with love or with all spritual forces. God, according to Gandhi is a force of power pervading all existence"[5], not only an entity belonging to transcendental sphere, and is also conceived as "living law in obedience to which the whole universe moves".[6] Love to all is the actual service of mankind. Thus we find that whole of Gandhian thought is the implication of his concept "spiritual humanism". According to Gandhi, the basic principle of life is spirit. So whenever we start to use it. That will be called spiritual use of life provided we use it to know its basis is spirit.

The spiritual humanism of Gandhi is different from material humanism of Marx and moral humanism of Buddha in the sense that it combines the values of the two theories. Man is, no doubt, the crown of this evolution. But he is a part of nature. The analysis of man's powers reveals the truth that man cannot be reduced to nature or equated with nature.

Today the technique of the old great philosophies of India are being revived in consonances with the modern-western emphasising but Gandhian thought so far as it concerned it such a philosophy that is suited for all ages because Gandhi assmilates modern India in thought, lives them in his life and gives them social and political shapes through his philosophy.

That is why Gandhiji also called "Hindu evangelical and puritan".[7] This message of Gandhiji having relevant to the twentieth century has significant also in the twenty-first century. If Gandhian thought is followed today, modern man will be in tune with nature and in complete harmony with his fellow-beings, living beings and non-living beings on earth in future, the twentyfirst century. We hope for the same.

REFERENCES

1. Donald, B. Conroy (quoted), *The Church Awakening to the Global Environmental Crisis in America*, February 17, 1990, p. 149.
2. N.K. Bose (ed.), *Selections from Gandhi* (Ahmedabad, Navjivan Publishing House, 1948), p. 223.
3. *Ibid.*
4. R.R. Diwakar, *Satyagraha: Its Technique and History*, Bombay, Hind Kitabs, 1946, p. 91.
5. N.K. Devaraja, *Philosophy, Religion and Culture*, Motilal Banarsidas, 1974, p. 207.
6. N.K. Bose, *op. cit.*, p. 3.
7. *Cf.* Arnold Kruger (quoted), 'Indian Philosophical Quarterly', Vol. XXII, No. 2, April 1995.

11

RELEVANCE OF MR. M.K. GANDHI AFTER HIS 125th BIRTHDAY AND IN THE 21st CENTURY

—MANORANJAN SARKAR

Many eminent personalities were born in the nineteenth century in India. Shri M.K. Gandhi was one of those great personalities who made substantial contribution in the socio-economic, political movement in India at the fag end of Nineteenth century and in the first-half of the present century. He received informally traditional but rich education in certain values like discipline, hard work, truthfulness, obedience to elders, character building etc. from both his father, Mr. Kaba Gandhi and mother Smt. Putli Bai. Both his father and mother were traditional casteist Hindus belonging to third order in rank named Vaisya. He learnt informally traditional Hindu values of tolerance, religious caste-practices, etc. After matriculation in 1887, at the age of about 18 years, he was sent to England to become Barrister and he became Barrister in 1891 from Grey's Inn, London.

As all traditional so called upper caste Hindus practised the ugly custom of untouchability towards *Ati-Sudras*, Gandhi family was not exception. His mother Smt. Putlibai was Vaisnavite and orthodox principle she practised including untouchability. Young Gandhi obeyed family injunction. He learnt informally from his father qualities like obedience to elders, skill and hard work and good character and from mother he learnt love kindness, respect and politeness. Gandhiji practised these values and preached. All these human values have eternal relevance in society.

As a barrister he could not do well in Bombay High Court and shifted to Rajkot for practising law. This time he got a case and went to Natal in South Africa to conduct that case there. He started his political career at Natal to protest against the colour discrimination (apartheid) policy of South African Government towards blacks of India and that of Asian's origin. To establish their right and dignity, he started peaceful *satyagraha*. This was *ahimsa* and non-cooperation movement against injustice.

The objectives of *Satyagraha* movement were for realising human rights through the process of peaceful demonstration thus hitting the conscience of the wrong doers, oppressors and maintaining maximum restraint even in the teeth of provocations. This *Satyagraha*, according to Gandhiji, would bring change of heart of the oppressors (wrong doers) and would compel them to bring an honourable compromise and solution with the wronged group. This non-violent agitation brought-spectacular results in South African to bring honour and dignity to blacks of India and Asia. Mahamati Gokhale invited Gandhiji to join in "Indian National Movement". Mr. Gandhi returned to India in 1915 and started *Satyagraha Ashram* on the bank of river Sabarmati at Ahmedabad to train volunteers for Non-violent *Satyagraha* movement. His non-violent agitational approach satisfied many. He appeared in the National Movement to give non-violent leadership to protest against "Roulat Law"/"Roulat Act" which intended to deal roughly revolutionary activities and terrorists for attaining home rule/self rule. Thus Mr. M.K. Gandhi gave a new life to the Indian National Movement through the Congress going to the masses through non-violent *Satyagraha* (*Ahimsa* and truth), new concept of protesting oppression and exploitation by foreign rulers.

Gandhiji though practised casteism and untouchability in early life, felt urgent need to reduce its rigour and gradually to remove it from Hindu society through act of moral atonement, change of heart of affluent section e.g., Brahmins and their associates, the Ksatriyas and Vaisyas (Bania-business and industrial communities). He felt need for social reform and also wanted the Congress party's involvement in it. "The Indian National Congress in its annual session in Calcutta in the year 1917, passed the following resolution "The Congress urges upon the people of India, the necessity, justice and righteousness of removing all disabilities imposed by custom upon the depressed classes, the disabilities being of a most vexatius and oppressive character, subjecting those classes to considerable hardship and inconvenience".

The president of the session was Mrs. Annie Besant and the untouchability resolution was moved by Mr. G.A. Watesan of the Madras. It intended to remove all inequalities and injustices before moving and attaining for self-government. Procondition of Home Rule was to shatter the shackles on our feet.

"You cannot be political democrats and at the same time social autocrats. Remember that a man is a social slave, cannot be politically a freeman", said Mr. Rama Iyer while supporting the resolution for social reform. Mr. Gandhiji's entry in Indian politics provided extra strength to social reform policy of the Congress which he learnt from great people like Annie Besant and others and experienced in Natal in South Africa. The Congress and the social reform group were compelled to pass the social reform and untouchability removal resolution because of the fact that the "Depressed classes at Bombay in two general-meetings passed resolutions in November 1917 showing loyalty to British throne, seeking removal of untouchability through socio-political reform making primary education free and compulsory for depressed classes. Resolution also urged the British Government to promote and protect the economic and other interest of the depressed/ untouchables and also the Indian National Congress for removal of all inhuman and disabilities imposed by religion and custom upon the Depressed Classes. So the Depressed Classes clearly intimated the Congress-League scheme (Muslim League) of reform and (capturing political power without removal of social disabilities of the depressed and untouchabilities as Negotiated through Sir Narayan Chanda Varkar. The Congress resolution and Mr. Gandhi's involvement in it became a dead letter and no good came out of it.

This social reform plea of the depressed classes—later on named as Scheduled Castes and *Harijan* by Gandhiji, remains still a big problem. Naming depressed classes as *Harijan* by Gandhiji was vehemently opposed by their leaders.

The social reform scheme of the Congress and Gandhiji was not found favour to those who demanded radical reforms to get themselves free from ugly, unscientific, illogical insulting social practices having sanction from religion.

Gandhiji trained his volunteers and likeminded friends in the Satyagraha Ashram since its establishment in 1915 and overhauled the Congress organisation for its objective functioning with grassroot people (masses). In the year 1919, Gandhiji fully took control of the Congress and established grassroot link and thus obtained sanction from masses. Before this time also social reform resolutions were passed but the same remained as dead letter and the Congress functioned as an elitist organisation and did not go down to the masses to secure their participation in the political movement. It did not believe in mass action. Under leadership of Gandhiji, the Congress took constructive programme of social amelioration. The new Congress was entirely transformed and started functioning as mass socio-political organisation.

In the present state of affairs Gandhiji's style of functioning at the Congress as a mass organisation for amelioration of socio-economic condition of poor/depressed has great relevance today.

The programme of the Congress under Gandhiji to organise depressed classes for a better life, to improve their social mental and moral condition, to induce them to send their children to schools and to provide them ordinary facilities which other citizens enjoy as per resolution of the Bardauli Congress in February 1922 still has great relevance even after 125 years of his birth since these people are still illiterate and poor and live as if they belong to 4th world in 3rd world India. The politicians/parties pass as before constructive resolutions like Bardauli Congress, radical election promises are made but they function like social theories not to meet out social justice to the oppressed. It will require many years to rectify injustice done to the depressed, hence its relevance in 21st Century shall remain. Gandhiji warned in the *Young India* of 29th December 1920—to quote him Non-cooperation against the Government means cooperation among the governed and if the Hindus do not remove the sin of untouchability, there will be no *Swaraj* whether in one year or in one hundred years.... *Swaraj* is as unattainable without the removal of the sins of untouchability as it is without Hindu-Muslim unity". This still has relevance as oppression and gross social injustice to the depressed in different forms continue in our unjust society and the need for Hindu-Muslim unity is still utterly wanting. Gandhiji considered the question of untouchability as mostly moral and religious as degraded by orthodox upper caste Hindus. This perception also has still relevance in the country in general and villages in particular. This was made clear by a letter to Sir Samuel Hoare on 11.3.1932 as a sequence of Second Round Table Conference and constitution of safeguards. The political equality cannot save them from oppression, exploitation, physical torture and other forms of socio-economic deprivation. Depressed classes (Scheduled Castes) could not even get place in the last tier of the fourth tier. Hindi system which Gandhiji wanted to place them in the greater fold of Sudras and named them as Harijan after abolishing rigour of untouchability. But social philosophy, outlook, traditions, vested interests of the so called upper castes and supported by Gandhiji acted as serious internal limitations of bringing social change through reforms. Present day social scenario of differences and discriminations in between upper castes with modern education and with illiteracy are so wide that one will be tempted to place the target group of beneficiaries of social reforms of Gandhiji as people belonging to another world i.e., fourth world in third world India. Indian limiting factors of the ruling class to which Gandhiji belonged has put the object of reforms as servile class and they have become poor and more illiterates.

Mr. M.K. Gandhi entered into a long battle with Dr. Baba Saheb B.R. Ambedkar on the question of emancipation of the depressed classes, social reform and total development of Indian Nationalism and society. Gandhiji emphasised on moral attainment, attitudinal change of the upper castes for removal of untouchability and social development by integrating them as *sudras* of the Hindu system while Dr. Ambedkar wanted social and National Development through abolition of Hindus graded inequality of casteism having implications of economic and political power attached with it and providing constitutional/legal safeguards to promote and protect their interests. "After having gone on fast unto death, he signed the Poona pact. People say that Mr. Gandhi sincerely believed that political safeguards were harmful to the untouchables. But how could an honest and sincere man who opposed the political demands of the untouchables who was prepared to use the Muslims to defeat them, who went on fast unto death, in the end accept the same very demands—for there is no difference between the Poona Pact and the communal Award—when he found that there was no use opposing, as opposition would not succeed? How can an honest and sincere man accept as harmless the demands of the untouchables which once he regarded as harmful? Wrote Dr. Ambedkar in his book *Mr. Gandhi and the*

Emancipation of Untouchables, (M.S. Govt. 1990).

Keeping four castes intact, abolition of untouchability is not only difficult but almost impossible proposition as untouchability is only an extended form of castes. Gandhiji was in favour of castes and social justice is not possible in vertically divided and graded inequal Hindu society. Hence the position is that atrocities on SC/STs and the illiterates and the poor mostly they belong to former depressed and untouchable group of Hindus, are going on and the programme of Gandhiji and the Congress for social reform has not taken place. So the deprived socio-economic groups generally do not like Gandhiji. 'On social problem, Gandhiji wrote in 1921-22 in the *Navajivan*, a Gujrati journal, that "Hindu society has been able to stand, it is because it is founded on the caste system. The seeds of *Swaraj* are to be found in caste system. Different castes are like different sections of military divisions. Each division is working for the good of the whole. A community which can create the caste system must be said to possess unique power of organisation.

The above situation lacked democracy in social front. Since caste system has linkage with economic and political system, Gandhian thought of social reform was not democratic and not relevant to social objective of socialism through democracy.

Gandhiji also assigned with the member of castes, the duty of spreading primary education, political and judicial function, defence, control and restraint on enjoyment with religious section. Inter-castes marriages and inter-dining were not according to Gandhiji, necessary for creation of better society and nationalism. He favoured hereditary occupation by different castes people; as soul of caste system. He decried western European social system and lamented that those countries. Consequently, have not derived from caste system the same degree of advantage which India has derived. This was rather very conservative views and convictions. In 1925, he changed his views and wrote that his support for caste system was for restraint as opposed to control—which he noticed in the society and compared the infinite number of castes as limitations like chain. He desired that small castes should fuse into one big caste and there should be four such big castes so that we may reproduce the old system of four *varnas*" write Gandhiji in *Navjivan* on 3rd February 1925. The ancient Indian *varna* system i.e. (i) Brahmins occupation was learning, (ii) Kshatriyas occupation was warfare/defence etc., (iii) Vaisyas occupation was trade, and Sudras occupation was services to other classes/*varnas* has some relevance even the modern society though not entirely relevant. Gandhiji's changed views were that though one *varna* people might learn the art, skill and knowledge of other *varnas*, and they could do it but they had to follow the occupation of their *varna* by birth. People of a particular *varna* must make a way of earning their living through the occupation assigned to them by birth. These views are conservative, illogical and unscientific though still are found in the system as such, have some relevance in the socio-economic systems—amongst Hindus.

In the field of economic life, Gandhiji stood for opposition to automation and idolisation of *charkha* (spinning wheel) and hand weaving as a matter of philosophy. This philosophy, Mr. Gandhi propounded in his presidential address at a Kathiawad political conference held on 8th January 1925. "Nations are tired of the worship of lifeless machines multiplied *ad-infinitum*. We are destroying the matchless living machines, viz. our bodies by leaving them to rust and trying to substitute lifeless machinery for them. It is a law of God that body must be fully worked and utilised. We dare not ignore it. The spinning wheel is the auspicious symbol of *sharier Yajna*-body labour. He who eats his food without offering this sacrifice steals it. By giving up this sacrifice we became traitors to the country and banged the door in the face of the goddess of Fortune".

Gandhiji's philosophy was also evident in his book *Hind Swaraj* written in 1908, in which he wrote that he was against modern civilisation. He affirmed this views even in 1921 and he opined that India would discard modern civilisation.

In Mr. Gandhi's view-expressed in *Dharma Manthan*, page. 65, is to quote:

> "Western civilisation is the Creation of Satan".

In *Navajivan* on the 8th June, 1921, Gandhiji wrote that "Two paths are open before India, either to introduce the western principles of "Might is right", or to uphold the Eastern principle that truth alone conquers, that truth knows no mishap, that the strong, and the weak have alike a right to secure justice". Even if the labourers legitimate rights are enforced violently, the industry would suffer in the long run and labourers would be affected. According to Gandhiji in caste of European people, possession of wealth does not argue the possession of any moral or spiritual qualities.

These above views of Gandhiji have lost relevance by and large in the present situation of industry and commerce where regional, national and international interaction and competitions exist. Gandhiji's not favouring strike as means of realising labourers demand goes in favour of rich and propertied class. This is not relevant and permitted by the Indian constitutional objectives.

Scientific and technological competition improves production and productivity. Gandhiji's views would protect interest of the moneyed and propertied class if labourers cannot agitate reasonably to improve their lot. The economics of Gandhism are fallacious. Though machineries and western civilisation have brought many evils, these are because of wrong social organisations which have made private property as matters of absolute sanctity. If the machineries and western civilisation have not benefited any section, the remedy is not to condemn them but to alter the structure/organisation of the society so that the benefits will not be usurped by the few but will secure to all. In this sense Gandhiji views that the western civilisation is a "Satan" cannot be treated as relevant in these days of automation and international cooperation for the benefit of society and labourers. The machineries are not only labour saving devices but they have also given relief from drudgery of human labour.

Gandhiji's conception of village *Swaraj* and rural reconstruction cannot be fully achieved in the present time of regional, national and international interaction and competition. Development of at least one trade through caste (*varna*) experiences informal family education is not wholly justifiable and possible. The work of hand spinning, weaving by *charkha*, oil pressing by *ghani*, rice from paddy by *dhekhi* and the like vocation cannot bring self sufficiency. However, these activities have partial relevance in cases of seasonally unemployed labour and women who perform household duties and can save time. "Give back the village and take back the city". Call of Gandhiji was too much conservative and lacked social justice by depriving the villagers from the fruits of modern education. His concept of no modern education through formal system to the villagers had no relevance even 100 years back not to speak of present day relevance. If one section of the nation receives modern education science and technology and rural section is kept confined to informal, and traditional caste vocation, the society will be divided and great injustice will be done to villagers who produce real wealth. In fact this policy has been working resulting division of our polity into ruling class and servile calls one, most educated scientifically developed section and another rural and slum section—caught by the viscious circle of illiteracy and poverty.

He was secular and democrat in his political thought excepting social democracy among Hindus. His secular views of religious co-existence has great relevance now in Indian national life and society.

Gandhiji's views of funding higher education through linkage with industry and user group have great relevance now-a-days. Government and public agencies are now unable to finance huge non-plan budgetted expenditure. All higher and technical education should be linked with industries, trade, commerce and the like profession and those sectors which receive the benefit of such education should be accountable to bear cost and the poor folk should not be burdened by paying such cost of Higher education from Public fund. At present rich, urban sectors receive major benefit from higher and technical education at the cost of illiterate and poor villagers and slum dwellers who contribute more than 90% government revenue. That is the rich receives best and good education at the cost of the poor, servile class people and Gandhiji did not like that. Here is the great relevance of Gandhian thought about educational funding in India. Dignity of labour work-culture, education through work experiences are other relevant areas from which the present society can derive immense benefit as education system have lost values and youngsters are suffering from wrong western values.

To quote Gandhiji:

> "The manner in which Higher Education is given in India is not desirable and I am its enemy. My plan is to create higher level library system, laboratories and research centres where batches of researchers, engineers, chemists and specialist will work. Their responsibilities will be to meet and serve

> the growing needs of the nation. They will work and confer in Indian languages. The fruits of their research will be national property and the work will be Indian original and the cost will be borne legitimately by all". Wrote Gandhiji in the paper "*Harijan* on 9.7.1938".

The University system is still functioning as an ivory tower of knowledge and skill and has not been able to establish linkage with industries etc. Dignity of labour and human values viz., cooperation, support, good character, love, kindness, constructive competition, truth, *ahimsa*, hard labour etc. are utterly lacking resulting violence and disregard for human rights. Here is the greatest relevance of Gandhiji in the 125th year of his Birth and these shall remain relevant in 21st Century and for ever.

12

CONTEMPORARY CRISIS AND GANDHIAN INSIGHT

—D.M. DIWAKAR

Industrial civilization has created an extra-ordinary situation of global crises and has brought the modern world at the crossroad. Today there is fierce competition among advanced countries to control over non-renewable natural resources of the world conquering through advanced technology and military power. Advanced technology has introduced a new kind of taste, pleasure and culture by producing new goods and services to attract the people. This weapon has even worse effect on human civilisation. Arms race has reached almost to non-reversible point. It is difficult to a country to opt out of the competition of war technology even if she wishes to isolate herself. In this process man, for the first time in the history, has captured the kay of power to destroy mankind and human civilisation. In the light of historical facts, as early as 1931, Gandhi warned against industrialisation. Industrialisation is, I am afraid, going to be curse for mankind. Expoitation of one nation by another nation cannot go for all time, and if the future of industrialisation is dark for the west would it not darker still for India."[1]

There is growing realisation that trickle down theory has failed and the benefit of modern industrialisation could not percolate to the lower rung of the society which was supposed to attend the problem of unemployment, poverty and inequality. This is the situation even in the industrially advanced countries of the world. Jobless growth and inequality remain a significant feature of the global economy. Problem of unemployment has been getting compounded with the increasing use of labour saving devices in production. Moreover, estimated workforce of the world which is about 2.5 billion in 1995 is projected to increase further by 2.1 billion by 2025 AD. Thus, future of humanity with this industrial civilization remains darker than ever before added with environmental degradation and ecological imbalances. World Social Summit or Poverty Summit took serious note of it. However its prime concern was on ecological balance and sustainable development.

In a situation of gradually integrating world none of the countries can afford to overlook the world phenomena and her internal contradictions within the country either. It is particularly difficult to those countries of Third World which are dependent on advanced countries for their technology and development aid. In fact many of Third World Countries have already surrendered their economic sovereignty to the neo-imperialist and others are in the process of doing so. Since large numbers of Third World Countries today (in order to overcome their foreign exchange crises which has arisen on account of ever increasing foreign indebtedness and concomitant debt serving, foreign trade deficit, etc.) are literally begging for foreign investment and offering concessions after concessions, it is, therefore, easier for the neo-imperialists to invest in the non-renewable natural resource sectors and acquire monopoly control over them. This has historical evidence: "The more capitalism is developed the more strongly the shortage of raw materials is felt, the more intense the competition and the hunt for resources of raw materials throughout the whole world, the more disperate the struggle for the acquisition of colonies.[2]

India which is second most populous country in the world and the home of about one-sixth of mankind has hardly different conditions than other such developing nations. It is not only that British colonial rule deliberately destroyed its self-reliant and self-sustained economy and production structure to make India a hinterland of British manufactured goods. Even after independence, a wishful copy of western development model of heavy industries, centralised planning and bureaucracy was introduced. Nehru was convinced that rapid development of Indian economy can be made only through big machinery and industrialisation. I am all for tractors and big machinery and I am convinced that the rapid industrialisation of India is essential to reduce the pressure on land, to combat poverty and to raise standards of living, for defence and variety of other purposes.[3]

Contrary to that Gandhi had a different view. He was opposed to mass production by big machines, rather he advocated a system where production is handled by masses: "We have no need for big mills and heavy machinery. If one machine does the work of a hundred men then where are we to employ those hundred men? In a country with such a huge population proliferation of machanised industries will surely lead to large scale unemployment."[4]

The catastrophic blunder was committed when Gandhi who was a mass mobiliser par excellence and who successfully waged freedom struggle against the strongest imperial power was isolated on the question of model building for Indian development on the eve of independence. The power structure, accepting Nehruvian model of development, though shared the spirit of self reliant growth with social justice, summarily rejected Gandhian model for nation building and suffered from inherent contradictions which forced India to give up even Nehruvian model and to enter the arena of dependence paradigm in the year 1991.[5]

It is not that India has not moved ahead after independence. During last 47 years per capita income of the country in real terms has been growing at an annual average rate of 1.5 per cent. There has been marginal improvement in some indicators of development also, i.e., of per capita consumption of coal, steel, petrol and petroleum products, electricity, etc. Per capita availability of foodgrains has grown at an annual average rate of 0.5 per cent. Not only that these material gains to the society have been extremely low but also that they have accrued mainly to the top 20 per cent. 10 per cent engaged in the organised sector and other 10 per cent consists of adults of the rich farmers' families. Remaining 80 per cent of the workforce are either unemployed, underemployed or in disguised unemployment. Moreover, every year about 70 lakh persons are adding to the workforce. Over 40 per cent of the population struggle for square meals amidst poverty. Besides unemployment and poverty, national economy is badly trapped in foreign debt. Latest data available so far, outstanding external debt has increased to Rs. 28,4000 crore by 1993-94 which is 36 per cent of our national GDP. Every Indian on an average owes Rs. 3177 burden of foreign debt. There is no let up of decreasing foreign debt burden even in the financial year of 1994-95. Debt servicing has increased to Rs. 19,160 crore in 1993-94 from Rs. 9,550 crore in

1990-91. The proportion of total revenue used to make interest payment has increased continuously from 40.3 in 1991-92 to 41.9 per cent in 1992-93 and 49.2 per cent in 1993-94. Total debt servicing consisting of interest payments and repayment of debt constitutes 100.7 per cent of total receipts.[7]

Amidst the situation of increasing debt and unemployment huge mass of unemployed and underemployed, enmessed in feudal tradition and ethos has been getting increasingly associated with the dons of underworld (who not only possess black money in abundance but also are the prime mover of the parallel economy running the length and breadth of India and, therefore, wield considerable power) and contributing mainly to the ever increasing organised violence in the country. The issues related to such violence may be anything ranging from petty feuds to communal passion linguistic identities, caste contradictions, ethnic questions etc.

Gandhian Insight

As early as in 1925 analysing the roots of all these evils Gandhi said: "Idleness is the great cause, the root of all evils, and if that root can be destroyed, most of the evils can be remedied without further effort.[8] Again in 1947 speaking on evil effects of unemployment he said: "It there are riots in India today, the cause is to be found in idleness and unemployment."[9] Today we may and may not accept Gandhi but his perception to the future of India and Indian has come true. It is not the question to save Gandhi but to ourselves. He has an aspiration to live for 125 years to evolve a self-reliant and self sustained non-violent social order in India of his dream where no one is first and none is last. Mere political independence from the British colonial rule was only one of the lowest ladder for him. This become obvious when he says: 'unless poverty and unemployment are wiped out from India, I would not agree that we have attained freedom. Real wealth does not consists in jewellery and money, but in providing for proper food, clothes, education and creating healthy conditions of living for every one of us. A country can be called prosperous and free only when its citizens can easily earn enough to meet their needs.[10] His concept of freedom does not and with political and economic manifestations but it goes further to the question of education, culture, and way of life of Indians, when he says: "for me real freedom will come only when we free ourselves of the dominating of western education, western culture, and western way of living which have been in us, because this culture has made our living expensive and artificial, both for men and for women. Emancipation from this culture would mean real freedom for us."[11]

As early as in 1934 suggesting Congressmen at a conference held in Patna, Gandhi warned them who were interested in parliamentary activities: "the Congress will commit suicide if its attention is solely devoted to legislative work. *Swaraj* will never come that way. *Swaraj* can only come through all-round consciousness of the masses."[12] And mere 'legislative work cannot rouse the masses'[13] to their consciousness. In this context besides his prescription of eleven vows, eighteen constructive programmes and *satyagraha* he suggested constructive work organisation to keep the parliament under check by educating and guiding voters."[14] It is unfortunate that Nehru and his successors ignored his perceptions of nation building. He was torn after independence and says "Everybody is eager to garland my photos and statues. Nobody really wants to follow my advice."[15] Consequences are obvious. Elapsing half a century after independence none of the parliamentary party at the national level is in a position to win the confidence of people and to claim its strength as they have failed to identify themselves with the constructive work programme for the society so far.

There will be hardly any disagreement so far as the deterioration in polity and socio-cultural milieu is concerned. All these deterioration on political, economic and socio-cultural front bring the facts home that the diagnosis of the disease from which Indian society suffers, forwarded by Mahatma Gandhi was closer to accuracy. It implies further that his insight to understand the Indian society and its problems was very profound. Even today the only significant change that one may perceive is of compounding problems of unemployment and poverty added with environmental degradation as a product of modern industrialisation. Moreover, these prescriptions of development and nation building which were forwarded in terms of mass production and trickle down theory to address the problem of unemployment, poverty and inequality, almost failed in solving these problems. It is irony of the facts that despite nard realities of stagnation and non-development Gandhian prescriptions have not received proper attention.

When one starts questioning Gandhian relevance, questions need rather to be asked to the problems of unemployment, poverty, inequality, exploitation, communal strife, organised violence, so on and so forth, for which Mahatma Gandhi fought until his last breath and aspired to live 125 years to wage struggle against these evils in order to restore complete independence, peace and nonviolent social order free from exploitation and discrimination. It seems immaterial to ask whether Gandhi as a man is relevant or not but it is very important to ask whether his ideas are relevant. However, personality and thoughts seldom differ. Thus Gandhi or some one else may differ in approach but the ends are almost similar, i.e. to rebuild a society free from coercion, exploitation and discrimination. The issues for which Gandhi mobilised masses for non-violent struggle through *Satyagraha* against the British rule and later, i.e., after independence when he planned to work for mass awareness to take away the encrustation of Indian villager, remove his chronic poverty and illiteracy through constructive work programme in order to have the finest specimen of what a cultured, cultivated, free citizen should be,"[16] are still relevant or not. He was aware of the facts that without cultivating living interest of the masses in nation building work freedom cannot be attained. As he says: "whether the British remain or not, it is our duty always to wipe out unemployment, to bridge the gulf between the rich and the poor, to banish communal strife, to exercise the demon of untouchability, to reform dacoits and save the people from them. If crores of people do not take a living interest in this nation building work, freedom must remain a dream and unattainable either by non-violence or violence."[17]

Unfortunately unemployment, poverty and inequality have lost the place in today's political agenda of the country. So-called liberalization is infact only one way traffic for multinationals. There is no trade off in which India can penetrate global market. Non-tariff barriers are getting stronger, and gradually difficult to enter into the world market. Undoubtedly, developed world is widening its market either through GATT or through New Economic Policy. Small scale industrial sector which was the basic unit for supplementing rural employment and income has been now captured gradually by the capital intensive technology through which human labour is bound to be replaced. Capital-output ratio has gone up remarkably. This process has been faster since late eighties and now the exemption limit to invest in this area has been extended to Rs. three crores.

It is not that arguing idea of Gandhi means to push back to backwardness or stagnation. It is a dynamic one which embodies latest current with such technology as *charkha* of those days through which employment can be ensured without displacing labour. If one interprets *charkha* properly it symbolises to such technology which can be brought easily to the millions of masses as a means of production and the skills of workers can be improved so that the product will find its market even outside in natural process. Modern sophisticated labour saving devices may produce cheaper goods with better quality but neither it is affordable by the masses nor it is sustainable. One should not forget in this context that the benefits of all the development and progress can be harvested only through employment and income. If there is growing unemployment irrespective of technological efficiencies and economies of scale, demand for industrial production is bound to stagnate. Worldwide recession of today is not a different case but an example of similar cases.

Before Gandhi, Ricardo in the early nineteenth century (when the capitalist mode of production had taken firm roots in England) had perceived the limits to growth on account of negardliness of nature in his famous formulation known as the Law of Diminishing Return. It was the post-Keynesian growth theorists who neglected this aspect of 'limits to growth' and propounded the thesis that given the technological level of progress, the economic growth in any society is an increasing function of the saving rate, i.e., the rate of accumulation. They went even beyond this formulation and provided evidence to show that technological progress is positively correlated with accumulation. They failed to take into account of the limits to growth caused by non-renewable resources and the high probability of ecological and environmental degradation inherent in present techno-cultural syndrome available to the world. Increasing use of non-renewable resources of the world coupled with environmental and ecological degradation at a faster pace led to revival of 'limits to growth' theories in recent past. The essential implication of the revived thesis of 'limits to growth' is that the development of mankind is not possible unless the existing techno-cultural syndrome is abandoned.

Gandhi was far ahead and aware of these facts when he said, "In fact, India when it begins to exploit other nations as it must if it becomes industrialised, will be a curse for other nations and menace to the world."[18] He had a firm belief and vision of complete political and economic decentralisation through which self-reliant and self-sustained agro-industrial village republic and village economy can be reconstructed on permanent basis. This economy would be based on local and regional resources, human and material to the satisfaction of local and regional needs, conducted on co-operative basis. In a fully developed village of his dream "there will be no dearth in them of men with a high degree of skill and artistic talent. There will be village poet, village artists, village architects, linguists and research workers. In short, there will be nothing in life worth having which will not be bad in the villages."[19]

This reflects a complete picture of a village-local to Global Village in an Oceanic Circle of a non-violent social order. This can neither be seen in isolation nor can be achieved without living interest of the people which in turn needs consistent struggle and modification of strategy in the light of people's insight and confidence. There are only a few freedom struggles in the history in which common masses were taken into confidence and considered wiser and only a few leaders of the world has accepted their (people's) wisdom. Gandhi is one of them who had profound insight and confidence in masses. Replying to Maurice Frydman in 1939 he said: "The moment you talk to them (the Indian peasant) and they begin to speak, you will find wisdom drops from their lips."[20]

Given the present objective and subjective conditions prevailing in India, it is of a great relevance and provides a catalyst's role for many of us who can learn from them about the social and economic problems and also the solutions as perceived by them. In this process numerous scattered ideas can be gathered from the villagers and a concrete action plan can be made in such a way that it is accepted by them as their own. When it is identified with them they act upon the plan without any aid or support from the outside. The basic assumption behind this hypothesis is that this process once initiated, not only brings the dormant wisdom of the masses to the surface but would also cultivate living interest and enthuse them to take pride in their self perceived unaided actions and, thus make them move from the dependence paradigm to a self-reliance."[21]

REFERENCES

1. Gandhi, M.K., *Young India*, Nov. 12, 1931.
2. Lenin, V.I., *Imperialism the Highest Stage of Capitalism*, Progress Publishers, Moscow, p. 78.
3. Nehru, Jawaharlal (1956), *Discovery of India*, p. 430.
4. Gandhi, M.K., *Collected Works*, Vol. 88, June 26, 1947, p. 213.
5. Diwakar, D.M., 'In Service of Neo-Imperialism', *Mainstream*, March 13, 1993, See also by the same author 'India and Non-Development Paradigm', *Mainstream*, October 2, 1993.
6. Diwakar, D.M., 'Joblessness Syndrone in India', *Gandhian Perspective*, Vol. I, No. 2, Fall, 1993.
7. *Economic Survey*, Government of India, 1994-95, p. 21.
8. Gandhi, M.K., *Young India*, August 27, 1925, p. 299.
9. *The Collected Works of Mahatma Gandhi*, Vol. 88, p. 213, See also Vol. 89, p. 488.
10. *The Collected Works of Mahatma Gandhi*, Vol. 87, p. 463.
11. *Collected Works of Mahatma Gandhi*, Vol. 87, p. 310.
12. *Ibid.*, Vol. 58, p. 11.
13. *Ibid.*, Vol. 58, p. 4.
14. *Ibid.*, Vol. 90, pp. 510-11.
15. *Ibid.*, Vol. 88, p. 33.
16. Gandhi, M.K., *Harijan*, 28.1.1939.
17. *Collected Works of Mahatma Gandhi*, Vol. 77, p. 120.
18. Gandhi, M.K., *Young India*, November 12, 1931.
19. Gandhi, M.K., *India of My Dream*, Navjivan Publishing House, 1947, pp. 97-8.
20. Gandhi, M.K., *Harijan*, January 28, 1939, emphasis from *India of My Dreams*.
21. Prasad, Pradhan H., Self-Reliance Progress versus Dependence Paradigm, *Mainstream*, Vol. 32, No. 11, January 29, 1994 and *Gandhi, Marx and India*, Manak Publications Pvt. Ltd., Delhi 1994.

13

NEW ECONOMIC POLICY: AN ASSESSMENT IN A GANDHIAN PERSPECTIVE

—JAI NARAIN

Good economics is bad politics as the saying goes, an erroneously conceived grabling. Some spontaneous adverse responses may emerge as misplaced reactions to a good policy regime that may be aimed at long-range structural corrections of the growth path as well as the development course of the economy. These policy alternates are like a minor, and sometimes major, surgery that may be painful for a while. Yet, if these pain persist too long and turn out to be too severe, the well intended surgical operation may ricochet to spell disaster. An effective and rational economic policy regime entails sensitive balancing process and amounts to walking on a tight rope of tradeoffs between economic logic and political sensitivities of affected sections of society. Characteristically in the context of political economics, if good economics is not viewed as good politics, it is no economics at all. It is the violation of logical politico-economic parameters that generate antipathy to the ruling authority.

The present economic policy of liberalisation, privatisation and globalisation was launched in the middle of 1991. At the time the economy was at the verge of financial disaster threatened by precarious balance of payment and current account deficit as well as huge monetised budget deficit. The popular economic dole-out without providing the required level of acceleration to the growth of the economy, especially in respect of primary and secondary sectors, had led the nation to the brink of bankruptcy. Foreign exchange, were not enough to meet import need for a week even.

As a result gold had to be mortgaged to the Bank of England in order to save the country from defaulting on international debt repayments that had fallen due. Without restructuring of economic policy, there was perhaps no alternative available that could stem the drift.

In favour of economic polity it was suggested that it was no use being out of step with the given socio-economic conditions in India and global developments. The Prime Minister and the Union Finance Minister promised when they launched the programme that with the assistance of the World Bank and the IMF adjustment credits and investment of foreign capital on a large scale, India will return to the high growth path and prosperity all round.

Giving the *swadeshi* touch to the New Economic policies, the Prime Minister said on January 30, 1995 that it was not different from what was advocated by Mahatma Gandhi, "The economic programme that are being implemented in India since 1991 have been on the lines shown by the Mahatma although they may not be carbon copies adapted as they are to suit changed circumstances."[1] A few days earlier in Calcutta, the Prime Minister stated that the NEP presented a "bypass model of development to take care of poverty in the countryside, as an adjunct to the mainstream middle path.[2] The bypass model was perhaps perceived to provide a human face to the government's developmental forays. But the Prime Minister's Gandhian developmental disguise, and the bypass paradigm to serve the countryside present an oxymoronic confusion.

To begin with the new economic policy gave rise to the much, excited talk about the 'middle class boom' which would provide the social base for it to succeed in contrast to the failed effort of planned, socially based, economic development. The strength of the middle class in India was, variously estimated to be 150 to 200 million, which it was argued, was more than the population of many developed countries and therefore, could provide a social base for rapid economic growth. How exactly was the middle class in India defined or identified, however, been a curious exercise. The official poverty line definition is well known. It was drawn at per capita monthly consumption expenditure of Rs. 20 at 1960 prices. Taking inflation into account this corresponded to Rs. 6400 per household of five per annum in the rural areas and Rs. 7300 in the urban areas in 1982-83. This needs to be further updated to about Rs. 12000 in the present context. So far as those above the poverty line subsistence living are concerned; provision has to be made for the education of children, non-slum housing, decent clothing and other requirements which would put an individual or household in the middle class category. It was estimated in the mid eighties that an annual income of Rs. 35000 was necessary for a household of five to be so counted. For entry to the category of upper middle class, an annual income of Rs. 1,20,000 was found necessary in terms of the price level of 1983-84. Inflation has since eroded the real value of incomes and not less than double—the income calculated on the basis of 1983-84 prices would be necessary for different categories of the middle and upper segments of the population to maintain their standard of living.[3] The top, the extremely thin crust in society can be left out of any such reckoning.

Going by whatever criterion is chosen to determine the number of those in middle class in India—those who pay income tax, those who own a car or even a scooter—it can be safely suggested that this segment cannot possibly comprise more than 15 per cent of the population. Those in the upper middle class who can provide a viable market for high tech items of consumption—consumer durables, private transport or entertainment gadgets will be much less, hardly 5 per cent of the population. The number of those in the middle class is just not adequate to provide a stable social base for an upswing in industrial production on a sustainable basis, let alone contain social tensions when the middle class is so alienated from the mass of the people. It too is not surprising that effective demand in the market has tended from time to time to be quickly satisfied and industries producing the items of middle class interest so often run into demand recession. It is also a characteristic of the middle class that every one belonging to this category work hard to improve his position in society and tried to rise from the lower to upper levels in the hierarchy, while a handful do succeed in entering the ranks of the upper middle class, many are liable to be pulled back to the lower middle and even poor classes, especially if the economy does not grow fast enough and generate new opportunities for gainful employment as has happened in the last four years when indigenous impulses of growth within the economy have been strangled by allowing foreign capital to take over the commanding heights over the economy.

In this condition of stagnation the middle class is very vulnerable and its rank thin very fast. The Indian market has actually been shrinking since the launching of the new reforms.

Another justification for the new economic policy is that it is one of the moves to increase the Gross National Product (GNP), a measure in which human suffering does not figure. Only goods and services that are bought and sold for money count. Music or dance unless they are marketed have no meaning here. This leads to strange conclusions. A housewife's dawn to dusk labour at keeping the home going, however, essential to the family and society, has no value, because she is not paid in money. If she does the same work in another house for payment and someone else is employed to work in her home, they contribute to the country's standing in the GNP race, irrespective of the social cost.

If the estimates of community and voluntary services are included in the calculations of GNP, India would rank much higher. But economists are uncomfortable with consideration of family and community sentiments and pay no regard to culture, craftsmanship and tradition. An underlying objective of the present western oriented model of economic enrichment, hidden from even some local enthusiasts, seems to be to eradicate all values that cannot be exploited monetarily.

Some economists too few, have come to realize the limitation of their prescriptions. Paul Samuelson, one of the best known American economist, eases his conscience in the introduction to his textbook on economics by asking, "Must modern economics make a fatish of quantity at the expense of quality of life? Or can we correct the official statistician's measure of GNP so that it becomes more of a measure of what people will consider to be Net Economic Welfare?"[4] He reproduces a chart showing the wide gap between GNP and NET in the USA, as calculated by two other economists who take into account pollution and other disamenities of urban living. But this is as far as he gets. Economists are out of their depth in non-statistical waters.

In a country with as much poverty and unemployment as our own, it is evident that employment should be the primary objective of economic development. Gandhiji faced this issue squarely "we should be ashamed of resting or having a square meal so long as there is one able bodied man or woman without work or food."[5] He wrote as long as 1921, when the total population of United India was less than the number of Indians below the poverty line today. He was driven to identify himself with them by dressing like them in a loin cloth. Employment unlike voluntary work is measurable. Yet it is scarcely mentioned in official documents like annual economic survey, indicating the low priority it is given in contrast to GNP. But it cannot be taken for granted that employment will rise with GNP. Data for the period after the new economic policy was formally implemented in 1991 show that while GNP has risen, the rate of employment has fallen noticeably meaning thereby that the benefits of increased GNP are being appropriated by a few. By this way we are driving millions of people to desperation and compelling them to do things that militate against their elementary sense of decency, self-respect and human dignity. Our elite is going the Latin American way turning against those very people who sustain its prosperity.

In parallel, another phenomenon is coming into existence among the rich and powerful according to Dr. Manmohan Singh no less. He calls it "Crony Capitalism" (Address at the Centenary Celebrations of Punjab National Bank on January 28, 1995).[6] This is a system of dispensing undue favours at Public expense to friends and relations and build a coterie of scamsters on the basis of which to run a government. Dr. Singh referred to Crony Capitalism in the context of telecommunications, power and oil as examples of how rackets are operated in the name of liberalisation and promoting consumption.

Even if belatedly, Dr. Manmohan Singh has at last recognized some real dangers of mindless marketisation and privatisation. If he were to look more closely at other sectors, he will find equally eloquent examples. The same crony capitalism has been at work in the way the government has treated several Non-Resident Indians, whose involvement in several scandals should serve as a deterrent to anyone who remotely aspires to legitimacy.

The logic is plain: If you are a poor man with no access to a public tap, you are liable to be kicked to death, if you are a petty criminal; you might become a victim of the Bhagalpur syndrome; if you are a corrupt but powerful bureaucrat or banker, you are unlikely to be punished, if you are a mega crook and` a multinational swindler, then you are certain to be treated as a hero, a super patriot, God's gift to humanity. This dread logic can only have horrifying effects on the legitimacy of the political system, the credibility of the elite and stability of the democratic order. This is precisely why some members of our establishment are seriously worried. Dr. Shanker Dayal Sharma; our President, stressed the need to measure success by what policies do for the majority of the people. .

Arjun Sengupta, member-secretary, Planning Commission, and earlier our director on the IMF, has been at pains to warn of the pitfalls of the structural adjustments and argued against the liberalisation of financial sector. Since he had been in IMF and had the first hand knowledge of the working there, this attitude may be the result of that. Similarly, Geethakrishnan, our present director at IMF and former Finance Secretary, has written a remarkable letter to Montek Singh Ahluwalia, our Finance Secretary, expressing the fear that the New Economic Policy could lead to an Indian version of the Mexican disaster. Geethakrishnan had actively supported economic liberalisation in his previous appointment as Union Finance Secretary. He was Mr. Ahluwalia's immediate predecessor. Now he has suggested that India should learn from the turmoil in Mexico due to free market policies. This change in attitude can be attributed to the first hand information in IMF. The letter says, "In free market politics there is no place for compassion or sympathy for the poor while there may be much at stake for the western countries pushing these policies. One did not seem to notice such extreme harshness in all those long years of relationship with USSR but that perhaps is a bygone era. Mexico's development demand that we recognise that we are not a rich country but a nation of serious needs and shortages, we cannot, therefore, identify ourselves with pattern of consumption in wealthy societies that have already resolved the disparities that still afflict up. There is a clear signal for us in India."[7]

Convinced by the truth of contents of the latter, someone took an enormous risk in the public interest by leaking the letter to the media so that the country is acquainted with the state of affair. Clearly, the establishment is now seriously divided over our social and economic policies, and worried at the disparities and the social strife they are creating. Because we cannot have a sustainable economic order in a society riven between the prosperous few and the restless many.

The Mexican crisis comes as great embarassment to the US

Administration and the IMF World Bank combine which had earlier held up Mexico as a show case for structural reforms to the rest of developing world. A quick look at the state of affair in Mexico can put the facts straight.

Mexico adopted the world first socialist constitution in 1917 and during the eighties became the world's most enthusiastic converts to the cause of economic liberalisation. It declared national bankruptcy in 1982. Mexico is a country of 86 million people with 30 per cent of people living in rural areas and agriculture accounting for only 7 per cent of GDP. Over 40 million live below the poverty line and 70 per cent of them inhabit the country side.

Under the economic liberalism it took care to correct the macro-economics to attract investor's attention and became a candidate for stardom. It joined GATT in 1987 and is a member of rich countries club OECD (organisation for Economic Cooperation and Development). Inflation was brought down from 159 per cent in 1987 to single digit and the ratio of the government debt to the GDP fell by more than a half. The Central government deficit was 15 per cent in 1987 and since 1991 its books have been in surplus Exports have been growing at 20 per cent.

Mexico's current account deposit rose to 8 per cent of the GDP, which was higher than the 1982 debt crisis. This was financed by foreign capital. Much of the capital went in consumption and speculative investment in equities and the country over depended on this 'hot money'. Lowering of tariff under NAFTA (North America Free Trade Agreement) gave a fillip to the consumption of consumer goods, reducing saving ratio.

Neglect of micro-economic relations have cost it heavily, small and medium companies were totally neglected and direct bank finance stopped. Only in October 1994 did it allow 40 foreign banks, securities firms and insurance companies with a big bang. Skewed distribution of income received no attention. There is polarisation of wealth with one-fifth of the population getting only 4 per cent of the income. It has about 15 billionaires (in dollar terms) compared with one in 1988. It had built exchange reserves of the 29 billion dollars after more than a decade of economic reforms which with in a span of 10 months last year fell to 7 billion dollars. The financial crisis, triggering capital flights and loss of investors' confidence for an indeterminate future have been caused by huge current account imbalance, resultant pressure on Peso galloping inflation and mismanaged currency devaluation. The devaluation went up 40 per cent and shares crashed beyond 30 per cent. Out-flow of capital is continuing with an increasing rate in the wake of billions of dollars lost by USA and other investors in Mexican stocks, panic gripped financial and stock markets both in North and Latin America. The USA and Canada, the two partners of Mexico in NAFTA have pumped billions of dollars to stabilise Peso and blister confidence. The speed with which these countries have once again put together a rescue package for Mexico is dictated by their own stakes in the economy.

An interesting fact is not out of place here the Mexico has the most economically literate government in the world with many ministers and officials having postgraduate degrees in Economics. A visitor coming for a meeting is greeted with the question: "Are you an economist"?

What can flow in can flow out. Investors have already started putting out from all over the globe. Argentina, Brazil, Philippines, Thailand, Sweden, Spain and Italy are the early victims. Whatever, the cause, immediate and underlying, for Mexico predicament, it is a warning for all countries, set on broadly identifical strategies of market led development of economics.

What has happened in Mexico can happen in India because we have close parallels with it. India has at present 22 billion dollars of foreign exchange reserve after 4 years of reforms. It can be no consolation much less assurance that a similar relapse will not take place, and India will not be pushed back to a vulnerable position as in 1991. Because this 22 billion have not been earning of foreign exchange the hard way by competitive exports and for a surplus in current account but by reckless borrowing, combined with opening the doors for inflow of hot money (portfolio investment) for foreign capital to extract speculative profits by operating on the stock markets. The long term direct investment has been small and much of it has been made either in shortgestating high profit making areas or on onerous terms with guarantees of high returns and free repatriation of profits. Since the policy relies on foreign capital as the chief engine for investment and economic growth and looks upon it not as a complementary and additive to but a substitution for optional utilisation of domestic resources, human, material and financial investment and growth are bound to be fitful and sluggish. This has been shown to be the case both in industry and agriculture.

We are indeed so obsessed with the access to dollars that we are unwilling and unable to recognise that it is not dollars that the mass of India want. They are concerned with access to essential commodities and services at affordable prices in rupees. They want employment oportunities and decent return for their labour and are not reconciled to being pushed out of productive activity by capital intensive, labour saving technologies which fascinate a small crust of elite in Indian society. They want gains of growth to be equitably shared.

The irony of the situation is that our elite have become the chief spokesman of the present system. They are initiating the life-styles of the west and of classes which have been once attacked as the expression of exploitation of the colonial people. Indeed, there is double irony. The same instrument of ideology and class consciousness which were important inputs in the national independence movement become precisely the instruments and legitimiser of the present moves. Instead of thinking for themselves, they let the IMF, World Bank MNC combine think for them and provide them with the vital justifications for the new moves.

During the freedom struggle, Gandhi's campaign for the boycott of British goods stirred the entire country. The enthusiasm for the boycott movement was infectious a sort of assertion for our Independence from the stranglehold of foreign goods. This campaign gave a new impetus to Indian entrepreneurship apart from rousing patriotic fervour as part of the freedom struggle. Not only were the first steps taken towards setting up industries, particularly small industries under Indian ownership, but also opening the floodgates of a mighty cultural upsurge in which literature, art and education were overwhelmed by a new sense of Indian nationalism. It inspired a whole host of writers and thinkers, from Tagore to Aurobindo. The rich among the nationalists came forward to provide the resources and whole band of educationists and top engineers and doctors volunteered their services for the nation's cause.

The intellectual ferment led to concrete actions. If Dadabhai Naoroji wrote about the poverty under foreign rule and the way to overcome it, Jamshedji Tata engaged a young Bengali geologist to go deep into the interior of Bihar and Orissa to prospect for iron ore and other minerals. Out of such a search came the pioneering nationalist endeavour to produce our own iron and steel at Jamshedpur looked a small step at the time but turned out to be a giant leap forward in asserting India's economic Independence. Those were the men of vision and ardent patriotism who made this country great, instilling into us a sense of self confidence.

It is precisely this sense of national self confidence which is being mortgaged by our present economic strategy or virtually handing over all the key sectors of national economy to giant multinational corporations from abroad. At that time also, there were critics who felt that this was a movement with a narrow, insular outlook—an extension of Gandhi's Khadi fad. But soon it was clear that it generated a new wave of self-confidence, a feeling that we must be masters of our own economic destiny sought to be crushed by the East India Company and its progenies. The ideological contribution of *swadeshi* movement was that it unmasked the economic exploitation behind political domination of the foreign ruler. Today there is an urgent need to expose the same economic exploitation as leading to the road to political dependency.

Professor J.D. Sethi has termed this phenomena as 'International Economic Darwinism' (I.E.D.) which is a set of relations between nations and peoples on the principles of the survival of the fittest, except that nations or peoples do not disappear, if only because it a neither in the interest of the fittest nor in their power to make the unfit completely disappear. They are obliged to make the least fit survive, but only marginally or as destitutes living in ghettos."[8] If some developing nation tries to break this vicious circle all types of pressures are put on it. Modern Darwinism assumes that peoples and nations will generally remain intact. The North-South distinction is derived from this Darwinism, showing that under all assumptions made so far, no matter how the present order is reordered, it will allow the weaker and more unfit to survive but not to participate in and certainly not to decide the global order. All energies are concentrated to make the weak and unfit dependent on the strong and fit for all the times to come.

We will have free ourselves from this vicious circle. The economy is not a matter of bargain. Nor is it a free play of statistics. Economic rejuvenation requires hard headed decisions. We cannot of course live in isolation. India has to be a part of global market forces with the due stress on the competitive spirit for growth with quality. But economic revival is an exciting proposition. It has to be invigorating self-generating and mass based. Here in lies the test for the nation's nerves. Indeed India's future depends upon the rational choices made today and those to be made from now on. History is full of examples of countries which got crushed under their own follies—just by ignoring the basic human values and cultural roots. Every economic philosophy gains or loses its creditability by its conduct and approach to human beings, especially the have-nots. The liberalisation have to address itself to the liberation of these have-nots from the clutches of poverty and deprivation. Swami Ramkrishna Param-hansa once remarked, 'while seeing good' in all persons and all things, do look for the hole in the pot you purchase." While embracing the World Bank, IMF, economic creed of liberalisation privatisation and globalisation, we should not overlook the 'holes' in the foreign pot and discard the time tested *Swadeshi* pitcher.

REFERENCES

1. *Indian Express*, Chandigarh, 31.1.1995.
2. *Ibid.*, 28.1.1995.
3. *The Tribune*, Chandigarh, 9.2.1995.
4. Samuelson, Paul A. and Nordhaus William D., *Economics* (New York, McGraw-Hill Book Company, 1985), p. 4.
5. *Young India*, 13.10.1921, p. 325.
6. *The Tribune*, Chandigarh, 9.1.1995.
7. *Indian Express*, Chandigarh, 9.1.1995.
8. Sethi, J.D., *International Economic Disorder*—A Theory of Economic Darwinism and A Gandhian Solution. (New Delhi, Vikas Publishing House Pvt. Ltd.), 1991, p. 16.

14

PRAGMATISM OF GANDHIAN VALUES IN CONTEMPORARY WORLD

—K.B.K. SINGH

Gandhi, the embodiment of truth and non-violence is that great thinker of modern times whose thought has added a new dimension to the history of thought. In fact, "Every social epoch needs its great men and when it does not find them, it invents them."[1] The great man of the age is the one who can put into words the will of his age, tell his age what its will is, and accomplish it what he does is the heart and essence of his age; he actualizes his age.[2] By all standards Gandhi is a great man.

But he is not only a great man rather more than that. He is a genius, a thinker, a saint, a philosopher and a theoriest par-excellence. His thought, is comprehensive. It is because of his multi-dimensional thought that the people around the world have remained engaged in exploring, explaining and evaluating the relevance of Gandhian thought for the last five decades. But, the more we explore Gandhism, the more we feel ignorant and thus get involved in knowing about Gandhian thought and its relevance.

It, however, is not possible for anyone to evaluate and present judgement about the relevance, utility and value of one or the other theory of Gandhi. Scholars, intellectuals and leaders throughout the world appreciate and praise Gandhian theories and consider them as the most valued gift to mankind by a naked *Fakir* of India. But there are a few who do not consider Gandhian theories and principles as pragmatic and relevant. Rather they consider them as outdated which do not have relevance for the modern world of today. However, which of the above is justified or true is difficult to accept and assert. But judging from the point of view of the interest and the concern of scholars, leaders and people of the present world, it can be safely accepted that Gandhian thought is useful and relevant for the present world.

In every thought one can find and locate the presence and dominance of certain values which make it relevant and distinct. Gandhian thought too is based on certain values is undeniable. But do the Gandhian values have relevance in the present world? Are they pragmatic and worth acceptance and realization into practice by the people of today? are some of the basic questions which often are debated upon. This is an attempt to make a probe and evaluate the relevance and practicealism of Gandhian values in contemporary world.

But before I proceed to examine the central theme, it would be proper to present a brief discussion of the term value and the context of this chapter.

The term value has been attached different meanings and also defined variously. However, in sociological perspective value is defined as a set of principles whereby conduct is directed and regulated as a guide for individuals and a social group.[4] Mukherjee holds, "Values are socially approved desires and goals that are internalized through the process of conditioning, learning or socialization and that become subjective preferences, standards and aspirations."[5] In fact, values are socially shared and sanctioned ideas, goals and aspirations which are considered good, right and desirable. They find manifestations in the norms of society.[6]

Values work as the vital base of the society. They are essential to the very existence and perpetuation of human race and society. The sub-system of society and societal living of individuals are regulated by the values. In sum, society is the organisation and accumulation of values.

But values grow out of the felt needs. They are the product of human mind. The individuals when faced with problems invents values and adopt them into practice. Thus whatever values now the world have are the product of the minds of individuals or group.[7] However, it would not be an exaggeration and improper to state that the values which we accept and practice are the gift of deliberations on societal problems by the thinkers or philosophers, saints and reformers of different ages. But it is also a fact that the values propagated by one thinker or any other may be both similar and dissimilar to others. Apart from that, even if similar values are advocated by two or more thinkers the means suggested by them to attain and practice such values may differ.

Gandhi dwelt and deliberated upon societal problems and as a consequence propagated values is undeniable. But when we speak of Gandhian values, we must accept that it is an integrated whole composed of different values. In fact, whatever values Gandhi preached and asserted are not new to the world. Because, prior to him such values have been advocated and even remained in practice in human society. If we read *Gita, Ramayan, Veda, Upanishad, Bible* and *Koran* or if we make a probe into the thoughts of Buddha, Mahavira, Socrates, Nanak and many others we may confirm the presence of Gandhian values in all of them. For this reason, Gandhian values have been labelled as heavily influenced by earlier thoughts.

Notwithstanding that, Gandhian values are accepted as something distinct, something new to the contemporary world. It perhaps is due to the fact that the moral tone and the principles contained in the Gandhian values and the means through which Gandhi prescribed to realize such values into practice are quite different if not novel to all others. For instance, Bhattacharya rightly remarks, "Gandhi's social and political philosophy was grounded on certain fundamental postulates. He brought a new message, or, to be more accurate, restated the old truths. But it was his singular credit that he adopted a technique considered value in individual, spiritual and religious life to the secular and collective sphere of human life."[8] But to assert our point of view, let us examine the character and peculiarity of the values Gandhi propagated. It however, would be honest to confine our discussion to the most significant Gandhian values as it would not be possible and relevant as well to take up all the Gandhian values for scrutiny here.

The crucial values which Gandhi advocated, preached, practised and insisted for realization into practice by the human being are the following. They are: Truth, Non-violence, Kindness, Charity, Repentance, Self-purification, Sufferings, Attruism, Tolerance, Sacrifice, Benevolence, Fearlessness, Equality, Continence, Non-possession or voluntary poverty, Humility, Generosity, Freedom, Honesty and Simplicity.[9]

Gandhi preached and asserted only such values which have ever been eulogized by people in all the ages of history. According to him, only by practising such values maintenance and sustenance of human society is possible. Gandhi accepted truth and non-violence as the basic values. Gandhi says, 'Truth means that which exists and that in reality, logically, nothing exists except truth.'[10] He identified truth with God and considered devotion to truth as the sole justification for human existence. Gandhi tied *Ahimsa* (Non-violence) with *Satya* (truth). According to him truth and non-violence are the two sides of the same coin. He considered *Ahimsa* as means and truth as the end. But in Gandhian non-violence cowardice has no place. For Gandhi non-violence is the weapon for the brave. Further, he says that non-violence is meant for everyone as through it only harmonious social order is possible.[11] For Gandhi truth and *Ahimsa* require acceptance and nurturing of the values like kindness, suffering, love, sacrifice and humility.

Gandhi gave great significance to continence and suggested every individual to practise it. Non-possession is the most preferred value for Gandhi. Gandhi maintained that if each retains possession only what he needed for a simple living, no one would be in want and all will live in contentment. There shall be no disparity and exploitation. Wants of everyone would be fulfilling.[12] Gandhi gave highest premium to the practice of honesty, repentence and self-purification. He believed that only through these values a just social order is possible. As said earlier, fearlessness was Gandhi's favourite dictum and value as he believed that "the path of truth was for brave, not of the cowards."[13] Fearlessness for Gandhi meant freedom from all external fear. Fraternity and tolerance, Gandhi considered as essential values to be nurtured by mankind.[14] He said that only by commitment to such values, people irrespective of their caste, class and community can live together and maintain harmony as well as extend co-operation to each other. For Gandhi, equality, justice and liberty are fundamental values through which a perfect social order can be attained and established. In consonance to these values Gandhi cherished the ideal of *Sarvodaya* and *Ram Rajya* society. In such society there shall be no place of inequality, exploitation and injustice.[15]

The above values virtually found new interpretation by Gandhi. In addition Gandhi gave methods to nurture and realize such values into practice. Gandhi had firm conviction that only by inculcating such values among the people and adopting them as way of life by the people we can attain peaceful, perfect and progressive social order and a world free from various ills.

To repeat, with a view to make the aforesaid values effective, useful and to realize them into practice for the sake of well-being of the people and for a just social order, Gandhi gave and insisted upon adopting the methods like: *Satyagraha*, non-co-operation, fast and peaceful movement.[16] Observing on the Gandhian belief about *Satyagraha*, Singh writes, "Gandhi believed that he could bring about a fundamental change in the individual and the community through *Satyagraha* which may be defined as the struggle for truth. *Satyagraha* for Gandhi meant the exercise of the purest soul-force against all injustice, oppression and exploitation.[17] The methods referred above other than *Satyagraha* virtually are the weapons of Gandhian *Satyagrahi*.

On the other hand, Gandhi rejects and denounces all such values which are contrary to above discussed values. They are violence, individualism, materialism, dishonesty, fundamentalism, selfishness, inequality, cowardice, etc. which are as Gandhi considered them detrimental to the proper functioning of the society and the welfare of the mankind. They cause disequilibrium in the society.[18]

Now let us turn to the central issue of discussion that is pragmatism of Gandhian values today as well as for the future. The world in which we are living today is the world of development and progress. Mankind have attained remarkable success in diverse fields, such as science and technology, economy and in other fields which are definite indicators of developments. We have secured comforts, affluence and even command over nature. Nations of the whole world since last two centuries have only one concern and agenda that is to grab all-round development. The race for development is never bad as it brings happiness and welfare to mankind. But the costs which we have paid or paying for such developments are heavy and detrimental to the human society as a whole. Because, in the race of development we have alienated from ethical and universal values. Instead we adopted the new values like individualism, materialism and even conflict for grabbing development and happiness. Diwakar rightly views, "Unfortunately modern science does not care for what can be said to be the value system human beings have evolved through generations by experience. Human values such as peace, love, beauty, joy and so many other values do not come any where in the agenda of science and technology. On the other hand, science boasts that it is value neutral "and recognize quantifiable facts only."[19]

In fact the old order has gone paving way for a new order. But the new order is far from being satisfactory as the mankind has experienced more misery than happiness, more losses than gains, more problems than solutions. If we put a glance or make a probe into the contemporary social world, political culture, economic system and cultural milieu we can safely conclude that they are all gripped with various ills and stand at a cross-road. Individuals, groups and nations are found engaged in the game of self-development, economic hankering, political bossism (*Dadagiri*) at different levels, by breaking all the ethical and social values and rules. The means they adopt for securing their ends are violence or conflict, exploitation, suppression, dishonesty and others which suit the savage world.

Anarchism, terrorism, war, fundamentalism, ethnocentricism, intergroup conflict, prejudice, communalism, crime etc. reign supreme in the present world. In fact, all these have emerged due to erosion of values of the people as well as latter's commitment to the dis-values. Hence at different levels, national and international platforms, leaders, intellectuals and others are making appeals to make the world peaceful free from aggression, hatred, and any other values and actions which are responsible for all the ills. But to achieve a peaceful harmonious order and world free from violence, selfishness, narrowness, exploitation, inequality, injustice, the Gandhian values have been accepted as appropriate means. It is here that Gandhian values hold practical value. Because, such values contain welfare of all. Sorokin who dedicated his book 'Reconstruction of Humanity' to Gandhi has written in it that 'unless man becomes less egoistic and more altruistic, he has no future. To put it in plain words, man must rise above his many-sided egoism, and have regard more for the 'other'. He has condemned political power, and money power because he says, the concentration of these in a few hands is to bring about all kinds of inequalities as well as immoral activity."[20] In fact, the solutions of the problems with which the entire world is infected definitely lies in Gandhian value system. If they are adopted by the individuals and groups as well as the nations in the context of socio-economic and political milieus, that may definitely yield results and confirm the pragmatism of Gandhian values. Diwakar, Unnithan, Kumar and many other Gandhian scholars have examined the relevance of Gandhian values today. They unanimously have viewed that if you want to get rid of the ills of the modern world and intend to install a world free from any form of inequality, exploitation, deprivation and conflict, there is a need to adopt Gandhian values which find manifestation in different theories of Gandhi. Thus pragmatism and relevance of Gandhism is undeniable as they can only rescue human society from the present crisis. The Gandhian values are practical and useful. They will never become outdated. Lord Boyd thus, made an appeal to the world to understand the importance of Gandhian values and adopt them. He said, "Is it possible that these great principles, these wonderful ideals could be applied on a world wide scale? I think the time has come when they can be applied. They must be applied and they will be applied because people realise that there is no other hope with modern science and the abnormal powers which the scientists have let loose for destruction and which cannot be bottled up again. And if non-violent methods be sincerely applied, you create a new world, a world free from poverty or world free from preventable diseases where all mankind, all nations, the wealthiest as well as the poorest, have a very much higher level of cultural and spiritual well-being."[21]

In fact, Gandhian values are pragmatic not because they have ethical base but because they suit for universal application. They are simple, befitting human nature and above all they are logical. Desai rightly holds, "Gandhi's thought is India's most enlightened and modernising gift to the world, the basis for social action which enables each individual and each community to enrich the world's diverse cultural heritage without claiming privilege and hurting another's susceptibility or legitimate interest."[22]

It, now does not need to elaborate further about the pragmatism and utility of Gandhian values for the contemporary and future world as well. People all over world now accept that only by implementing Gandhian values we can solve various problems and ills with which the contemporary world is infected and also can prepare ground for a better future world. Therefore, national leaders, intellectuals and philanthropists are repeatedly stressing upon the need to adopt and realize Gandhian values into practice. But despite that they have failed to receive wide acceptance. None of the nations including even India and the people in general all over the world have been able to conform to the Gandhian values and make them as their norms. However, a tiny negligible fraction of people are there who adhere to and practice Gandhian values, whom we designate as impractical and out of date. In this sense, it can be said that Gandhian values are not considered pragmatic by the people. Perhaps because of the fact that we fear that adhering to Gandhian values would mean non-fulfilment of our selfish ends. Thus we prefer to adopt non-Gandhian values for the sake of self-amelioration and fulfilment of our goals. But on the other hand, we do not hesitate and fail in praising Gandhian values and suggesting others to follow them. Because, most of us are hypocrates we have dual personality. There exists contradiction in our thought and action. None of us, whether politicians, philanthropists, intellectuals or else, virtually have the capability and courage to practise Gandhian values. For this reason, the people in general fail to locate the model personality of Gandhian values.

In fact, there is the need not only to preach and praise but to become the model of Gandhian values like Vinoba Bhave, Gaffar Khan and a few other contemporary Gandhiates who by their deeds or actions can motivate and mobilise the mass to adopt Gandhian values and only by that we can make Gandhian values pragmatic and useful for the future generations.

REFERENCES

1. G.F.W. Hegel, *Philosophy of Right*, English translation with Notes, T.M. Knox, (Great Britain, Oxford University Press, 1958), p. 295.
2. Mary-Engels, *Selected Works*, Two-volume edition (Moscow, Foreign Language Publishing House, 1958), p. 194.
3. R.R. Diwakar, 'Reflections on Conflict Resolution and Gandhian Studies', in *Gandhi-Jyoti*, Journal of Gandhian Thought, Year 8, No. 1, (30th Jan. 1991), p. 1.
4. *International Encyclopaedia of the Social Sciences*, (ed.), Davis L. Shills, Vol. I, (London: The Macmillan Co. and the Free Press, 1968), p. 450.
5. R.K. Mukherjee, A. General Theory of Society, in *The Frontiers of Social Science* (Ed.), B. Singh, (London, Macmillan and Co., 1956), p. 23.

6. Ian Robertson, *Sociology*, (New York, Worth Publishers Inc., 1978), pp. 59-60.
7. For instance see, R.K. Mukherjee in E.S. Bogardus, *The Development of Social Thought*, (Bombay, Allied Pacific Private Ltd., 1964), pp. 635-37, B. Kuppuswamy, *Social Change in India*, (New Delhi, Vikash Publishing House, 1972), p. 67.
8. B. Bhattacharyya, *Evolution of the Political Philosophy of Gandhi*, (Calcutta, Calcutta Book House, 1969), p. 14.
9. *Ibid.*, p. 18 ff, T.K.N. Unnithan, *Gandhi and Social Change* (Jaipur, Rawat Publications, 1979), pp. 39-59.
10. M.K. Gandhi, *Hindu Dharma* (N.P.H. Ahmedabad, 1950), pp. 247-49.
11. See, Unnithan, *op. cit.*, pp. 45-46, *Harijan*, Sept. 15, 1948; S. Radhakrishnan, *Indian Philosophy* (London, George Allen and Unwin Ltd., Vol. I, 1923 & Vol. II, 1927).
12. See, Unnithan, *op. cit.*, p. 52; M.K. Gandhi, *An Autobiography: The Story of My Experiments with Truth*, translated from the Gujarati by Mahadeva Desai, (London, Poenix Press) MCMXLIX.
13. Gandhi cited in Unnithan, *op. cit.*, pp. 53-54.
14. Duncan Ronald, *Selected Writings of Mahatma Gandhi*, (London, Faber and Faber Ltd.), pp. 48-50.
15. K.B.K. Singh, 'Gandhi and Ambedkar on Social Justice' in *Gandhi Jyoti*, Journal of Gandhian Thought, Bhagalpur University, Bhagalpur, No. 1, 15 August, 1992, p. 61, M.K. Gandhi, *Sarvodaya: Its Principles and Programmes* (Ahmedabad, N.P.H. 1951), *et. al.*
16. For detail see, B. Bhattacharyya, *op. cit.*, pp. 281-346; T.K. Unnithan, *op. cit.*, pp. 50-51.
17. Imtiaz Ahmad, *The Hindustan Times*, Oct. 14, 1987.
18. K.B.K. Singh, *op. cit.*, p. 61.
19. R.R. Diwakar, *op. cit.*, pp. 6-7.
20. P.A. Sorokin, *Reconstruction of Humanity*, cited from R.R. Diwakar, *op. cit.*, p. 6.
21. B.P. Singh, "Gandhism Today", *The Indian Nation*, April 13, 1986.
22. M.V. Desai, "Relevance of Gandhi", *The Hindustan Times*, April 21, 1994.

15

MAN-MACHINE DILEMMA AND GANDHIAN VIEW ON SUSTAINABLE DEVELOPMENT

—VIJAY KUMAR

Each developing country that adopts new methods and value orientations has to face the question of what to do with its pre-modern traditional culture. In the great debate over this and related issues, three types of attitudes can be observed:

1 *Traditionalism*, which seeks to reject or to minimize the influx of new ideas and values;
2. *Iconoclasm*, which claims that the new can emerge only on the basis of the destruction of the old; and
3. *Syncretism*, which seeks to create a viable synthesis between new and time-transcending old ideas and values. While Khomeini may be considered as typical traditionalist and Kamal Ataturk and Mao Dze-Dong as typical iconoclasts, Gandhi represents a classical example for a selective syncretist approach. Gandhi was firmly convinced of the time-transcending validity of many ethical concepts of classical religious literature on Hinduism which he regarded as lasting roots of India's cultural greatness. Here he saw a sphere of India's genuine superiority over the west. He explicitly believed that one of the most important steps in the restoration of original greatness of India lay in the regeneration of moral values of our nation. He emphasised that we ought to preserve the old morals that are good and at the same time reform harmful traditions. Gandhi disliked the typically 'colonial' self-contempt of those culturally

uprooted Indian intellectuals who frantically and superficially sought so hard to become westerners without ever really achieving that objective. For him, Indian nationalism included the ability of identifying oneself with lasting values of India's great cultural heritage without a simultaneous rejection of new, useful and dynamic impulses coming to India from across the world. Being well versed in western as well as Eastern culture, he appeared to be a living symbol for the changing times in which he lived as well for the syncretism which he advocated. Regardless of the disputable and indeed often hotly disputed merit of his system or its single component parts, Gandhian philosophy, as developed by himself until the end of his life, represents the base and most systematic Third World ideology of development which are so typical for aspirations and issues that are even now being shared by so many developing countries and the western developed countries are coming to realise their significance.

II

It was Harry S. Truman who truly inaugurated the era of development in his January 25, 1949 speech. He announced a plan for economic growth and prosperity unlimited for the entire world, explicitly including the underdeveloped world. To quote him:

> We must embark on a bold new programme for making the benefits of our scientific advances and industrial progress available for the improvement and growth of underdeveloped areas. . . The old imperialism—exploitation for foreign profit has to place in our plans. . . Greater production is the key to prosperity and peace. And the key to greater production is a wider and more vigorous application of modern scientific and technical knowledge.[1]

This message of Truman has been proclaimed for nearly forty years in countless statements by the political elites of both the East and West. Greater prosperity calls for increased production and more production requires scientific technology remained the powerful *mantra* of the ruling elites in developed and developing countries alike these past four decades. John F. Kennedy, for example, exhorted emphatically the Congress on March 14, 1961, for authorization of financial resources necessary for the Alliance of Progress in the following words:

> Throughout Latin America millions of people are struggling to free themselves from the bonds of poverty and hunger and ignorance. To the North and East they see the abundance which modern science can bring. They know the tools of progress are within their reach.[2]

Truman's grandiloguent idea of development became the fashion, a towering lighthouse guiding sailors towards the costs of prosperity for one and all. But this "beacon on the hill', making science and technology the demigods of the earth, failed to hold the key to prosperity and stand on its feet as the tools of progress to lead the countries of the world toward the sunny uplands of the future.[3]

Today, only in four decades, no one knows how to live with the frightening new Horsemen of the Apocalypse let loose by development of which four are clearly identifiable—a changing climate, genetic depletion, pollution, the breakdown of various immunities and their side effects. Even more difficult than to survive with these environmental changes is the horror of living with the habits of fulfilling the needs (or the 'habits of needing') which the four decades of development have established.[4] Besides, a number of fundamental questions have now arisen. Did the new orientation, in which the 'other' cultures of the world declared as 'developing countries' and given assistance to raise their productive capabilities through science and technology really bring about an end to colonialism? Is our present era definitely a new and effective period in our development or a new stage of West in Imperialism? If that is the case, then how is it that the leaders and intellectuals of 'developing countries' accepted so readily the imperial message of the blessings of science and technology without realising the international political upmanship of the game? and are they in fact, finding the promises of material prosperity fulfilled through the import of modern technologies from the West? Or are they simply inviting destruction of their culture, their natural habitat and a modernized version of poverty? Is the fundamental assumption in regard to the industrial countries that the western wealth was created by modern science and technology valid? Or was it fed from other sources?[5]

III

The assumption 'bewitching the self-conception of modernity' is increasingly being recognized as 'the great illusion of the epoch'. Before we begin to examine the views of Mahatma Gandhi on the development of science and technology, let us examine the view of two Western scholars.

Bertrand Russel, in his book *The Prospects of Industrial Civilisation*, examined the effects of science and technology and found that application of science has been 'in the main immensurably harmful' and it would only cease to be so 'when men have a less strenuous outlook on life'. Russell further asserted:

> Science, hitherto, has been used for three purposes: to increase the total production of commodities; to make wars more destructive; and to substitute trivial amusements for those that had some artistic or hygienic value.[6]

In retrospect, the harmful effects of science Russell complained about shortly after the First World War have all gathered momentum in an explosive fashion since second world war. Their impact in the developing countries has been highly negative—it has increased hunger and misery, it has hindered independent development and it has secured corrupt regimes against popular revolutions in many countries.

The second observation coming from historian Rolf Peter Sieferle is thus:

> Juxtaposed to the 10,000 year. duration of the agrarian system, the industrial system appears as a brief, one-time paroxysm of intoxication in which the resources gathered over many millions of years are used up in a couple of hundred. . . . There is much to suggest that this paroxysm will be followed by a bad hangover.[7]

In the race for development the use of science and technology with the sole objective of economic growth, did neither bring peace on the earth nor prosperity. The concept of development encouraged consumerism that has kept the individual in a state of perpetual dissatisfaction. The dealers of development thrived on two big lies— (1) Nature is a commodity, and (2) Society is exclusively of human beings—which are not true. Nature is not a commodity, and we are including all creation a part of Nature and society is not only of human beings alone as all life is interdependent. Thus a truly developed society is one in which human behaviour is in tandem, equipoise or equibalance with Nature—a state of affairs in which Nature is used to fulfil the basic needs of all beings. Gandhi was true when he said, "Earth provides enough to satisfy every man's need but not every man's greed."[8] The objective of a developed society should be achievement of permanent peace, happiness and fulfilment.

From the beginning development's hidden agenda was nothing else than the westernisation of the world. Decision and disappointment, failures and crimes have been steady companions of development and they tell a common story; it did not work. Piles of technical reports show that development failed, political studies proved that development was unjust, an imposition to perpetuate western dominance on Eastern minds. It was only a myth full of fantasies, which unleashed a lot of passion, a story full of sound and fury signifying nothing. Truman's project was a blunder of planetary proportions. In 1960 the Northern countries were 20 times richer than the southern and in 1980 46 times.[9] Again, "the gap between the rich and the poor is widening. The world has 200 billionaires and perhaps three million millionaires, but 100 million people around the globe are homeless, living on side walks, in garbage dumps, and under bridges."[10] Though average "calories per person has risen from 2,290 calorie a day 30 years ago to 2,700 calories a day in 1990. Despite this advance, the number of chronically undernourished in Africa has grown from 101 million to 168 million in the past two decades. . . . Nearly 13 million children under the age of five died every year as a result of hunger, malnutrition or related diseases and about 2000 million people suffer from a lack of vital micro-nutrients, such as iron, iodine and vitamin A."[11] In India, the per capita income in 1980-81 was Rs. 1,630 and in 1990-91 it was Rs. 2,227 (based on 1980-81 prices), but the rich gained 20 per cent of the top share and 50 per cent of the national income, while the bottom 20 per cent got only seven per cent. In Brazil, top 20 per cent got 67 per cent and the bottom 20 per cent only two per cent. The industrialized rich countries have to face another kind of poverty."[12] "Death by suicide in man under 24 and frequencies in young teenage girls are continuing to rise. . . . Suicide in youngmen aged 15 to 24 have continued; the increase started in mid 1980s. In 1990, the rate was 100 per million of the population compared with 50 in 1950,"[13] a 100% rise in just 40 years.

IV

It is in this context that Gandhian view of a sound and sustainable development is a matter that attracts the attention of the people of the non-western world and right thinking people in the western world. Gandhi was more concerned with the moral regeneration of the Indian people and his concern for political struggle for freedom was secondary. He was deeply convinced that the internal factors are more important than external circumstances in the development and decay of societies; and if the Indians took proper care of their internal and intrinsic conditions, the external causes of slavery, poverty, malnutrition and dependence upon others would disappear. For Gandhi the nationalist movement in India was more than a liberation movement to get rid of the British rule. The struggle for freedom was indeed a response to the encounter with the material western civilization and education as well as political domination and exploitation by the British Gandhi saw in the British occupation of India not merely an alien political domination but also a cultural and economic stranglehold of the western civilization over the Indian people which he wanted to do away with. His ideas about the dangers of western civilization have assumed significance in the context of several issues concerning the survival of the Earth and evolution of a just and viable world order. In fact, long before the west awakened to the perils and limitations of unrestrained economic growth through science and technology, Gandhi pointed out the pitfalls of industrialism:

> Industrialism is, I am afraid, going to be a curse for mankind. Exploitation of one nation by another cannot go on for all time."[14]

Mahatma's objection to the machine was not to machine *per se* but to the use of the machine for displacement or exploitation of human labour:

> I am uncompromisingly against all destructive machinery. But simple tools and instruments and such machinery as saves individual labour and lightens the burden of millions of cottagers I should welcome.[15]

Replying to Rabindranath Tagore, who criticized him for rejecting machinery with all its potentialities for all violating the hard economic lot of man, Gandhi wrote:

> I do want growth, I do want self-determination, I do want freedom, but I want all these for the soul. I doubt if the steel age is an advance upon the flint age. I am indifferent. It is the evolution of the soul to which the intellect and all our faculties have to be devoted."[16]

And on another occasion, he asks:

> Does economic progress clash with real progress? By economic progress, I take it, we mean material advancement without limit and by real progress we mean moral progress which again is the same thing as progress of the permanent element within us."[17]

In answering his own query, be suggests a sharp conflict between the two kinds of progress:

> I hold that economic progress in the sense I have put it is antagonistic to real progress. Hence the ancient ideal has been the limitation of activities promoting wealth. This does not put an end to all material ambition. We should still have, as we have always had, in our midst people who make the pursuit of wealth their aim in life. But we have always recognized that it is a fall from the ideal. . . . I have heard many of our countrymen say that we will gain American wealth but avoid its methods. I venture to suggest that such an attempt, if it were made, is foredoomed to failure. We

cannot be 'wise, temperate and furious' in a moment....[18]

Man are put under a spell by complex technology even when it deprives them of work. Therefore:

> What I object to is the craze for machinery. . . . Men go on 'saving labour', till thousands are without work and thrown on the streets to die of starvation. I want to save time and labour, not for a fraction of mankind, but for all. . . . Today machinery helps a few ride on the backs of millions.[19]

Labour intensive, not capital intensive production, we might interpret him as saying, would often be the best way to show respect for human personality. 'The machine should not be allowed to cripple the limbs of man,'[20] complex technology breeds centralization and violence, as an ideology of economic growth it breaks up "organic" ways of structuring society and destroys the basis of genuine human community. By promoting high mobility it promotes uprootedness, undercuts social stability and creates a bad environment for the nourishment of the soul. Random and widespread introduction of complex technology deprive human beings of the opportunity to do significant manual work; and while material goods and their needs may multiply, the soul shrinks in the process. And he also observes that manual work "will serve to improve. . . . the quality of. . . . intellectual output,"[21] by making life more meaningful and relevant.

V

The Brundtland Commission on Environment and Development in its report *Our Common Future* submitted in 1987, warned the world of the lurking fears and dangers of development caused by irrational use of machines and spread of consumerism and called forth that in order for "development to be sustainable, it must meet the needs of the present without compromising the ability of the future generations to meet their own needs."[22] This report in itself is probably the highest tribute to Gandhi. Though without reference to him it upholds the ideas of Gandhi in various respects. The sustainable development pleaded for by the Brundtland Commission has been subjected to a variety of interpretations but what this actually means is that:

(i) It cannot be achieved in the short run;
(ii) It is based on equity and justice;
(iii) Its approach is balanced and integrative;
(iv) It has common goals—meeting the basic needs of all—but different routes;
(v) It accepts nature not only as resource but as the earthly womb for survival and development of mankind;
(vi) Sustainable development is participatory in nature.
(vii) There should be equity among nations, regions within nations, people and generations.
(viii) There should be balance between economies, ecology and technology; and
(ix) A proper admixture of material and spiritual in human behaviour and conduct.

Gandhian approach to development took care of all these ingredients of sustainable development. He made an attempt to preserve the traditional socio-economic structure to fight poverty and idleness of the masses, to ensure independence and self-respect among people, banish economic exploitation of human beings and nature, to rescue labour intensive means of production from onslaught of capital-intensive based industry; preserve local culture and wisdom accumulated over generations of living within a region; in sum, from all evils of materialism and western civilization which were ruinous for society and humanity. It is really a wonder how he could foresee and forewarn of the dangers of the western way of life, even before its results were visible to the practitioners. One wonders at the relevance of his ideas to the contemporary world.

REFERENCES

1. H. Truman, Inaugural Address, Washington D.C., 20 January, 1949.
2. J.F. Kennedy, Special Message to the Congress, Washington D.C., 14 March 1961.
3. See for details, Wolfgang Sachs, Introduction, in Sachi (ed.) *The Development Dictionary*, London: Zed Books, 1992, pp. 1-6.
4. Ivan Illich, "Needs", in Sachs (ed.), *ibid.*, pp. 88-99.

5. These questions are adapted from Otto Ullrich, "Technology". Sachs (ed.), *op. cit.*, p. 276.
6. B. Russell, *The Prospects of Industrial Civilization*, New York: The Century Company, 1923, pp. 186-87.
7. R. P. Sieferle, quoted in Ullrich, *op. cit.*, p. 280.
8. Pyarelal, *Towards New Horizons*, p. 12.
9. Sachs, 'Introduction', *op. cit.*, p. 3.
10. Alan Thein Durning, 'Income Distribution Worsening" in World Watch Institute (WWI), *Vital Signs, 1992*, New York, W.W. Norton & Co. 1992.
11. FAO, *Fighting Hunger*, Rome: FAO, 1993.
12. Quoted in S. Bahuguna, "Development Redefined", in (*JPA*, July-Sept. 1993, pp. 232-33.
13. *Independent* (daily Newspaper) London, 30.9.1992.
14. M.K. Gandhi, *Hind Swaraj*, p. 37.
15. *Young India*, 12.11.1931.
16. *Young India*, 10.12.1919.
17. Lecture at the meeting of Miner Central College Economic Society, Allahabad, 22.12.1916, in *Speeches and Writings of Mahatma Gandhi*, 4th ed. Madras: G.A. Natesan & Co. n.d. p. 349.
18. *Ibid.*, pp. 353-54.
19. D.S. Tendulkar, *Mahatma*, Bombay: Vullabhai K. Jhaveri and D.G. Tendulkar, 1952, VII, p. 212.
20. From an article by Shri Mahadev Desai in *Harijan*, Reprinted as preface to the edition of Gandhi's *Hind Swaraj* in 1938.
21. *Harijan*, 23.2.1947.
22. *Report of World Commission on Environment and Development*, Oxford, Oxford University Press, 1987.

16

AHIṀSĀ IN THE BUDDHIST AND THE GANDHIAN PERSPECTIVES: ITS RELEVANCE IN THE 21st CENTURY

—BAIDYANATH LABH

Scientific inventions and material developments have brought a revolution in the human life. Today even a middle class man enjoys more ease and comforts because of these developments than what a king of yester years did. Latest developments in the fields of communication, computerisation of more and more means of public and private sectors, medicines etc. are the well recognised examples in this regard. However, there is another side of the coin, too. These ease and comforts and material gains, have intensified the feeling of narrow mindedness, intolerance, mutual distrust as exhibited in the society, as well as at the national and international spheres. International rivalry, tendency of usurping each others' territories, economic sanctions and dominance against other countries etc. have become order of the day. If seen at individual and social level, people have lost peace of their mind. They want to regain the same but do not hesitate in disturbing others for their own sake. Therefore, peace becomes a must for a healthy mind and prosperous society, nation and even for the whole world.

This chapter on *Ahiṁsā* in the Buddhist and Gandhian perspectives is an attempt to search a means for bringing peace in the mind of an individual, and mutual understanding and harmony in the society, nation and even at the international level in the time to come.

With the passage of time and development of civilization, man gradually realized the value of conquer over attachment and aversion. In India, this factor got prominence particularly after the rise and development of the Vedic civilization. The first such conqueror (Jina) *Ṛṣabha* is mentioned in the Yajurveda and the *Śrīmadbhāgavata* besides a galaxy of *ṛṣis* mentioned in different Vedic texts. Later on Mahāvīra, Buddha etc. became conquerors and enlightened the human race with such conquers.

The Buddha, a non-believer in Brahma or *ātman* (permanent soul) thrusted upon the notion that there is no master other than the moral law that governs the whole world. Further he establishes that what one sows one reaps; what we are at present is the result of what we did previously, and what we shall be, is determined by what we do at present—"*Bhāsitaṅ petaṅ, mahārāja, Bhagvatāṃ Kammassakā, māṇavā, sattā, kammadāyādā, kammayonī, kamma-bandhū, kammapaṭisaraṇā. Kammaṅ satte vibhajjati yadidaṅ hīnappanītatāyāḷ ti.*"[1] We know that pain is disliked by us, so it must be by other beings; as it is with us, so it must be with others. The Buddha has told that violence or injury is ignoble. He clarifies that a person indulged in such acts cannot be a noble man.

Na tena ariyo hoti, yena pānāṇi hiṁsati/
Ahiṁsā sabbapāṇānaṅ ariyoḷti pavuccati//ṅ[2]

The Buddha does not approve or support ethics of war and violence. In the Dhammapada he says that victory generates enmity and a defeated person feels pain but only a person who has overcome passion for victory and defeat, enjoys peace within and without:

Jayaṁ veraṁ pasavati dukkhaṁ seti parājito/
Upasantaṁ sukhaṁ seti, hitvā jayaparājayaṁ//ṅ[3]

Anguttaranikāya makes this concept more specific. A violent person creates hell in the world, whereas a non-violent one creates heaven. A person who is either himself indulged in violence or approves violence is considered to be a sinner, an inhabitant of hell. On the contrary, a person who restrains himself from violent acts, discourages others from such acts, and does not approve them, creates heaven on this earth.[4]

However, one point is to be made clear here. Violence may become a necessity in extreme cases. So the Buddha does not teach that evil doers should not be punished. He tells that when evil is spoken of us, or when we are subjected to cruel and unjust treatment (e.g., a group of robbers looting passengers in a train, or a person indulged in outraging chastity of some woman) we should not simply remain silent resenting it, or be offended threat in mind, thinking that hatred is not pacified by hatred in return but by non-hatred and friendliness, as preached by the Buddha:

Na hi verena verāni sammantīdha kudācanaṅ/
Averena ca sammanti esa dhammo sanantano//ṅ[5]

On the contrary, without malice towards those evil-doers, with no resentment, they should be caused to be punished.[6] This is illustrated by the Buddha's own life. When Devadatta tried to create schism in the Buddhist *Saṅgha*, the Buddha rebuked him severely and excommunicated him. When Devadatta won the support of Prince Ajātaśatru and tried to create schism in the *Sangha* again, the Buddha remarked that gains, favours and flattery would destroy a fool. Just as to crumble liver on a mad dog's nose would only make it madder; and that those who are obsessed by evil conditions are doomed to a state of woe.[7] For the sake of good men, bad men must be punished appropriately, as the life and happiness of good men is infinitely more valuable than that of bad men, and for the sake of the just rights of the majority those of the minority may have to be sacrificed. These implications follow directly from the impossibility of not injuring any life and the necessity of causing pain to some life or other.

In the *Mahāparinibbānasutta*, the Buddha has pointed out merits of Vajjian Republic and dissuaded Varṣakāra, the minister of Ajātaśatru from attacking Vaiśālī but has not mentioned anything about immorality of war.[8] However, the Buddha's aversion to war is clear from his statement, that conquests engender hate, the conquered live in misery, but he who is at peace and without passion, lives happily.

The great Buddhist emperor Aśoka, on whose edicts are based the legal systems of the Buddhist countries of South East Asia, does not enjoin 'forgiveness' for each and every time: 'He who harms is to be forgiven, if he is fit to be forgiven.' Only that who can be forgiven, should be forgiven. This is the policy which he thinks is appropriate to inter-personal relations as well as to relations between peoples of different societies, states and nations.[9]

He also concedes that 'victory through arms' may be necessary sometimes, in which case he counsels moderation and peace as far as possible.[10] Indiscriminate forgiveness and peace always and at any cost were not advocated by Aśoka.

Thus, the Buddha gave a pragmatic interpretation of *ahiṁsā*. He improved this concept by adding to it compassion *(Karuṇā)*, urge to do good works. A true Buddhist, always feels concern seeing others in distress and tries to do at his level best to rescue them from that distress. 'May the good done by me alleviate pains of all the beings'—this is the Buddhist ideal.[11]

Ahiṁsā in the Gandhian Perspective

In the 20th century, basing himself on *ahiṁsā* and the doctrine of returning good for evil, Mahatma Gandhi led the Indian nation to independence. During the Second World War and even earlier, Gandhi said and wrote much about the use of non-violence in preventing external aggression, besides using it for liberating oppressed people.

According to Gandhi, love is the source and end of life and the law of human race. While he admits that this cannot be proved by argument, he puts forward five suggestions in this regard, such as, (i) All great teachers have preached love; (ii) had love not been the law of life, we would have perished long ago; (iii) for its execution and exhibition there can be no distinction between man and beast; (iv) all the saints have been living illustrations of the law of love; and (v) what is possible for some men should be possible for all.[12] Many of the developments in science show that what was once impossible became possible later on. Given proper training and leadership, love or non-violence (Gandhi popularised 'love' for *ahiṁsā*) can be practised by the mass. Non-violence is not passivity, but the most active force. It is a quality of heart. The effects of non-violence are not overtly visible, but are lasting and can be experienced and witnessed. Gandhi thinks that while the effects of the Buddha's non-violent activity still persist, that of Chengis Khan's slaughter do not.[13] Non-violence involves fearlessness and ability to resist. Nobody, thinks Gandhi, can practise perfect non-violence, still it can be used in politics as we do it in the domestic sphere.[14]

Non-violence, according to Gandhi, is of three types, such as, (i) that which is used against constituted authority; (ii) that which is applicable during internal disturbances; and (iii) that which can be used against external aggression.[15] So far as internal troubles like communal riots were concerned, the method discovered by Gandhi could not prove to be that much effective. His attempts to form Peace Brigades for this purpose could not succeed. India succeeded in applying passive resistance against an external power. However, India's struggle for independence was not unadulterated non-violence, Gandhi admitted.[16] His non-violent action was not fully successful even in the domestic field in India nor even against constituted authority.[17] India, said Gandhi, has no experience of the non-violence of the strong, so she has not a good example to furnish the world, and no contribution to make to the peace movement.[18] The technique of unconquerable non-violence of the strong, declares Gandhi, has not yet been fully discovered. It was evident from the fact that he had to terminate *satyagraha* movement many a time.

Gandhi's application of non-violence in the international affairs is based on the supposition that human nature is one in its essence, and responds positively to love. Even dictators and aggressors have feeling of tenderness and affection, as seen in their dealing with their family members.[19] 'They have the same soul that I have', remarked Gandhi. Further, a non-violent man does not depend upon the good-will or positive response of dictators, but on God's unfailing assistance. He cannot succeed without a living faith in God.[20] Gandhi thinks that non-violence of the strong can successfully resist external aggression. Complete sincerity, faith in non-violence God's unfailing help are necessary for non-violent resisters.[21]

Gandhian technique is not altogether new for India. As we have seen earlier Jainism, Budhism, Vishnuism etc. have produced outstanding personalities who exemplified non-violence in their life. Gandhi took many good points on *Ahiṁsā* from Buddhism. He went one step further and held that unearned income and living on the physical labour of others is also a form of violence. He brought out full implications of this principle when he said that a truly non-violent man will refuse to be a party to any kind of exploitation.

As seen earlier, Gandhi relies on two assumptions in his

advocacy and practice of non-violence: (i) it is the law of life and the fundamental moral virtue; and (ii) human beings are alike in nature, which is essentially godliness. In the day to day life, these assumptions are not found totally practical or true. However, efforts may be made and target may be achieved to a great extent, if practised sincerely.

Non-violence in the 21st Century

The two clinching arguments against non-violence as conceived by Gandhi are provided by himself. If defensive warfare is wrong, is it right to have the police, law courts and prisons? Non-resistance to evil must not be in foreign affairs, but also in home affairs. Gandhi's answer is that a modern state based on force cannot non-violently resist internal disorder or external disorder. Secondly, can genuine and lasting pacifism be based on a technological civilization which believes in fundamental restlessness, discontent with what one has, perpetual progress and constant increase in material standards of life? Are not strife and discontent implicit in the contemporary civilization itself? Gandhi's answer is honest: 'you cannot build non-violence on a factory civilization but it can be built on self-contained village.'

He envisaged the perfect society as such, where each individual is a law unto himself, living peacefully and with goodwill towards all, controlling all his passions, and living by his own labour. The Buddha calls it the sublime state of living (*Brahmavihāra*) which has four steps, namely *maitrī* (universal life, good-will or friendliness), *karuṇā* (compassion), *muditā* (blissful joy or more clearly joy seeing others prosperity) and *upekṣā* (equanimity).

Of course, Gandhi's perfect non-violent society seems to be a romantic idea, but he himself realized it to a great extent by living a life of such ideas and ideals.

Though Gandhi talks of decentralized and rural economy, for non-violence, which many modern thinkers ridicule, but it is true that despite technological progress in a cut-throat competitive world, it requires adoption of accommodative outlook and thinking for well-being of other's interests for a stable, peaceful and prosperous society. Gandhi himself had said that the reason for the lack of a genuine spirit of love in those who participated in the struggle for Indian independence was lack of their training.[22] Without chastity, adoption of poverty, truth and fearlessness, Gandhi held, non-violent resistance would not succeed. Use of village economy and crafts is the pillar of *ahiṁsā*; and *ahiṁsā* has to start at home, then extend to one's community and country and ultimately to the entire world.

Love, compassion, non-violence, hatred, ill-will, violence etc. are all contradictory attitudes, but they all are creations of our mind only or they all are psychic factors (*caitasikas*) as termed by the Buddha. These factors are universal and common to all the times—past, present and future. Mighty personalities like Hitler, Musolini, Idi Amin etc., and many such other powers perished and their coercive techniques failed ultimately. They are remembered with hatred and disregard but messages of non-violence propounded by our great seers including Buddha, Mahāvīra, Gandhi etc. are still remembered with reverence. It is the biggest proof of its relevance not only in the 21st century but for all the time to come.

REFERENCES

1. *Milindapañho*-Ed. Swami Dwarikadas Shastri, Bauddha Bharati, Vanarasi, p. 22.
2. *Dhammapada*-Ed. & Tr. Bhikshu Dharmarakshita, Motilal Banarasidass, Delhi, verse, 220, p. 85.
3. *Ibid.*, verse 201, p. 65.
4. *Aṅguttaranikāya* III/153.
5. *Dhammapada*, verse 5, p. 2.
6. *Majjhimanikāya* I, PTS, London. pp. 128-29.
7. *Vinayapiṭaka*, II, PTS, London, pp. 7-287.
8. *Dīghanikāya* (Hindi Tr.)—Rahul Sankrityayan, Bauddha Shiksha Parishad, Lucknow, 1979, pp. 275-76.
9. Edicts of Aśoka, the Adyar Library, Madras, 1950, pp. 43, 63.
10. *Ibid.*, p. 49.
11. K. Sacchidanand Murty, Evolution of Philosophy in India, pp. 172-73.
12. M.K. Gandhi, Towards Lasting Peace, Bharatiya Vidya Bhawan, Bombay, pp. 14-15.
13. *Ibid.*, p. 17.

14. *Ibid.*, p. 138.
15. *Ibid.*, p. 132.
16. *Ibid.*, p. 105.
17. *Ibid.*, p. 134.
18. *Ibid.*, pp. 99, 241.
19. *Ibid.*, p. 73.
20. *Ibid.*, p. 64.
21. *Ibid.*, pp. 1, 9, 62, 271.
22. *Ibid.*, p. 137.

17

RELEVANCE OF GANDHIAN THOUGHT IN 21st CENTURY

Rural Development: The Gandhian Experiences

—C.P. SINGH

Development in developing countries like India, necessarily implies rural development, as the real India is seen in her 5,76,126 villages where hunger and disease stalk the land and about half of the population lives below the poverty line. The landless and homeless, agricultural labourers, small and marginal farmers, Scheduled Castes and Scheduled Tribes are among the destitutes and poor. Economic deprivation is compounded by social discrimination and poor hygienic condition making for a helpless and hopeless situation. Alarmed by the magnitude of mass poverty and unemployment, particularly in the rural areas of the country, various poverty eradication programmes with integrated rural development were started as one of their major planks.[1]

In the absence of a participative culture caused by indifferent and apathetic attitude of the masses, the State came to play a lead role in development. Being committed to democratic socialism, India believed in development through planning. Accordingly five year plans were formulated for the balanced and effective utilisation of the country's material, capital and human resources. The development of rural areas and generation of employment to alleviate poverty have been the major concerns of planning[2] process since its formulation in 1952. In the early fifties, the government of the United States offered to finance any programme that India initiated to develop her country-side. To give shape to this offer an agreement was signed in early 1952. It was under this agreement that the first scientific and systematic programme of Community Development was initiated. The goals of C.D. Programmes were set as follows:

(i) to increase substantially the agricultural production in the country,[3] improve nation's communication system, health, hygiene; and promote education in villages; and

(ii) to generate and direct a process of integrated social, economic and cultural changes with the ultimate aim of transforming social and economic life in the villages. Suitable administrative machinery was created at all levels to guide and assist the planning and implementation of the programme. The main responsibility for improving the socio-economic conditions in the villages, however, was rest with the people themselves. It was argued that unless people considered community development as theirs, and valued it as a practical contribution to their own welfare, no substantial result could be gained.[4] Optimum utilisation of scientific and technical know-how was also envisaged under the programme. The central objective was, to develop the capacity of the common man and woman and to organise themselves for working for their own development and the progress of the country, making the best possible use of the technical know-how.

The actual participation of the rural people in activities of their own development was contemplated under the programme. It was sought through the Village panchayats, Cooperative societies, Block Advisory Committees, later known as Block Development Committees and District Planning Committees. Of course, the philosophy and institutional arrangement of Community Development Programme was based on the past experiences of rural development efforts specially before independence. The conceptual aspect of Community Development Programme owes much from the Sriniketan Project of Rabindra Nath Tagore (1921), Marthandam Project of Young Men's Christian Association (1921), Gurgaon Project of F.L. Brayne (1920), Baroda Project of V.T. Krishnamachari (1932) and above all the Sevagram Project of our Father of Nation Mahatma Gandhi (1936), in its two important basic elements. The first was that all aspects of rural life being integrated, we cannot improve one part of it unless we regard rural life as one and indivisible and seek to improve all aspects of it. Sense of self-help, cooperation and participation of the people in this effort of improvement consisted the second element. In other words, people's participation in the process of development and a wholistic perspective to solve the problem were devised as the main elements of the C.D. Programmes.[5]

The scheme seemed to work in the early years of its introduction. However, in three to four years, it lost its initial momentum and the participation and involvement of the people showed a considerable. It was noticed that the Community Development Programme, instead of being people's programme with government's assistance was becoming more and more government's programmes with varying degree of people's participation.[6] The village Panchayats were found weak and ineffective in mobilising masses in support of the programme. The Block Development Committee, created as the main body to enlist popular support and participation in the programme, lacked capacity, vitality and power to represent people's point of view on development matters of their areas. The District Planning Committee was also powerless and ineffective.[7]

The failure of the officially planned, organised and guided C.D. Programme to evoke people's participation provided the basis for what is popularly known as the Mehta Committee Report.[8] It observed that the popular participation in the C.D. Programme enlisted through *ad hoc* advisory bodies was not adequate. The Team recommended setting up of a Three-tier system of elected and organically linked democratic bodies of Panchayati Raj. When the evaluation of Panchayati Raj started, it was felt that the vast majority of weaker section stand isolated from the process and, therefore, they are not in a position to recap the fruits of development. This realisation of the ineffectiveness of Panchayati Raj Scheme led to the 73rd amendment of the Constitution to strengthen the Panchayati Raj bodies and made it more meaningful specially for the weaker section of society.

The Panchayati Raj Scheme was supplemented by the various schemes of Poverty Alleviation Programmes, Integrated Rural Development Programmes, and now Jawahar Rojgar Yojna in the form of centrally sponsored schemes and states sponsored schemes. International agencies also provided huge fund for rural development programmes to support area development, minimum needs, rural employment (NREP), Landless employment guarantee (RLEGP) and other programmes of social services and social utility.[9]

Inadequate Impact of the Programmes

The strategy followed for these programmes of rural development is one that bases all initiative for development on the government and its administration. This approach is a "topdown" pattern of rural development activity in which rural people are always the "objects" or 'recipients' of the ideas, plans, schemes and services from above. Under the Plans various schemes were launched. During the First Five Year Plan priority was given on the transfer of technology or to provide adequate technology for development. In 1960 the priority was shifted to resources and in 1970 to the building of organisation, without any desired impact on rural poverty, unemployment and equitable distribution of development benefits.[10] In the late 70s local capacity, power and motivation of rural people and their meaningful participation in the process of development was emphasised.

However, the total picture emerging out of all these efforts does not, seem to be encouraging. More than four decades of development have not had the desired impact on the socially, economically and educationally handicapped groups of rural people. Their problems could not be resolved through the percolation of general economic growth, and even the special programmes and schemes to equip them with technology, resource, power and motivation could supplement to their living.[11] The majority of Scheduled Castes and Scheduled Tribes, for whom these schemes were specially meant for, are below the poverty line and also face special problems particular to them. They are still continuing to pursue traditional occupation, unable to avail the fruits of economic growth and participate fully in the process of modernisation.[12] The majority of rural people are agriculturist despite the fact that majority of them do not own land or have marginal holdings. Over 33 per cent of S.C. population are agricultural labourers. If the marginal and small farmers are classified among rural poor and are considered together about 1.6 million families per year added to the group classified as rural poor.

The number of landless agricultural labourers increased from 47.5 million in 1971 to 55.5 million in 1981, an increase of 8 million in the period of ten years. Social and economic impoverishment of the rural poor merge to form a single basic factor of backwardness.

In spite of constitutional directives, Legislative enactments, Executive decisions in the form of various programmes and schemes and the efforts of eight plan periods, the basic problem of their poor economic base has remained almost untouched so far.[13] The search for alternative approaches and schemes, administrative innovations and experiments are still going on. The right scheme and strategy is still a far cry.

The basic defect in our planning process lies not in our planning process, but in our thinking for the planning, in a way already laid down by the western thinkers. To solve the problems of rural development in Asian countries, we have to adopt the strategy best suited to the rural needs and rural people who cannot work for their development alongwith the bureaucrats, trained, oriented and directed through the Weber's concept of bureaucracy and bureaucratic style of working. The Gandhian approach and experiment of rural development is a product of his matured and practical wisdom based on the real observation of rural India. His approach to rural development is meaningful to serve our purpose.

Gandhian Approach to Rural Development

Rural development for Gandhi is a "Self-sufficient village economy and self-sufficient village community." He emphasised the utilisation of local resources for development. He endeavoured to set up society that is self-supportive and self-governing. Gandhi wanted to make the affairs of the rural development the work of the rural people itself. On the basis of past rural development experiences of Sriniketan, Mathandam, Sevagram and others, from the Community Development to the present efforts of amended Panchayati Raj bodies people's participation was made the corner stone in the whole process. However, the participation of the people could hardly been achieved. Several field surveys has revealed that in a large number of cases, the beneficiaries are not even aware of what their legitimate rights are. "How much does one get out of the fruits of local social efforts"?, the answer to this question depends very much upon the fact that "How much does one contribute to the local decision making process." The social section contributing maximum to the process will naturally receive maximum from the decision and its implementation. And as the things are, the vast majority of the rural poor stand isolated from the process and, therefore, are not in a position to reap the fruits of development.[14]

Their participation is highly relevant to the effective implementation of programmes and schemes having direct, immediate bearing on their socio-economic life. The Sevagram Project established by Mahatma Gandhi is the answer to all the problems of rural development. The project was a scheme of rural development for a self sufficient and self-governing village community, managed by the rural people themselves.

The Sevagram Project

Mahatma Gandhi started this project in 1936, when he settled in Sevagram, a village near Wardha. It is said that there is no comparison between Gandhi's experiment with other experiments, considering the motivation, objectives, scope and activities. Let us attempt a brief analysis of this programme, to assess its relevance to the present rural development efforts in the country.

The Objective of thc Project[15]

The Sevagram project was based on the four main objectives:

- — Provide services to the less privileged fellow men;
- — rebuilding the villages and regenerating the village resources for the village needs;
- — promoting village industries; and
- — developing all aspects of human life for the purpose of achieving the objectives. Thus, material as well spiritual development of the village community was contemplated as the basic objectives of rural development. Whereas in the present efforts of rural development material well-being is regarded as the basic need of a good and happy life. Spiritual life, has been ignored leading to the moral degradation of our society. Gandhi contemplated a healthy growth of human life, a balanced life so that moral and

material life can be adjusted for the balanced human life.

Programme Strategy

Gandhi considered people's participation and mutual support as the vital requirement for any programme of rural development. To set-up a society that is self-supportive and self-governing he endeavoured the following schemes and strategy:[16]

(i) In order to realise the scheme he began to organise volunteers from all over India. One worker per village was his goal.
(ii) The project spelled out every strategy and technique that is to be utilised while implementing the programmes. Each strategy was planned in such a way that every villager becomes socially responsible.
(iii) One village worker from each village was selected, trained and appointed in his respective villages.
(iv) Each worker was trained in spinning, health, sanitation etc. and he had to promote cottage industries, rural education, environment sanitation and health practices.
(v) The village worker was also to preach the moral and ethical values, the principles of non-violence and self-reliance.
(vi) Production of village consumption goods and removal of untouchability (social evils) was another part of his project, and
(vii) This project also introduced improved agricultural practices and new varieties of crops.

Gandhiji, thus, fully believed on the utilisation of rural people's talents, skills and participation. Gandhiji blended the sense of people's power with spiritual sanctity through his project which was the reflection of his own life style. He presented his life to be followed.

The main lessons derived from the experiments can be listed as follows:

(i) It is entirely a new and balanced concept of rural development encompassing economic as well as spiritual aspects of human life.

(ii) It gave much importance to the basic principle of self-help instead of depending on the government and other financial assistance.

(iii) The inspiring life of Gandhiji was a driving force for all the workers engaged in the task.

The Relevance to the Present Context

The present efforts for rural development is criticised for its much dependence on governmental assistance rather than the self help; for its spoon-feeding approach than the self-reliance and cooperation. It was also said that, despite the administrative innovations from the Balwant Rai Mehta Committee to the Present 73rd Constitutional Amendment Act, people's participation in the process of development could not be ensured and above all, the whole process was taken to task as it failed to provide proper leadership to the rural poor.

This situation clearly explains that the rural poor, specially the Scheduled castes and Scheduled tribes are dependent upon their exploiters for their sustenance and are largely denied opportunity to develop capability of attaining an independent livelihood. The tribals, who have remained somewhat aloof, have to be integrated in the mainstream of national life. To break the vicious circle and isolation therefore, the crying need for these communities is development. In fact, now there seems to be a genuine desire in the country to atone for the mistakes of the past. The general population has now realised what President Kennedy observed,

> "If a government cannot help the many who are poor, it cannot save the few who are rich."

It goes without saying that it is too difficult a task for government agencies to develop the vast majority of weaker section of our society at par with the socially, economically and educationally developed group, until they strive hard for their own development. "The work of the government is to allow scope for individual to undertake action in a national society, independent of state." This is the lesson of Mahatma's experiences of rural development, the practical solution of the problem.

REFERENCES

1. Sharma Sudesh Kumar, "Revitalisation of Panchayati Raj", *IJPA*, New Delhi, Vol. XXXI, July-Sept. 1985, p. 745.
2. Pints R. Marina, "India's Drive Against Poverty", *IJPA*, New Delhi, Vol. XXXIX, No. 2, 1993, p. 147.
3. The objective was emphasised later on, under the C.D. Block Programme leading to the "Green Revolution".
4. Dubey, S.N., "Organisational Analysis of Panchayati Raj Institutions in India", *IJPA*, Vol. XXVIII, No. 2, 1972, p. 254.
5. *First Five Year Plan 1952*, Planning Commission, Government of India, N. Delhi, 1952, p. 106.
6. Dayal Rajeshwar, *Panchayati Raj in India*, Metropolitan, Delhi, 1970, p. 6.
7. Dubey, S.N., *op. cit.*, p. 257.
8. Gaikwad, V.R., *Panchayati Raj and Bureaucracy*, National Institute of Community Development, Hyderabad, 1969, p. 1.
9. Singh, C.P., *Tribal Development Administration in Santhal Parganas,* Mittal Publication, New Delhi, 1991, p. 18.
10. *Fourth Five Year Plan 1969-74*, Government of India, Planning Commission, New Delhi, 1970, p. 415.
11. *Fifth Five Year Plan, 1974-79*, Government of India, Planning Commission, New Delhi, 1974, p. 84.
12. *Sixth Five Year Plan*, Government of India, Planning Commission, New Delhi, 1981, p. 419.
13. *Ibid.*
14. Hooja, B., *Rural Development Administration in India: Some Policy Reforms*, Associated Publishing House, New Delhi, 1985, p. 148.
15. Tiwari, Jaikant, *Rural Development Administration*, Chugh Publication, Allahabad, 1984, p. 105.
16. *Ibid.*, p. 265.

18

RELEVANCE OF GANDHI'S THOUGHTS TO NEW WORLD ORDER

—LAKSHMI BISWAS

The light that has illumined this country for these many years will illumine this country for many more years and a thousand years later that light will still be seen in this country and the world will see it represented the living truth.

These were the memorable words of J. Nehru on the day Gandhi was shot dead. Today we have to consider to what extent the light still shines. The Government of India followed a path that was manifestly divergent from Gandhi's teaching. What then is the reason that makes Gandhi's ideas relevant to day? Today we notice a widespread tendency to brush aside Gandhian ideas as irrelevant to the needs of the modern world. But some of the problems facing the world today have made the world look towards Gandhi once again. In the backdrop of those problems let us switch on to analyse the relevance of Gandhi to new world order.

I shall begin with the problem of war and violence. We are living in an age of mounting tensions—tensions between group and group, class and class, nation and nation. In thought humanity has advanced. Never before perhaps has the acceptance of the ideals of equality, brotherhood and world peace been so ubiquitous, and yet never has humanity or human values stood nearer to the brink of total destruction than they do today under the menace of the atomic bomb. The reason behind this paradox lies in the contradiction between the ends and the means that characterizes the present age.

When we use brute force to settle a problem it sets into motion an opposite force of a like character. This in its turn necessitates the use of greater force, and so the chair of retaliation and counter-retaliation lengthens and strengthens. Here a question arises—Is there a way of breaking this vicious circle? Is there a force different from and better suited for resolving tensions than brute force? Gandhiji shows one i.e. *Satyagraha*, which he called Soul force because it preached against the material force of the opponent the power of thrift. Gandhi was still alive when the first two nuclear bombs dropped on Hiroshima and Nagaski. Undeterred by these monstrous weapons of destruction, Gandhi had said:

> "So far as I can see, the atomic bomb has deadened to finest feeling that has sustained mankind for ages"[1]

Gandhi had not only given warning of doom to mankind, but also asserted his firm faith in non-violence thus.

"One thing is certain. If the mad race of armaments continues, it is bound to result in a slaughter such as has never occurred in history. If there is a victor left, the very victor will be a living death for the nation that emerges victorious. There is no escape from the impending doom save through a bold and uncondition acceptance of the non-violent method with all its glorious implications.[2]

According to Gandhi the real breeding ground of war is in the heart and consciousness of man and it is there that the final battle for peace has to be fought. Hence to the current predicament and the conflict in value systems that underlie the struggle between the industrialized world and the developing world, one has to consider how Gandhi would have looked at this issue and what approach he would have adopted to develop a solution to this highly complex problem. In order to evolve a Gandhian approach one has to understand what non-violence meant to him: how he was able to carry on a continuous struggle without compromising with unacceptable values and how resistance to dominance central to his thought and action. Narayan Desai has rightly opined:

> "With the destructiveness of weapons increased a thousand fold since Hiroshima, the relevance of Gandhi has increased a thousand fold too for mankind."[3]

Secondly, the world is facing the problem of scarcity of resources, we are today threatened with the prospect of shrinking food supplies with a steady increase in the world's population. Soil-erosion and impairment of soil fertility have become world problems. Our present day economy based on money values and desire to exploit nature for quick profits and ultimately it leads to the decline of civilisation. In order to avoid the decline the experts have prescribed the economy of conservation in place of economy of exploitation. And this very prescription had already been suggested by Gandhiji. His system of economy is one of conservation. Pyarelal has analysed Gandhi's system as follows:

(1) Intensive, small-scale, diversified farming as opposed to mechanized, large scale or collective farming, the total yield, as against yield per agricultural worker being the highest under this sytem.
(2) Development of cottage crafts as ancillary to agriculture.
(3) Cattle-based economy, with strict enforcement of the Law of Return viz. to the soil in organic form what is taken out of the soil, without which the health and fertility of the soil cannot be fully maintained.
(4) Proper balance and relationship between animal, human and plant life—social health and stability being essentially the product of a symbiosis of the three; and
(5) Voluntary protecti of both human and animal power against the competition of machinery as the price of social insurance.[4]

These features of Gandhi's economic policy should not be misunderstood as the policy of poverty but the aim of it to uplift the rural economic condition. His economy of non-violence is very much useful for the all-round economic development of the village, nation as well as of the world. He wanted to bring a reconciliation between capital and labour.

The other important 'Gandhian direction' is the close association of the people of an area with their plan. Local planning must be done at the local level by the local people. This will ensure that planning will be able to take care of the real local needs, it will enable the local population to relate their needs to local resources, and impress and on the people the importance of raising resources to meet local needs.

The problem of pollution and ecological imbalances is

another set-back of modern civilization. Today, not only the mother earth is being robbed of its riches but the whole atmosphere is being polluted by poisonous wastes of nuclear experiments, gases produced by burning of petrol and other oils, and industrial wastes poured into rivers, lakes and oceans. According to Gandhi our country has plenty of natural resources, which must be properly expressed and utilized. In a similar tune our modern economists opine that in present situation natural resources are either not put in use or put in wrong uses. Gandhi's love for nature made his ideas the very antidote to the problem of pollution.

The fourth problem of modern time is the problem of over-population, unemployment and disparity of wealth, production is increasing by dint of automatic machines at the same time unemployment and disparity in distribution of wealth are correct social order can be brought about when there was extreme decentralisation in respect of most of the necessities of life. The village should be self-contained producing most of the goods that the village requires for consumption. For only a few needs the village should depend upon centralised production.

In fact, in an age highly devasting weapons, widely scattered small scale industries can be a nation's best industrial defence against surprise serial attack. If on the other hand a nation's industrial power or potential is concentrated within a narrow range of territory, it would be relatively easy for the invader to paralyse the nation's economy at one stroke and secure early victory. Whereas a simple decentralised village economy has far greater spontaneous recuperative power than a more complicated one has.[6]

In this context it is notable to say that even the great industrial, pioneer, Henry Ford came to the conclusion towards the close of his life that his greats centralised factory of Detroit was a dinosaur an absolute monster.[7] And he began advocating economic and industrial decentralisation.

Centralised society of modern era leads to the problem of alienation of human personality. The man acting as a mere cog in the large machinery of centralism feels himself alienated from his world and from himself. Today, industry and science are developing rapidly, emphasis is being laid on man's material needs but man is lacking the feeling of co-operation and love at the same rate. Our scientists say that without the property of coherence the atoms and molecules will fail to be attached with each other and as a result the material world will be smashed just in the same way the force which unites all the living developing. Gandhiji tried to solve these two problems in order to eradicate the problem of unemployment Gandhi emphasised small scale industry. Gandhi's opposition to machines was based on two grounds:

(a) Machines meant large-scale production which resulted in the exploitation of labour by capital. The machines also destroyed the simplicity and harmony of village life, and
(b) Machines were not likely to provide full employment to the Indian millions.

In order to get over the income inequalities, Gandhiji also suggested the introduction of the Principle of Trusteeship. A person should use his talent and the bulk of his earnings not for himself but as a trust for the good of society. As 'trustee' he should be entitled to retain a reasonable rate of commission in recognition of his service or usefulness to society. The decentralised production, will also help in this direction.

Gandhiji thought of attacking the problem of population only from the narrow point of view of population but from a much wider perspective. According to him the effective method of birth control is to raise the standard of living and education. And Gandhi's method of raising the standard of living was to give the means of production to the masses instead of mass production.

Fifth problem is the problem of centrism which is just against the individual dignity, greed and harmful for the social welfare. Today the mentality of a nation is to run after power and wealth even at the cost of humanitarian values. This is why Gandhi said: Centralization as a system is inconsistent with non-violent structure of society.[5] Gandhi believed that a being is called "love". That is why, Gandhi's philosophy of non-violence of pure love is a solution for the problem of alienation. Gandhi's answer to this problem has been laid in his educational philosophy which strove to bring forth the best in the child's personality by giving him opportunities of using his hands by giving him complete freedom, love and self-expression. Experts of the UNESCO came to the same conclusion in their report based on the study of the educational pattern of a score of countries.

Thus it appears that the permanent value in Gandhi's thought and programmes of reform lies in the fact that he views life as an integral whole and not divided into separate water tight compartments. It is, therefore, necessary that only one set of moral laws and values should guide and regulate the various activities of man in the different departments of life which necessitates of the following:

(a) Morality to politics,
(b) Equality to society,
(c) Purity to economy,
(d) Righteousness and simplicity to life, and
(e) Brotherhood to world.

Thus, it seems to me that if we stick to Gandhism in its so-called pure form, it would probably become static, stagnant and even doomed. It may become irrelevant for the simple reason that it may lose touch with the changing reality. For this reason, it would perhaps be true to say that the orthodox Gandhians are the greatest obstacles to the spread of Gandhian ideas. The fundamental essentials of Gandhi's teaching are of abiding value. They are not only relevant today, but shall continue to be relevant for as long as we can foresee. The Gandhian light will continue to shine and to illumine this country for many years.

REFERENCES

1. *Harijan*, 7 July, 1946, p. 212.
2. *Harijan*, 12 Nov., 1938, p. 328.
3. Narayan Desai, *Gandhi's Answers to Central Problem in Gandhi and the Contemporary World*, 1981, p. 43.
4. Pyarelal, *Gandhian Techniques in the Modern World*, 1953, pp 39-40.
5. *Harijan*, 18 January, 1942.
6. Arnold Toynbee's article in *International Affairs* (London, October 1947), p. 468.
7. Herbert Read, *Education for Peace* (London, 1950), p. 26.

19

GANDHIAN THOUGHT IN 21st CENTURY

Relevance and Limitations

—RAM BINOD SINGH

> "The mother earth provides sufficient for the need of the people but not for greed".

The contribution of Mahatma Gandhi to the theory of economic planning and development can hardly be described in words. Gandhi was a rare admixture of a great humanist, a master strategist, a veteran politician and a down to earth economist. Above all Gandhi was realist as well as pragmatist who saw not only the present generation but also posterity.

Gandhian thought is non compartmentalised rather he held the synthetic and holistic view of the man, society and nature but man was the main thrust of his consideration.

Science of economics is in crisis. Rarely would an economist not talk about the crisis while dealing with contemporary issues. When a science is in crisis, it begins to question its own philosophical assumptions and methods and begins a search for alternative paradigms. Unfortunately, the century old reign of positivist economics which included famous models and their numerous versions such as neo-Keynesian, Keynesian and even Marxian economics, lost track of its philosophical assumptions. The disease of economic science have spread to other social sciences also. Technological revolution created more problems instead of solving them. The science of economics ceased to be dismal, it rather became an art of rat race. J.K. Galbraith talked about private affluence and public poverty as the central crisis of the developed capitalist system. It has been of no help to modern economists for raising the discipline of economics to the level of science to keep the value out of their analysis. Values without philosophy lead to vulgarisation of theory and corruption of practice.

If new wants can be generated at a rate faster than the existing ones are satisfied, not only will there be a feeling of deprivation and poverty but society would be obliged to become an arena of rate race among the human beings.

Explosion of knowledge and rapid progress in technological development, instead of solving the old problems, are creating new ones. Technology has taken the shape of Philosophy and it threatens to become the Supreme value. Technology is also looked upon as the answer to crisis created by technology itself. But by changing the structure of production, labour force and demand, technology has also eroded many old economic theories and paradigms. This crisis is getting circular and the curve of economics is a vicious circle.

Notwithstanding all the developments in the field of science and technology human organisation lags behind in capturing and controlling their essence. On the contrary, human beings are becoming victims of science and technology. The greater the thrust of new innovation, the greater the threat of human enslavement. There is bound to be reaction towards total anti-technology which is equally dangerous. To remove an old misunderstanding, it must be affirmed that Gandhi was neither anti-science nor anti-technology.

There are limits within which science and technology can be neutral. Once those limits are crossed, science and technology will become 'Frankenstine monsters'.

In the backdrop of above discussion and focus on the basic transformation that economics undergoes with the fresh metaphysical outlook, credit goes to Gandhi. Not supprisingly, the radical formulation is reflected in Gandhian elements in terms of *swadeshi*, bread labour, *Aparigrah* or non-possession, trusteeship, non-exploitation and equality which form the core of Gandhian economic thought.

During the last few decades, the global economy has been in perpetual crisis. The International monetary system is under stress. There has been energy crisis leading to rethinking about the mode of production and energy-induced technological development. The dialogue between the North and South is more and more full of conflict and suspicion. Capitalist system is suffering from stagflation and persistently high levels of unemployment accompanied by increasing number of poor, hungry and malnourished people. The future is not optimistic.

In the words of the Global 2000 Report to the U.S. President: "If the present trends continue, the world in 2000 will be more crowded, more polluted, less stable ecologically and more vulnerable to disruption than the world we live in now. Despite greater material output, the world's people will be poorer in many ways than they are today".

The crisis in global economy and in economic theory have precipitated a number of fresh ideas. The basic proposition is that the thought and practice of Gandhi also provide a fruitful area for fresh thinking specially in the changed scenario of the world. It is a fact that Gandhian ideas present a complete basis of economic theory. One point should be clearly borne in mind that Gandhian Economics and thought, in spite of its emphasis on the local level, relates to the global economy. In other words, global issues are necessary for the solution of local problems. This follows from the following Gandhian proposition: (1) there is an elite-mass contradiction in every society and (2) the national elites exploit national masses and international elites exploit masses all over the world. It can easily disrupt and destroy a society operating on Gandhian ideas elsewhere. Ramesh K. Diwan and Shushila Gidwani,[1] have suggested that there are six basic concepts that are essential in Gandhian economics. These are all related to each other. There is no hierarchy among them. These are equally important. They are (i) *swadeshi*, (ii) bread labour, (iii) *aparigrah* or non possession, (iv) trusteeship, (v) non-exploitation and (vi) equality. A votary of *swadeshi* will carefully study his environment and try to help his neighbours wherever possible by giving preference to local manufactures, even if they are of an inferior grade or cheaper in price than things manufactured elsewhere. But even *swadeshi* like any other good thing, can be ridden to death if it is made of fetish. To reject foreign manufacturers marely because they are foreign, and to go on wasting time and resources in the promotion in one's country or manufacturers for which it is not suited, would be criminal folly and negation of the *swadeshi* spirit.

Throughout Gandhi's writings run the thread of the importance of work in men's personal growth. The doctrine of bread-labour was inspired by Ruskin, Tolstoy and the *Gita*. In *Young India*, 10 October, 1921, Gandhi asserts:

> "I cannot imagine anything nobler or more rational than that, for, say, one hour in the day, we should do all the labour that the poor do must do and thus identify ourselves with them and through them, with all mankind. It asserts not only the dignity of labour but also avoids alienation which create classes leading to tension, conflict and distrust.[2]

The economic laws have discussed value-in-use and value-in-exchange but in the present day society value-in-threat has engulfed all other considerations. It is imperative for creating power base which is ultimately supported by them.

People concerned about the deprivation and poverty of a large part of humanity question such values of materialism, rationalism and selfishness. Gandhi argued for a different set of values.

To quote:

> "The moral law also requires that the strong men of a community or nation should regard it as their paramount duty to protect the weak and the oppressed. If all men realise the obligation of service, they would regard it as a sin to amass wealth and then, there would be no inequalities of wealth and consequently no famine or starvation".

The concept of non-possession is based on a different morality on the idea that all human beings are equal and that person is not to be exploited by another. The principle of *aparigrah* is an answer to the problems created by the acquisitive society. This society has set impressive records in the expansion of productive capacity, advances in technology, exploitation of resources, affluence and abundance of goods and services. But the same society has also generated severe strains and stresses on life and powerful tendencies towards the degradation of the total environment, social, economic, ecological, political and last but not the least moral. This is not accidental, it is quite natural.

Gandhi has serious doubt about the ability of modern societies to serving on its present course. To corroborate Gandhi the Limit to Growth Study, 1972 asserts:

> "If the present growth trend in world population industrialisation, pollution, food production and resource depletion continue unchanged, the limit to growth on this planet will be reached some time within next one hundred years. The most probable result will be a rather sudden and uncontrollable decline in both population and industrial output".[3]

Similarly, the Cocoyoc Declaration of 1974 observes:

> "The failure of the world society to provide a safe and happy life for all is not caused by any present lack of physical resources. The problem today is not one of physical shortages but of economic and social maldistribution and misuse of these resources. We believe that ways of life and social systems can be evolved that are more respectful of the whole planetary environment. The road forward does not lie through the dispair of doom watching not through the easy opportunism of successive technological fixes".[4]

Trusteeship

Gandhian thought argues that in virtually every society there is an elite mass contradiction. Generally, the elites exploit the masses, consequently every society is divided into two sub-societies. The elites, consisting of small part of population, are politically powerful, economically rich and by and large urbanised while masses are exploited, politically powerless, economically poor and generally rural based.[5] These two societies exist side by side. Privileges are the main characteristics of the elite society.

The Gandhian solution involves, *inter alia*, the concept of trusteeship. Trusteeship is based on the idea that "what belongs to me is the right to an honourable livelihood", no better than enjoyed by millions of others. The rest of my wealth belongs to the community and must be used for the welfare of the community. Here trusteeship implies relationship between privilege and power or the access to power and also involves decentralisation.

Finally, the two elements of non-exploitation and equality can be either explicitly or implicitly encountered throughout the discussion of Gandhian economic thought. Thus the decomposition and analysis of separate aspects and elements of Gandhi's economics, although necessary, is not without problems due to the interrelated and holistic nature of Gandhian thought.

Equality meant to Gandhi primarily two things: First, everybody has a basic right to live, is to meet the basic needs and live a dignified life integrated in community with one's fellow. He was averse to doles and charity. He advocated guaranteed employment for everybody who wants to work. Secondly, equality is absence of exploitation. He endorsed non-exploitative capital labour relation as well as non-exploitation of manual by intellectual labour and above all non-exploitation of the countryside by the city. Now it is clear that the core of Gandhi's economic thought has to be seen in the wider context of his view of human nature reflecting the whole of psychology, philosophy and religion. His system represents a radical departure from the mainstream of economic thought. It becomes remarkably coherent and logical as soon as we accept the axiomatic premises of his world view. Here equality means equality of opportunities open to all in order to be self-supporting and finally self-reliant.

Gandhi observes that democracy and violence can ill go together. The capitalist society is exploitation personified and the essence of all kinds of exploitation is violence. In order to root out exploitation, therefore, non-violent society or state is to be established. Such a society, of necessity, must be based on economic freedom and equality because without economic equality there can exist no real political democracy. Centralisation breeds violence and essence of non-violence is decentralisation. He advocated such decentralisation of economic and political power in the form of, more or less, self-sufficient and self-governing village communities.

In short, the above principles of Gandhian economy are the only practical and rational solution of various ills that harass the modern world. They point out the middle path between blood thirsty capitalism and freedom thirsty socialism.

Gandhian thoughts are economically viable, politically sound, sociologically desirable and ecologically sustainable. The use of violence both invites and suppresses further use of violence, but finally the violent victor is himself vanquished by the power unleashed by him or he becomes a victim of his own institution of violence, allowing the means to swallow the ends (Pakistan and Bangladesh).

The question of relevance of Gandhian thought in the 21st century appears to be absurd as it is universal and relevant for all times to come. But the forces which operate in the national and international fields, it has become imperative to rethink about Gandhian thought. When society is in trouble and deep distress, it has to find out the ways to extricate itself from the crisis. Every revolution has a child in its womb and when revolution succeeds, the child is born and by the passage of time the child attains maturity and ultimately devours the mother. This is exactly true in case of U.S.S.R.

Similar development of science and technological revolution has created situation which is posing problem even for the survival of mankind in terms of its destructive power and all engulfing impact. Now it is being realised by individual thinkers and various institutions that the present mode of production which is energy based and technologically-induced is not sustainable in the long run. Nuclear catastrophe like Bhopal Gas Tragedy, Chernobyl Nuclear Blast in Russia, rising temperature on this planet, hole in the ozone layer, ecological disruption and environmental pollution are posing challenges before the survival of human civilization and existence of mankind. This is true globally and India cannot escape from the final destruction even it it may not be responsible to a great extent.

India presents a different picture as it suffers from absolute poverty, structural unemployment, disparities in the wealth and income and consequent social tension, conflict and unrest. This destatulises social structure and administrative setup. To cap it all, it is rendering the political system irrelevant. Then all the channels for the redressal of genuine grievances are disrupted people are constrained to resort to direct action which generates extremism, terrorism and subversive activities. Ultimately the very foundation of nationhood is threatened. This is the realistic assessment of existing scenario of India. After independence, process of politicisation of crime was started as it was beneficial for the politicians and ultimately it resulted in the criminalisation of political system. Muscle and money power became the main ingredients of not only political system rather it engulfed the administrative structure as well. Consequently corruption has been institutionalised. Instead of inbuilt provision of justice, equity and fair distribution, there is in-built provision of corruption in the process of development itself. Less said is better in the present scenario of the country. In this context Gandhi's views are pertinent. Gandhi said:

> "A violent and blood revolution is a certainty one day unless there is a voluntary abdication of riches and the power that riches give and sharing them for common good".[6]

Almost similar opinion was expressed by Dr. B.R. Ambedkar in his speech in the Constituent Assembly:

> "On the 26th of January, 1950, we are going to enter into a life of contradictions. In politics we will have equality and in social and economic life we will have inequality. How long shall we continue to live this life of contradiction? How long shall we continue to deny equality in our social and economic life? If we continue to deny it for long, we will do so only by putting our political democracy to peril. We should remove this contradiction at the earliest possible moment or else those who suffer from inequality will blow up the structure of political democracy which this Assembly has so laboriously built up".[7]

The above assertions remind the government to be aware of its responsibility for not only for the present generation but also of the well-being of the future generation and Gandhi neatly fits in this scheme in terms of long term survival of minkind with peace and prosperity.

The task, then for the governments of the developing countries is to reorient their development policies in order to attack directly the personal poverty of the oppressed and depressed segments of the society. This the government can do without abandoning their goal of vigorous overall economic growth. But they must be prepared to give greater priority to establishing growth targets in terms of essential human needs. Such a reorientation of social and economic policy is primarily a political task, and the developing countries must decide for themselves if they wish to undertake it. It is obvious that there is no rational alternative to moving towards policies of greater social equity. The situation cannot be ignored when the highly privileged are few and desperately poor are many, and when the gap between them is worsening rather than improving, it is only a question of time before a decisive choice must be made between the political costs of reform and the political risk of rebellion. That is why policies specifically designed to reduce the deprivation among the poorest 40 per cent in developing countries are prescriptions not only of principle but of prudence. Social justice is not merely a moral imperative. It is a political imperative as well.[8]

Mahbub Ul Haque is of the opinion that time has come when we have to take decisive stand to serve the people and thereby the nation as well.

"I have always believed that those who make a virtue out of institutional conformity and loyalty serve their institution far more poorly than those who are willing to express their dissent and pay the necessary price for it.[9]

In India Gandhi paid the price in terms of his life for the conviction which he held and opinion expressed. Thus principles upheld by Gandhi offer solution to the present predicament of mankind and his views were shared by E.F. Schumacher, Myral, Laski, King Martin Luther etc. Not only in India, he is now remembered all over the world and people think, Gandhian thought will lead the humanity to peace and prosperity. There is no rational alternative to Gandhian principles for the salvation of humanity and solution of the problems on long term and sustainable basis. Let us hope and pray for the peace and prosperity of mankind.

If there is one single issue on which there is unanimity among the otherwise badly divided intelligentsia of this country, it is the profound nature of the moral crisis of contemporary Indian society. This was termed as crisis of conscience by Rajendra Puri. There are many dimensions to this crisis, rampant and increasingly visible corruption, decline in ethical standard among the individuals as well as social groups and classes, rapid erosion of morality in public life, collapse of number of institutions that could be termed guardians or Social "Conveyor belts" of morality.

This crisis consists not so much in a generalised degradation of ethical norms in society, as in the absence of a coherent, consistent and viable morality, both individual and public, and hence the prevalence of moral chaos. Praful Bidwai called it acquisitive hedonism.[10]

Acquisitive individualistic hedonism represents the most important of the many moral doctrines that hold sway over Indian society in particular the one-fifth of the population that comprises its best represented, most powerful, most articulate, relatively more privileged elite social strata. This doctrine puts pleasure above all other possible criteria of what is morally right, the individual pursuits of material pleasure is justified. In reality, callousness and cynical unconcern for social consequences of one's pleasure maximising actions, indeed for any aspect of social reality, are the usual concomitants of hedonism.

This kind of acquisitive culture has distorted the economy and society. Prof. K.N. Raj has recently analysed as a essential duality the Indian "Twin nation" in which co-exist a low-growth near subsistence-level majority economy and a high-growth minority elite sector marked by a sharp rise in expendable incomes that fuels the consumer boom. Credit-induced consumption has replaced austerity and Gandhian ideals in India. Consumerism has become all pervasive and it is disrupting the social cohesion and structure.

But question arises what is the wayout. If nothing can be done, then the situation is irretrievable. But where there is a will, there is a way, Gandhi offers solution.

If we take the holistic view of man and society, hopes can be rekindled amidst doom and dispair. According to Gandhi, economics, ethics and religion constitute an indivisible whole. Economics is the science of human welfare, hence, its goal ought to be *sarvodaya*, the welfare of all. The supreme consideration has to be man. The human welfare economics focusing on what Gandhi called the human element, implies the crucial importance of decentralised social economy. Finally, economics has to respect the law of *swadeshi*.

Humanistic approach is needed for the eradication of all the ills which affect mankind all over the world. Even today there is no real physical scarcity of resources to feed the mankind and to keep them in peace and happiness provided the leaders of the world think, work and consider the world as single homogeneous unit.

The concentration of economic and political power will be avoided, tension relaxed and unrest and other social ills finally, eliminated making this planet safe, happy, peaceful and harmonious for the entire mankind. Crisis is our own creation hence, we have to solve it amicably.

In the changing global scenario, modernisation is inescapable even for the third world country like India but rational and selective approach to technology is essential. In the words of Plato, poverty results from increase of man's desires, not from diminution of his property. A new approach based on Schumacher's philosophy of appropriate technology advocating the Small is Beautiful certainly caught the people's imagination. It is pragmatic also for the poor country. His assertion confirms Gandhian concept of self-sufficiency and work for all. He advocated production by masses as against mass production. This implies that appropriate technology should be the basic component of development strategy and where necessary capital-intensive technology may be preferred but selectively in the larger interest of the nation. Man being the main focus reiterated by Gandhi, there is no escape from this strategy in India. This is empirically proved on the basis of Planned Process of economic development. Principle of justice and equity cannot be ignored in the larger interest of the people.

Ideologies are almost always lonely, more adored and admired than followed. Similarly, Gandhi has been more worshipped than followed. Political ideologies are no substitute for self-realisation. One example may suffice the purpose. Atheist Jinnah created theocratic Pakistan while religious Gandhi created secular India. This is mainly due to inner and self-realisation and not due to ideology.

REFERENCES

1. Ramesh Diwan and Shushila Gidwani, *Elements in Gandhian Economics*, Gandhi Marg, Vol-I, August 1979.
2. *Young India*, 10 October, 1921.
3. Limit to Growth Study, 1972.
4. The Cocoyoe Declaration of 1974.
5. Ivan Illich, *Employment, Growth and Basic Needs: A One World Problem*, New York.

6. Mahatma Gandhi: Constructive Programme, Its Meaning and Place, pp. 20-21.
7. Dr. B.R. Ambedkar, Speech in the Constituent Assembly on 25th of November, 1949.
8. Robert McNamara, Annual Speech to the Board of Governors, September, 1972.
9. Mahbub Ul Haque, *Poverty Curtain*, Oxford University Press, Cal. 1978, p. 6.
10. Praful Bidwai, Acquisitive Hedonism, *The Times Magazine*, November-December, 1988.

20

EMERGING WORLD ECONOMIC ORDER AND GANDHI

—R.P. SINGH

Mahatma Gandhi was the greatest leader and reformer of the 20th century.[1] His greatness lies in the fact that by thought and action, by views and deeds he was the perfect followers of truth and non-violence in private as well as in public life. As Gandhi was a practical idealist, he diagnosed the real and deep maladies of modern civilization and prescribed their solutions fully based on truth, simplicity and non-violence.[2] His personality had multi-facets. He ceaselessly worked for the improvement of exploited and suffering masses till his death. His efforts were not limited to a particular aspect of life rather to all aspects—political, social, economic, spiritual and religious, i.e. wherever he found the cause of suffering of humanity he jumped there instantly and fearlessly to serve and help the people suffering.[3] In reality the whole life of Gandhi was constant struggle against social injustice, economic inequality, political suppression, religious fundamentalism and discrimination against humanity.

Gandhi entered politics to emancipate the suffering masses in India in particular and elsewhere in the world in general. Politics according to him and political freedom of India were not an end in itself but a means of welfare of the exploited, deprived and suffering people of the country.[4] The main instrument of exploitation of Indian people during British rule was its economic policy under which there was provision of import of goods manufactured by the British industries and export of raw materials from Indian. This resulted in the destruction of Indian cottage industries. In this regard Pt. Nehru remarked: "the old order of cottage industries was killed, and its rebirth was not permitted by the British authorities in the interest of British industry. In the same way, the old village system was also ended without any rebirth of a new village system."[5] The hint was towards beginning of the zamindari system which robbed the ownership right on land of actual tillers preventing them to bring any permanent reform on their land holdings. As a result of decline of cottage industries and establishment of zamindari system in villages a large number of rural work force became unemployed. The gulf between poverty and prosperity started increasing to alarming level. This situation led to the emergence of rural migration of rural people towards towns where also they were exploited by capitalists. Slums started growing in the cities. Poor people both in rural and urban areas were subjected to abject poverty, inhuman economic and social exploitation by the indigenous as well as British capitalists and ruling classes. The self-reliant village economy was destroyed by the economic policy of the British Government. This situation had sentimentally hurted the soul of Mahatma Gandhi as a result of which he criticised the evils of western civilization and economic system. He suggested to discard them and attempted to get rid of this situation through the adoption of his concept of *swadeshi*. The economic thinking of Gandhi was properly been explained in his Constructive Programme, *Hind Swaraj, Young India, Harijans* and his speeches.

The essence of his economic thinking are non-separation of economies from ethics, non-violence, purity of means, sanctity of labour, simplicity, equalitarianism, emphasis on production of masses in place of mass production, economic decentralisation, regeneration of villages, human values, *sarvodaya* and trusteeship. Gandhi strongly favoured, propagated and adopted in practice the idea of *swadeshi*[6] as an effective and non-violent means for economic and political emancipation of the country during the period of freedom movement. According to Gandhi *swadeshi* is a way of service of the motherland. It does not include competition or opposition to any other nation.[7] Again *swadeshi* does not mean to confine its followers in their own world. It does not teach to hate others, rather it is a religion growing out of love and non-violence. As such it is not a narrow religion. It teaches only to produce goods what can be produced easily within the country and to import those goods which can be produced easily by them. They should also demand for the goods easily produced by us.[8] Thus it is clear that Gandhi's concept of *swadeshi* does not oppose international econcmic co-operation for the genuine cause but it certainly and vehementally opposes the intervention of foreign capital, technical know-how and entrepreneurship. Its purpose is exploitation of weak economy as in case of exploitation of India with the help of economic policy during British rule.

It is essential to present in brief the possible form and nature of the world economic order to be emerged in the 21st century and also its effect on the Indian economy in particular and the weaker economies of other countries in general so as to examine the relevance of Gandhian economic thought in the coming century.

After independence India adopted the policy of mixed economy under the framework of planned economic development. It was more influenced by Nehru's westernised socialistic view than that of Gandhi's realistic and *swadeshi* based model of development. Despite Nehru's view being unsuitable to Indian condition it continued till 1984 and thereafter late Rajiv Gandhi started inclining towards liberalisation of the economy. But after the disintegration of U.S.S.R. and signing the GATT proposal framed by Mr. A. Dunkel. India along with more than 120 countries of the world adopted the policy of economic liberalisation since the early nineties of the present century. Now the entire globe has become one as a result of this policy from the view point of world trade and commerce breaking all the geographical and trade related barriers.

The policy of economic liberalisation predominated by capitalist and developed nations will shape the form, nature and direction of world economic order in the 21st century. This policy will have both good and bad effect in the coming century. As claimed by the developed nations, international economic organizations and supporters of the New Economic Policy, the main gains to be obtained from it will be increased in industrial investment, inflow of foreign exchange in developing countries which will help cure their balance of payment problem, import of new technology, increase in healthy competition, improvement in management and quality and quantity of production.[9] It also aims at providing larger employment opportunities, better and fuller utilisation of natural resources, increase in export through providing larger and unrestricted markets to developing countries, creating incentives and opportunities for adoption of improved and better technologies, environmental protection, modernisation of farm sector and improvement in quality of life etc. For the attainment of above mentioned objects the 1993-94 GATT proposed provides for general agreement on trade in services, reduction in subsidy to farm sector, adoption of Trade Related Investment Measures (TRIMS), substitution of Multifibre Arrangement (MFA) by Agreement of Textiles and Clothings (ATC), gradual privatisation of economy and free entry of multinational companies in the field of trade and production in developing nations.[10] But according to Valentin Shetinin this policy will open the door of gradual exploitation of developing nations through export of capital, technology and consumer goods to them. Such doubt has been expressed by him in 1988 even before the adoption of this policy,[11] which has also been supported by W. Applenan Williams.[12]

India adopted the policy of economic liberalisation in July 1991 and since then it has obtained capital inflow of Rs. 136.58 arabs in 1994-95 from different countries like U.S.A. (Rs. 32.12 arabs), Japan and other Asian countries (about 29 arabs) and the rest was invested by European countries such as Germany, Holland and England in 203 projects. Japan and Germany are more keenly interested for making investment in India due to cheap availability of resources here. They have been planning separately to compete with U.S.A. in this regard. Recently Germany and India have agreed to abolish double tax system on their trade. Our trade relation with Singapore, South Korea and Thailand has improved and attempt is being made to make our trade relation better with France and South Africa. International Finance Corporation related to the World Bank has placed India in the list of Big Emerging Market countries. The report has registered the rate of investment in India as 6.5 per cent in terms of dollar in 1994 which is a significant indicator of better avenues of investment.[13]

The reason behind adoption of policy of economic liberalisation was two fold (i) economic and (ii) political. As per economic consideration liberalisation will help the country in reducing the burden of foreign debt. In 1991 the debt burden of short period was to the tune of 8.10 arab dollars which reduced to 3.60 arab dollars in 1994.[14] In addition to reducing the debt burden the policy of liberalisation has helped us to come out of the trap of poverty, inflation and stagnation in growth rate as claimed by the

Ministry of Finance, Government of India. The Ministry claims that in 1991-92 the growth rate of Indian economy had reduced to even below 1 per cent which rose to 4.3 per cent in 1993-94 and further it touched the height of 5.3 per cent in 1994-95. Likewise industrial growth rate rose from 5.1 per cent in 1991-92 to 8.7 per cent in 1994-95. Rate of inflation had declined from 17 per cent in 1991-92 to 7.3 per cent in 1994-95. Production of foodgrain also increased from 16.80 crore tonnes to 18.50 crore tonnes during the period under consideration. As a result the buffer stock of foodgrains has touched the record height of 3.10 crore tonnes.[15] In June 1991 the stock of foreign exchange was about nil which rose to 21 billion dollars in 1994. Likewise in 1991 the foreign investment was of Rs. 3.51 arabs which rose to Rs. 6.75 arabs and 17.86 arabs in 1992 and 1993 respectively, which is expected to cross the level of 50 arabs by the end of 1995. From April 1994 to December 1995 the total inflow of foreign capital in India was Rs. 4 arabs consisting of 20 per cent direct investment and 80 per cent portfolio and share investment. In 1995 also real investment is only one-fourth of the total approved investment.

The rosy picture of Indian economy presented by the Finance Ministry has been rejected by the Planning Commission and doubted by the Industrial Development Bank of India. The Planning Commission in its mid-term appraisal (1995) has termed the economic reforms under New Economic Policy as directionless. The appraisal alleged that budget deficit is mounting, prices are rising, non-economic expenditure by the bureaucrats and government is unrestricted. Profit earning units of public sector are being sold to private entrepreneurs in the name of its reform. The Planning Commission has exposed that the six major considerations of economic reform policy have not been implemented on proper line and significant scale. These considerations are:

1. The fiscal reforms are to be kept continued to control the possibility of inflation effectively;
2. Public expenditure is to be controlled so as to develop and encourage fiscal expertise;
3. The uncertain industrial revival is to be transferred as strong industrial regeneration;
4. Export should be given the direction of national effort;

5. Balance of payment position is to be corrected without foreign help, and
6. Import is to be restricted to bare minimum.[16]

The Planning Commission expressed regret over non-fulfilment of none of the above considerations significantly. Industrial Development Bank of India too has cast doubt over the gainful effect of the policy of economic liberalisation on the following grounds:[17]

(1) Due to defect in domestic capital market double amount of internal investment of the amount of foreign investment in a project relating to infrastructure is not coming forth. The norm relating to ratio of such internal investment to external one has been laid down by the Government Policy.

(2) The IDBI and other financial institutions have set forth the norm that the internal share should be to the extent of 40 per cent of the total investment in a project of which 25 per cent will be spent in meeting the establishment cost and the remaining 15 per cent will be utilised for expansion of the project. It will be difficult for the IDBI including commercial banks to meet this high percentage of internal capital requirement. In such a situation if foreign investment in huge projects is to keep continued, the country will have to depend on external sources for this 40 per cent capital requirement which will have adverse effect on our balance of payment position and the priorities of infrastructural sector.

(3) During the period 1991-95 (till October 1995) the ratio of Direct foreign investment to total foreign investment is only 20 per cent; the rest 80 per cent consists of loan and portfolio investment which may be withdrawn any time and the fate of the Indian economy may meet to that of Mexico.

(4) Recently the working committee of the R.B.I. has suggested that the non-residential Indians and foreign investors who have invested in fixed assets should be allowed to take away the principal amount of investment as well as profit earned on it to their own countries. The Committee also suggested that the time limit of 3 years to hold this capital in India should also be abolished. If the suggestion of the RBI's

working committee is accepted, there might be sudden outflow of capital from India giving its economy a serious blow.

The liberalisation of economy is based on market economy or capitalism the essence of which is the propagation of the culture of consumerism without any consideration of its evil social, moral and economic effect on the general mass. The main consideration in market economy is not benefit of the society but maximisation of profit. The human touch between consumers and producers is lost. Since the last four years as a result of liberalisation of economy India is suffering seriously from the outbreak of consumerism which seems to be fatal for its family, social and national integration as it will tell upon human values and morality of the citizens of the country. This policy apparently may turn us into a world citizen worldly but in reality we shall be completely materialistic self-centred men. The people's resentment against this policy is revealed by the tooth and nail opposition against Enron contract, Kentucky fried chicken, Pepsi, Dabhal project and Kargil projects.

Despite several evils inherent in economic globalisation it is a brutal reality that it will shape the form and nature of economies of the world in the 21st century. It is so because nearly two-third countries of the world will be capital deficit economies who will need foreign economic and technological assistance to develop their economies and to maintain their rising population. Poverty and unemployment will be their main challenges in the coming century. To meet this challenges inspite of their moral degradation, social degeneration, economic exploitation of the poor by the rich and national disintegration they will have to resort to the course of economic liberalisation. Under such situation Gandhian ideas of simplicity, equality, non-violence humanitarianism, *sarvodaya* and trusteeship will be of great relevance to the suffering masses in the 21st century. Specially in India, villages shall be happy and prosperous only when they will be freed from the capitalistic way of exploitation,[19] emerging out of the policy of economic liberalisation. Again there will be need of taking precaution for India to protect her village dominated economy from the evils of cities dominated western civilization.[20] Gandhi considered public ownership of means of production of goods satisfying primary needs of the people[21] essential which the market economy will negate in the coming century. His idea of simplicity and equal distribution of income will also be essential to fulfil the basic wants of the society and providing maximum happiness to the common mass. Abundance of goods and wealth cannot make man happy if they are not satisfied mentally. According to Gandhi, "we notice that the mind is a restless bird; the more it gets, the more it wants and still remains unsatisfied. The more we indulge our passions, the more unbridled they became." The Gandhi's idea of *sarvodaya, swadeshi* and trusteeship will play a significant role in the field of economic distribution deciding welfare based pattern of production, ecological balance and exchange of goods and services in the 21st century, likewise adherence to the principle of non-violence will be the unavoidable condition of the survival of human race in the coming century due to presence of highly destructive nuclear weapons as well as perfect degree of interdependence between the production and distribution system of different nations.

The policy of economic globalisation will be a certainty in the 21st century. But to make it beneficial to the societies developing nations it will be necessary to modify them on Gandhian lines in respect of selection and adoption of technology, deciding pattern of production and distribution, taking consideration of ecological balance in resource use and environment pollution, rising population, providing employment to all capable, economic self-reliance, encouraging people's participation in economic development and creating basic infrastructure to initiate and sustain the process of economic growth. As emphasised by Gandhi Cooperative and village panchayats shall also play a significant role in the field of securing sustainable and comprehensive growth pattern and obtaining the goal of distributive justice in the coming century. As such Gandhi will be more relevant specially to the developing nations in view of the nature of the world economic order likely to be emerged in the 21st century.

21

GANDHIAN THEORY OF COMMUNAL HARMONY

The Question of its Utility and Acceptance

—R.R.P. SINGH

There is no dearth of writings and literature on Gandhian theory and thought. In fact, during the last five decades most of the relevant issues, problems and phenomenon on which Gandhi dwelt and in regard to which he propagated theories have been examined, discussed and deliberated by numerous people belonging to different disciplines and professions. R.R. Diwakar rightly holds, "There is no dearth of literature on Gandhi in almost all languages of the world. Even after 40 years of his passing away, Gandhian is still pouring out of the world press. He is also the most documented person in all history. Humanity cannot afford to ignore him and/or what he said and did and taught."[1] However, the more we read, think and deliberate on Gandhi's writings, the more we become enlightened and reduce our ingnorance about his thought.

In this paper a very crucial subject—Gandhian approach to communal harmony—has been taken up for scrutiny because Gandhi not only propagated theories of communal harmony rather he sacrificed his life for the cause of the same. But at the outset, it would be proper to explain the term communal harmony.

Communal harmony is the reverse or communal disharmony and conflict. In the strict sense, the term communal harmony may be taken to mean as a state or condition of peace, normal or good relation and presence of fraternity relation between any two communities. But in the Indian perspective communal harmony is almost always taken to mean the persistence of fraternity relationship between Hindus and Muslims. Opposed to communal harmony is communal conflict which refers to a state of hostility or antagonism in the relationship and interaction pattern of any two communities. Bhattacharyya and many others preferred to use the word communalism instead of communal conflict. In fact, communalism is always there at the root of inter-community conflict and thus by defining former the meaning and context of the latter becomes clear. Cantwell Smith holds, "Communalism in India may be defined as that ideology which emphasizes as the social, political and economic unit the group of adherents of each religion, and emphasizes the distinction; even the antagonism, between such groups; the words 'adherents' and 'religion' being taken in the most literal sense."[2] However, Bhattacharyya and most others accept that communal disharmony and conflict in India is taken to mean the antagonistic relation between Hindus and Muslims. Because, communalism or Hindu-Muslim disharmony viewed and appeared as a big problem in first part of this century during British rule and virtually the said phenomena is a gift of latter to the Indians. Bhattacharyya says, a Survey of the political history of India during British rule more particularly of this century, would reveal how the contagion of communalism perverted the social context of the anti-imperialist people's movement and frustrated the genuine aspirations and logical culmination of the nationalist struggle[3] Mehta and Patwardhan also viewed, "the Hindus, Muslims and the British governments constitute the three arms of the communal triangle. From other considerations also, the question assumes a triangular shape. The political arm of the triangle is generally the best known, since it is the most obvious."[4]

Communalism, tensions, conflict and antagonism between Hindus and muslims became a very serious problem to solve the thirties and forties of this century. It was believed that this problem would be automatically solved after independence as constitution-makers declared India as a democratic and secular nation. Even then communalism has not been solved rather nurtured in the post-independence era. Thus Hindu-Muslim riot and tension which often occur constitute a challenging problem for Indian people to solve.

Virtually, the fact of persistence of communalism has affected the nation in different ways, but one of its disastrous role is the threat it poses to national integration.

It has been mentioned above that Hindu-Muslim conflict owes

its origin to the beginning of this century. But actually, although not prominently, Hindu-Muslim antagonism has its root in the arrival of Muslims during ancient and medieval time. Chopra correctly observes: "The coming of Islam was a challenge at the outset to this process of synthesis and fusion that has been going on for several centuries in the past. Unlike the earlier invaders—Greeks, Saythians, Parthians and Huns who were absorbed in the Hindu society during the course of a few generations—Islam came to India with a message of its own."[5]

Virtually, it was because of socio-cultural diversity of Hindu and Muslim that strained relations between these two communities has been continuing since ancient and medieval periods. But the form of communalism was not that prior to this century. In fact, clashes between Hindus and Muslims were not given significance as they were not significant in their disastrous effects.[6] But the Britishers for the sake of retaining their rule played the game of divide and rule. Although Britishers did not succeed in retaining their rule yet they became successful in making communalism as an ever lasting problem for Indian people.[7]

India during thirties and forties of this century experienced communal riots on massive scale. At the time of partition many thousand Hindus and Muslims lost their property and become homeless. The extreme form of Hindu-Muslim hatred and antagonism became a serious problem to solve for the then leaders of the country, or the nation as a whole.[8]

Gandhi, virtually, remained in pain and distress because of the persistence of communalism. Therefore, Hindu-Muslim unity was a part of his very being. It was the breath of his life. Gandhi was from his early youth a votary of amity between people of different denominations. It was rather at an early stage of his public life in South Africa that Gandhi felt the necessity of communal unity. 'Throughout his public life of fifty odd years he symbolized in himself the message of brotherhood among communities.[9]

Gandhi believed, preached and practised the principle of co-existence among people irrespective of their religions and faiths. Gandhi believed that without Hindu-Muslim amity well integrated and organised Indian society cannot be imagined and achieved. He continued his unceasing efforts to secure communal unity and peace till the very end of his life till he himself was consumed by the poisonous flame of communalism. Gandhi denounced and hated inter-community clashes and killings.[10] In order to realise his principles of communal unity into practice, Gandhi made every effort possible. He dared intervene at the time of clashes between Hindus and Muslims and if failed, observed *satyagraha* and fast unto death. Unnithan writes "With tears in his eyes and folded hands, fearlessly facing all dangers, Gandhi went to these treacherous scenes with his sole weapon of love. He reached all places, Calcutta, Noakhali, Boosari, Punjab and New Delhi. He walked long distances in these troublesome areas consoling the victims and appealing to the fanatics. He undertook his last fast as a self-imposed penance for his inability to bring about communal peace.[11] Gandhi, virtually, derived that Hindu-Muslim must live in peace with each other and abide by rule of faternity. For this cause, he was ready to sacrifice his very being. He wrote, "I am striving to become the best cement between the two communities. My longing is to be able to cement the two with my bloods, if necessary.[12] Gandhi was a great votary of religious equality and tolerance. He believed in monistic pluralism in religion as observed.[13] Gandhi identified religion with truth and non-violence. He said, "All faiths constitute a revelation of truth, but all are imperfect and liable to error. It is a travesty of true religion to consider one's own religion as superior and others as inferior. Just as a tree has many branches but one root, similarly the various religions are the leaves and branches of the same tree.[14] Since Gandhi believed in truth and non-violence, he accepted the creative forde of religion in human history. Religion signified, to him, belief in the ordered moral governance of the world. He condemned the Godlessness and violence associated with Bolshevism. He called himself a Hindu but he was no narrow sectarian. Like Buddha and Rama Krishna, he was above the bounds of creeds, cults, rituals and ceremonies. He accepted the spiritual and moral essence of Hinduism which according to him was the essence of all the great religions of mankind as Judaism, Christianity, Islam and Zoroastrianism. Hinduism signified a relentless search after truth. True religion, according to Gandhi, implied an emphasis on the moral values of man as spirit. He believed if the moral basis is lost, one ceases to be religious. Morality is always opposed to doing harm to others in any form. According to him "All religions are founded on similar moral laws. He declared "My ethical religion is made up of laws which bind men all over the world."[15] Gandhi emphasized the need to cultivate the value of religious tolerance and respect for other's religion not only among Hindus and Muslims but among all. Because, according to him, only through that any form of communal hatred would be eradicated. Instead, that would lead to unity of hearts. In his words, "I write in the name and for the sake of heart-unity which I want to see established among the people of this land professing different faiths. In nature there is a fundamental unity running through all the diversity we see about us. Religions are no exceptions to the natural law. They are given to mankind so as to accelerate the process of realization of fundamental unity. He preached equal regard for all religions throughout his life. The key to the solution of the tangle lies in everyone following the best in his own religion and entertaining equal regard for the other religions and their followers."[16]

In addition, Gandhi wanted to solve the problem of communalism by pleading and emphasising for cultivating and generating generosity among the majority. The Hindus, he believed unless Hindus treat the Muslims as their brethren but not aliens, the latter will not develop a feeling of brotherhood towards the former. In his words, "It would be a great thing for the Hindus to achieve this act of self-denial."[17] But simultaneously, Gandhi said, "It is essential for the minority to trust and treat majority of their brethren. He believed that it was the duty of the minority to assent to the majority decision except where it offended their moral sense; otherwise their could be no social life and no corporate social government. Gandhi considered it improper for a minority holding the majority to ransom or otherwise exploiting it.[18]

In order to attain mental communal amity, Gandhi advocated the need of secular state permeated by the spirit of democratic values. In such state recruitment to various posts and positions must not be made along communal line, because that would distort the ideal of secular state and would cause inter-community antagonism.[19]

In nutshell, Gandhi presented a theory of inter-community relation based on the principles of love, benevolence, equality, fraternity and peaceful co-existence. He also emphasised in his theory on the cultivation of morals of high order and sense of sacrifice among majority and minority for the sake of expelling communalism and maintaining communal harmony.[20]

Gandhian principles of communal amity have been accepted

by the peace-loving and secular people as very useful for solving the problems of communalism and Hindu-Muslim conflict.

After the death of Gandhi his principles of communal harmony were taken note of by constitution makers and accordingly India was declared as a secular state in which every religion has equal significance but none of the religion is a state religion. Further, Nehru, Lohia and Jai Prakash Narayan and afterwards most of secular minded leaders, reformers and intellectuals have accepted Gandhian principle as very pragmatic in solving the issue of Hindu-Muslim conflict.

In fact, Gandhian theory of communal unity is significant and useful from different points of views as stated below:

First, it provides a means method and approach to the realistic solution of communal discord.

Second, it is very appealing to the conscience and heart of human beings.

Third, it fosters humanism and fellow-feeling.

Fourth, it makes the people conscious of treating others faiths and religions as equal to their own.

Fifth, it makes a realistic appeal to the majority and the minority with a solution for living together and trust each other.

Lastly, Gandhian principles of communal unity are stable from the point of view of human nature because it recognizes the value of love, non-violence and fellow feeling to be internalized by the Indian people.

Gandhian principles and theory of communal amity have remained a source of inspiration and as means of solving the problem of Hindu-Muslim divide in post-independence era. Therefore, prior to and after the Hindu-Muslim riots and tension Gandhian principles have been adopted and they have worked too. Thus, the question of its utility is beyond any doubt.

However, the question of acceptance of Gandhian principles of communal amity has remained unsolved until now. Firstly, because communal violence erupts often in the country and in that way find the murder of Gandhian principle. Secondly, Gandhian principle is yet to get acceptance by people of both the community at large because of the tuff principles contained in Gandhian theory. It seems that Gandhian theory has not become universalistic in its character. It might be due to the fact that human being whether Hindus or Muslims are basically selfish egoist and thus generosity and broadness are lacking in them. Further every community treats its own religion as the most valued and appropriate which lie at the root of religiosity, fundamentalism and religious hatred. Obviously, such elements are hazardous for communal amity. The Gandhian principles also do not suit to the people and leaders as they stand in the way of their personal ends. The leaders and people in general accept and advocate the usefulness of Gandhian theory but when it comes to realise into practice by them they withdraw or deviate. The appeal to heart and conscience contained in Gandhian theory as well as the moral principles prescribed in it are so high that they are difficult for people to adopt in their life and code of conduct. It is because of the above facts that Gandhian ideals of communal harmony is yet to be accepted and realised into practice by both Hindus and Muslims and for that reason the problem of communalism has remained unsolved until now.

The foregoing discussion provides the basis to observe finally that Gandhian theory of communal harmony are realistic and useful as well for maintaining communal peace. The principles and ideals, however, are repeated and advocated by the country people and leaders only when the nation feels the necessity to make use of them. But Gandhian principles of communal harmony have not made their way deep into the thinking and behaviour of majority and minority or more particularly among Indian people in general. Despite the availability of golden principles, the nation suffers with the disease of communalism. Thus, the need now is to realise Gandhian techniques and principles of communal amity into practice. The methods of implementation which often are presented by Gandhian institutes must be taken into cognisance for the sake of attaining communal harmony in Gandhian way.[21]

REFERENCES

1. R.R.Diwakar, 'Reflections on Conflict Resolutions and Gandhian Studies' in *Gandhi-Jyoti*, Journal of Gandhian Thought, Year-8, No.1 (20th Jan. 1991).

2. Wilfred Contwell Smith, *Modern Islam in India: A Social Analysis.* (Lahore, Minerva Book Shop, 1942), p. 185.
3. B. Bhattacharyya, *Evolution of the Political Philosophy of Gandhi*, (Calcutta, Calcutta Book House, 1969), p. 193.
4. Ashoka Mehta and Achyut Patwardhan, *The Communal Triangle in India*, (Allahabad, Kitabistan 1942), pp. 7-8.
5. P.N. Chopra, 'The Impact of Islam on India" in *Studies in the Cultural History of India* (Eds.), S. Metraux and Francois Grouzet, (Agra, Shivalal Agrawala & Co. (P) Ltd., 1965), p. 281.
6. M.R.A. Baig, *The Muslim Dilemma in India*, (Delhi, Vikas Publishing House, Pvt. Ltd., 1967), p. 90; G.S. Ghurye, *Social Tension in India*, (Bombay, Popular Prakashan, 1968), pp. 1-9.
7. For Instance see, Jawahar Lal Nehru, *Discovery of India*, (Calcutta, The Signet Press, 1946), p. 263; R.P. Dutta, *India Today and Tomorrow*, (Delhi, People's Publishing House, 1955), p. 225, *et.al.*
8. Kamlesh Kumar Wadhwa, *Minority Safeguards in India*, (Delhi, Thomson Press, Publication Division, 1975), p. 83-94.
9. B. Bhattacharyya, *op. cit.*, p.193.
10. Jawaharlal Nehru, *Independence and After*, (New York, The John Day Co., 1950), pp. 17-38.
11. T.K.N. Unnithan, *Gandhi and Social Change*, (Jaipur, Rawat Publications, 1979), p. 83.
12. Young India, 25.9.24. in *Young India*, 1924-26, S.Ganesan, (Madras, 1927), p. 82.
13. K.B.K. Singh, "Gandhi and Ambedkar on Social Justice" in *Gandhi Jyoti*, Journal of Gandhian Thought, No. 4, 15 August, 1992), p. 66.
14. M.K. Gandhi, *My Religion*, (Allahabad, 1955), p. 2, 12; Gandhi of I.N. BISOPH, (Ed.), *Indian Thought*, (Delhi Wiley Eastern Pvt., 1975), pp. 374-83.
15. V.P. Varma, *Modern Indian Political Thought*, (Agra Lakshmi Narain Agarwala, 1961), p. 326.
16. *Harijan*, 4.1.48, p. 497.
17. *Young India*, 12.3.31, p. 36.
18. *The Hindustan Times*, 14.10.1987, Patna.
19. K.G. Mashurwala, *Gandhi-Vichar Dohan* (Hindi), (New Delhi, Sasta Sahitya Mandal, 1968), pp. 80-82.
20. For instance See, T.K.N. Unnithan, "Gandhian Techniques of Conflict Resolution and Ethnic Conflicts in *Gandhi Jyoti*. Journal of Gandhian thought, No. 1, 30th Jan, 1991, pp. 14-23; Allan Datta, "What Gandhi meant by God", In *The Telegraph*, Vol. III, No. 337, June 19, 1985, *et al.*
21. N. Radhakrishnan, "The Deepening Communal Divide and the Role of Gandhian Institutions. In *Gandhi Jyoti,* Journal of Gandhi Thought, No. 1, 30th Jan. 1991, pp. 55-60.

22

TO THE TWENTY-FIRST CENTURY WITH GANDHI

—V.S. HEGDE

Introduction

The many hazards of modern civilisation, increasing violence around us and misdirected political and economic programmes make us more and more helpless day by day. These make us look for a saviour. Some look forward to Gandhi not only for solutions to some of our problems today, but for the survival of mankind itself. Every paper of a seminar, every discussion of a symposium brings out the relevance of Gandhi, but what surprises us is that in spite of all these, we are actually and gradually moving away from Gandhi Obviously, there are some problems in our understanding of Gandhi and his relevance. If he has already become irrelevant how can he be relevant for our future?

The problems are not merely of one kind, partly it is our lack of seriousness in dealing with issues that also makes understanding and application of Gandhian principles difficult. But assuming that we can be serious enough about these things, the question is; how do we understand Gandhi so as to apply some of his principles to solve the practical problems of the day? While considering the relevance of great people, we generally do not take this or that aspect of their life in isolation, but we take the entire life and thought of the person together, integrally. Gandhi's experiment with truth embracing all the dimensions of his life, must be taken as a whole and comprehensively so that we understand his philosophy of life.[1]

But this kind of comprehensiveness is lacking in our present understanding of Gandhi. Some think that he was a saint, some others that he was a politician, and still some others that he was a social reformer. He was all these, but this is no way of understanding him. This is not seeing him comprehensively. So the question how is the saint in him related to the politician in him and to the social reformer in him? Of course Gandhi himself says, the whole gamut of man's activities constitutes an indivisible whole. You cannot divide social, political and purely religious work into watertight compartments[2] But, how can a saint be a politician as well? How can a politician be a saint at the same time These questions remained. The answer depends on the framework we accept. And Gandhi's framework not only permits this but it requires that one is a bit of both at the same time. Now, to see that it is not a confusion but a considered view of the matter, one has to see Gandhi in relation to Indian thought and its framework.

Gandhi and his Framework

What then is the connection between Gandhi and the Indian thought? In fact, one of the problems with Gandhi is that he is so firmly rooted in the Indian tradition; that we, in the modern times, cannot easily carry on with him. We are not so clear as to what is its significance. We have, therefore, almost rejected it. But the perils of modernity are also bacoming obvious, and the dilemma deepens every passing day. Thus we are in a way compelled to have a closer look at our own tradition which in any case is necessary to understand Gandhi and his framework.

The essence of the Indian Philosophical tradition may be stated briefly in terms of the doctrine of the *purusarthas*, which present the human goals in their interrelationship. The goals being *dharma, artha, kama* and *moksha*.[3] The interrelationship among these goals is often misunderstood and this has led to the misconception that to attain *moksha* one has to abandon or give up the pursuit of *artha* and *kama*. But the most important thing to remember is that *moksha* presupposes *dharma* and *dharma* presupposes *artha* and *kama*, because *dharma*, the moral goal, is to be pursued in the context of our pursuit of *artha* and *kama*, i.e., wealth, power and pleasure. Thus, *dharma* or *moksha* cannot be pursued in a vacuum.

This shows that one cannot ignore any of the *purusarthas*,

though the stress on one at any time may mean that one cannot give equal importance to all at the same time. This raises the question as to whether the stress is to be more on *artha*, or *kama* or *dharma*. If it is on *artha*, then *kama* and *dharma* become secondary and if is on *kama*, *artha* and *dharma* become secondary. But it is very clear that in the Indian tradition stress is always on *dharma*. If one wants to achieve *moksha* stress on *dharma* becomes necessary, and therefore the pursuit of *artha* and *kama* become regulated. Pursuit of *artha* without such regulation becomes mere greed, and pursuit of *kama* without *dharma* is nothing but lust. Thus, *dharma* not only sets limits to the pursuit of *artha* and *kama* it really makes their pursuit possible, for without *dharma* there is no *artha* or *kama* but only greed and lust. In short, *dharma* makes pursuit of *artha* and *kama* worthwhile human activity.

Gandhi's philosophy of life is to be understood in this framework which envisages no conflict between this world and the other world between one's material needs on the one hand and moral and spiritual requirements on others. Individuals may give different accents to the different goals but the framework is to be the same for all and a society cannot ignore any of these goals.

If we can understand and appreciate this framework,[4] then we can see better how we are unable to apply Gandhi's techniques to solve our problems today. We are not able even to properly understand Gandhi's principles in their inter-relationship because we forget this framework which appears outdated. But the fact is that we have not got an alternative framework we have not compared this framework with the modern framework which we intuitively feel is too fragmentary.

The relevance of Gandhi will then depend on: (a) whether we understand his framework, and (b) whether we find it acceptable. If it is not acceptable how can any one of his principles and techniques be adopted by us? How can we pick and choose any of his principles, techniques and programmes without accepting his framework? Gandhian programmes presuppose Gandhian principles, and Gandhian principles presuppose Gandhi's framework itself. We cannot have one without accepting the other.

Now, even if we understand and accept his principles along with his whole framework, it does not mean that we are to accept his programmes as such. Because the programmes will have to be determined on the basis of the changed circumstances. It is only the principles that remain unchanged. For example, the principle behind *charkha* may be valid without the programme of *charkha* being equally valid today.

Gandhi's Approach to Problems

A discussion of the relevance of Gandhi's principles will not be complete unless we take into account his approach to problems.[5] What is the speciality of the Gandhian approach to problems? It is its comprehensiveness and wholistic nature which is certainly very relevant today. We are not able to solve many of our present problems because some problems we do not want to solve and some problems we do not know how to solve. About the first category I do not know what to say anything. As regards the second category, our approach itself to these problems is wrong. For example, we think that our economic problem is not related to our political, social and other problems. This is where we go wrong.

The Gandhian approach presupposes that any problem has different aspects such as social, political, economic, moral, religious. A genuine solution to any problem must take all these aspects into consideration. Take for example, the evil of drinking. Many think that this is mainly an economic problem. We introduce prohibition because it ruins the poor economically. But then we drop it because it is not workable and it ruins the economy of the state. And we decide that the evil of drinking is to be fought not by legislation but by education. Thus we never take the problem in its totality. The question is not whether Gandhi is for prohibition or against it. It is that he always considered the issue in all its aspects—social; psycho-physical, economic, moral and religious. According to him what is not good for the individual cannot be good for the state and vice-versa. And what is not morally good cannot be economically sound. Legal and moral pressures should go hand in hand. Law by itself cannot tackle the problem. Thus Gandhi has tried to work out a comprehensive solution to the problem of drinking. And what is true in the case of drinking is true in the various other cases.

To realise the significance of the Gandhian approach we must distinguish between, what is difficult yet possible, and what is easy and expedient but not desirable as a solution in the long run. If we opt for quick solutions, well Gandhi would not be of much help.

But if we realise the immensity of the problems and are earnest in working out real solutions, then, Gandhi can certainly show us the way, the direction.

Not that Gandhi has readymade solutions to all our problems. But his importance is in his having provided us with a perspective. Which, of course, is at variance with the modern perspective, what may be called modern perspective has glamour; it creates the illusion that it is scientific, thorough and, therefore, good. But it is not a perspective because it takes us to a blind alley. This is the lesson we learn from modern science, modern medicine, modern economic and political theories. Gandhi can definitely provide a counterpoint to this perspective, a counterpoint which has been actually worked out in some details for the modern Indian who is torn between his past or his tradition and the west with its glamour and attainments. Hence the importance of Gandhi, his relevance and significance, for this century or the next.

Theory and Practice: A Unique Combination

Another important point in the understanding of Gandhi is the unique combination of theory and practice.

In Gandhi sometimes theory grew out of practice and practice throws light on theory though ridiculed consistency as the hobgoblin of little minds, he never meant to undermine the importance of theory. Theory without practice is useless and practice without theory is directionless. Theory gives proper conceptual foundation and proper direction telling us what to do and how. Practice is the necessary corollary to theory, and it is only through practice that one knows what is wrong with one's theory, and through theory what is wrong with one's practice. They bring out mutual limitations. The weakness and strength of one, will be tested by the other.

It is my considered opinion that proper understanding of Gandhi's thought can only be had if we understand the relationship between theory and practice in Gandhi and therefore, one should interact with Gandhian social workers continuously. This interaction can help mutually. Theoreticians can always stress on the theoretical aspect of Gandhi's thought, but they can do so without, at the same time ignoring the importance of the practical aspect. Gandhian social workers can always stress on the practical aspect of Gandhi's thought, but they can do so without denying the significance of the theory.

Sustainable Development and Gandhi's Framework

Dr. Martin Luther King once said, "This is an age of guided missiles and misguided men." Unless we have men guided by wisdom, proper development will not take place. Gandhian economics will help us distinguish between economy of needs and economy of wants. Unless we control our greed and minimise our wants, there is no scope for sustainable development. Gandhi would not at all want us to ignore *artha* and *kama*, because these are also human goals. Rather Gandhi would tell us to pursue wealth, power and pleasure in a befitting manner. That development is required cannot, therefore, be disputed. But the question is, what kind of development?

It is Gandhi and Gandhi alone who can show us the way out. His philosophy which harmonises the economic, political, social, moral-religious aspects of life assumes greater significance in the context of man's rising aspirations to live in harmony with other men and nature. Gandhi's philosophy of life can be an immense help in resolving conflicts between man and man and between man and nature, which are bound to come up during the process of development. Truly, sustainable development presupposes this kind of philosophy of life.

Mrs. Kamla Choudhry in her recent article, "Gandhi and Agenda 21," brings out the Gandhian perspective and its relevance for sustainable development very clearly. Referring to Rio Earth Summit in June 1992, she says, "This summit marked the largest gathering of nations to discuss the dangers to the future of our planet and life support systems and to evolve policies and institutional mechanisms for sustainable environment and development. . . . Also emerging from the Rio Conference was Agenda 21 a master plan of action for moving towards sustainable development."

She further argues, "If the Rio concensus is to have any future then issues of human rights, equality and access to natural resource must receive greater attention. These are moral and ethical issues. Consumerism and consideration of patterns of consumption and production in Agenda 21 takes us again to Gandhiji's door."

She concludes, "Toynbee, the historian had said most civilizations dies 200 years before they know they died. We hope the industrial civilization is not in that process and that we shall be able to move towards sustainable development as envisaged at the Earth Summit and in Agenda 21 with some help from the Mahatma."

REFERENCES

1. An elaborate account of Gandhi's experiments in various field are given in his *autobiography*.
2. Verma, V.P., "The political philosophy of Mahatma Gandhi and Sarvodaya", Agra, 1972, pp. 73-74.
3. Buhler, 1970, pp. 70-71, 224.
4. It is first worked out by Prof. K.J. Shah.
5. Hegde, V.S., "Gandhi's Philosophy of Law", Concept, New Delhi, 1983.
6. Louis Fischer, "The Life of Mahatma Gandhi", Granada, London, 1982.
7. Raghavan Iyer, "The .Moral and Political Thought of Mahatma Gandhi," OUP, 73.
8. Gandhi, M.K., "My Religion".
9. Gandhi, M.K., "Hindu Dharma".
10. *Young India* and *Harijan*.
11. Kamla Choudhry, "Gandhi and Agenda 21," *The Hindu* (5.3.95, 19.3.95).

23

GANDHIAN THOUGHT IN THE TWENTY-FIRST CENTURY

—N. SIVARAMAKRISHNAN

Gandhi—The Inevitable

"Gandhi is inevitable. If humanity is to progress, Gandhi is inescapable. He lived, thought and acted, inspired by the vision of humanity evolving towards a world of peace and harmony. We may ignore him at our own risk". . . . These were the words of Dr. Martin Luther King Jr., the Nobel Peace Prize winner and the one who tried to translate Gandhi into practice in the West.

This meaningful sentence is perhaps the answer to the question that we are considering today.

We are not dwelling upon the relevance of Gandhi now and for centuries to come. But we are considering whether his message and teachings will live through the ages, and stand the test of times.

There can be no doubt about the relevance of, or following for Gandhi at any time in future, for, as Pandit Jawaharlal Nehru thoughtfully said in great agony soon after the demise of the Mahatma, that "the light is gone, and yet it will shine for a thousand years."

Gandhi's message and example cannot be erased from the phase of this Mother Earth, so long as there is trace of violence, injustice and exploitation in this world. This, I do believe and have no hesitation to declare.

The Essence of Gandhi

What does Gandhi symbolize? What does he signify? To different people, Gandhi is symbolic in different ways. To the philosopher, Gandhi is a faithful seeker after Truth. To the religionist, he is a synthesis of religious thought. To the politician, he is the builder of an impossible system. To the economist of the present day, he is nightmare. To the sociologist he is an impractical idealist. To the peasant and the worker, he is a living example and way of life, and for us—his followers—he is yet a mystery, for, the more we study of him, the more we come to realize of the unending vastness of his philosophy touching all branches of knowledge and social life.

But what is it that makes him relevant for all times? Is it his utter simplicity, openness, receptiveness of truth or what? To my humble mind, the greatest lesson that Gandhi taught us was the challenge he hold out to untruth, violence, injustice and inaction. This challenge implied the presence in the challenger of a sterling character, fearlessness and piety combined with absolute obedience to the law of the Being, an unreserved openness and humble receptiveness to truth, and above all, a highly scientific and analytical mind. The challenge will remain incomplete and ineffective without these supporting qualities. Call it by any name, '*Satyagraha*', 'Civil Disobedience or 'Constructive Action'; the essence is most certainly the challenge held out to wrong-doings, to injustice and to the wickedness of society.

Inaction is Violence

Gandhi's life was action-packed, which no other leader, national or international, of his time did possess, or will ever possess in future. To Gandhi, inaction was violence; it was cowardice, it was suicidal. He was convinced that if the challenge has to be effective and productive of peaceful and lasting results, then it has to be the non-violent way.

Gandhi's actions were timely and thoughtful. They were always carried out with the best of intentions; they aimed at the change of heart of the opponent. It was not the militancy of the wayward, nor the belligerency of the impatient extremist mind; it was a positive and scientific analysis and identification of the cause of injustice, and the accurate treatment for the elimination of the cause, like the surgeon removing the cataract for better vision.

For every ill the society suffered from, there was a pill in Gandhi's laboratory, which was not an anti-biotic dosage calculated to arrest the malady immediately and allow it to emerge in a different way, but a pro-biotic and tested cure of the very cause of the evil. While non-violence was the process of its sterilization, a clear scientific analysis of the causes and effects of its remedy was the basis for making the pill. The name and dosage of the pill are contained in Gandhi's *Materia Medica*, the Constructive Programme. The political version of this is '*Satyagraha*'. Those of us who have closely seen Gandhi in action know and realise this as the absolute truth. Those who lack the character and the preparation the Gandhi prescribed for the use of these pills, shall use it only with no effect. It is the unified action of the combination of all the needed character that makes action successful. This, we fail to realize, and having used his weapon without the training or conviction to make it effective, there can be no justification for blaming him for our ineffectiveness.

This Challenge has been Forgotten

The tragedy is that this challenge has been lost sight of. We refuse to look at the evils that creep into every part of society. We do not act in time to remove them. We take no notice of them, allow them to have their sway, and in course of time, get used to them. The evil becomes co-existent with us.

Take the instance of *Swadeshi*. Although Gandhiji confined it strictly to goods that were manufactured with locally available material and labour and with the least of exploitation. But the All-India Swadeshi League found it difficult to accept Gandhiji's definition of *Swadeshi*. While Gandhiji was keen on supporting village and cottage industries, and numerous crafts which were made by hand, the Swadeshi League was eager to bring in all small industries into its fold. It, therefore, became necessary for Gandhiji to redefine *Swadeshi*. But before doing so, he visited, during his extensive tours, many *Swadeshi* organisations so as to acquaint himself with the facts. Gandhiji wrote in the '*Harijan*' dated 10.8.1934, thus: "I had the opportunity to visiting and observing things and of seeing how *Swadeshi* organisations were functioning. I came to the conclusion that the existing practice was an unconscious fraud upon the public and that many workers of ability were wasting their energy in a vain effort. They were practising self-deception. This strong language, whilst it correctly describes my mental attitude, is not intended to cast any reflection whatsoever upon the workers in Swadeshi organisations. They were doing their best without realizing that they were moving in a vicious circle and labouring under self-deception. . . .

"We may profess to gratuitously help textile, sugar and rice mills and, respectively, kill the village spinning wheel, the handloom and their product, khadi, the village cane-crusher and its product, the vitamin-laden and nourishing *gud* and molasses, and the hand-pounder of his product, the unpolished rice. . . . Our clear duty is, therefore, to investigate the possibility of keeping in existence the village wheel, the village crusher and the village pounder, and, by advertising their products, discovering their qualities, ascertaining the condition of the workers and the 'number displaced by the power-driven machinery and discovering the methods of improving them, whilst retaining their village character, to enable them to stand the competition of the mills!. . . . What is needed is protection of the village crafts and the workers behind them from the crushing competition of the power-driven machinery, whether it is worked in India or in foreign lands. . . . Surely, there is in this work enough for an army of patriots. The reader may say, 'But this is very difficult task,' I admit. But it is most important and equally interesting. I claim that this is true, fruitful and cent per cent *Swadeshi*."

The Congress Working Committee passed the following resolution when it met at Benaras on 30th July, 1934:

> "Doubts having arisen on the Congress policy in regard to *Swadeshi*, it has become necessary to re-affirm the Congress position on it in unequivocal terms. Notwithstanding what was done during the Civil Resistance Struggle, no competition is permissible on Congress platforms and in Congress exhibitions between mill-made cloth and handspun and hand-woven khadi. Congressmen are expected to use and encourage the use of only handspun and handwoven khadi to the exclusion of any other cloth.

In regard to articles other than cloth, the Working Committee adopts the following formula for the guidance of all Congress organisations:

> 'The Working Committee is of the opinion that the activities of Congress organisations relating to *Swadeshi* shall be restricted to useful articles manufactured in India through cottage and other small industries which are in need of popular education for their support and which will accept the guidance of the Congress organisations in regulating prices and in the matter of the wages and welfare of labour under their control.'

The formula must not be interpreted to mean any modification of the unbroken policy of the Congress to promote the *Swadeshi* spirit in the country and to encourage the personal use of only *Swadeshi* articles. The formula is a recognition of the fact that the large and organized industries which can or do command State aid are in no need of the services of Congress organisations or any Congress effort on their behalf.

It must be borne in mind that Gandhiji's concern was not merely providing employment to the masses. He wanted to eliminate exploitation of the masses and the consequent oppression. He was convinced that the *Charkha* was the alternative, and when he said the spinning wheel, it meant decentralized production, non-exploitation, local consumption and self-sufficiency. By a single stroke he wanted to see that exploitation is set at rest. All his actions were motivated by this basic conviction. He boycotted foreign goods on these merits. He challenged foreign cloth with home-spun and hand-woven cloth, however course it was. Similarly, he challenged every centralized product with a wholesome alternative village product. There was an ideological restriction on it, viz., no one's work should displace any other of his employment. He believed that all such products which eschew exploitation, and do not displace people out of employment and cover a wide range of useful articles of daily consumption made locally and consumed locally are *Swadeshi*. It was a matter of necessity, if we wanted to provide work for the millions and ward off their poverty to some extent.

It is true that this ideological restriction was strictly adhered to till Gandhiji lived. But when there was no one as vigilant as Gandhi to lead the movement, there was slackness, and today we find almost all goods made in India virtually being called '*Swadeshi*'. Where is the spirit behind *Swadeshi* today? No one realizes that the challenge which Gandhiji held out to the three basic maladies—exploitation, injustice, and lack of character—has been thrown to the winds.

The Revolutionary Aspect of Gandhi

Gandhi was not a visionary, given to reverie or fantasy. He was never out of touch with the reality. He was not a dreamer. He was a practical revolutionary. The late Acharya Kripalani said once that history was a witness to the fact that after every revolution, there was a period of lull, which only signified that the effects of the revolution were being studied, and future course was being thought of. This must be true of the silent non-violent revolution of Mahatma Gandhi. I most fervently entreat the indulgence of learned scholars who are assembled here, to quote extensively from the speeches of Mahatma Gandhi, which will lay before us clearly the revolutionary aspect of Gandhi's revolution, and what is lacking today in this period of '*Search for purpose*'. Gandhiji spoke at the Congress Exhibition Grounds on the 27th December, 1936, making a 'restatement of his faith', which many newspapers at that time reported as an apology, a challenge, and a revolutionary and electioneering speech all rolled into one and predicted that Gandhiji was thinking of re-entering politics, after a break. Some of the paragraphs of that speech, as reported in the '*Harijan*',[1] will throw enough light on the present issue that is before us:

> "I am going to say nothing new today. The cult of the spinning wheel is 18 years old. I said in 1918 that we would win *Swaraj* through the spinning wheel. My faith in the ability of the spinning wheel is as bright today as when I first declared it in 1918. It has become richer for the experience and experiment of all these years.
>
> "But you should know the implications of the wheel or Khadi, its product. It is not enough that one wears Khadi on ceremonial occasions or even wears it to the exclusion of all other cloth if he surrounds himself with *Videshi* in everything else. Khadi means the truest *Swadeshi* spirit, identification with the starving millions.
>
> "Let there be no mistake about my conception of *Swaraj*. It

is complete independence of alien control and complete economic independence. So at one end you have political independence, at the other the economic. It has two other ends. One of them is moral and social, the corresponding end is *Dharma*, i.e., religion in highest sense of the term. It includes Hinduism, Islam, Christianity, etc., but is superior to them all. You may recognize it by the name of Truth, not the honesty of experience, but the living Truth that pervades everything and will survive all destruction and all transformation. Moral and social uplift may be recognised by the term we are used to, i.e., non-violence. Let us call this the square of *Swaraj*, which will be out of shape if any of its angles is untrue. In the language of the Congress we cannot achieve this political and economic freedom without truth and non-violence, in concrete terms without a living faith in God and hence moral and social elevation.

"By political independence, I do not mean an imitation of the British House of Commons, or the Soviet Rule of Russia or the Fascist rule of Italy or the Nazi rule of Germany. They have systems suited to their genius. We must have ours suited to ours. What that can be is more than I can tell. I have described it as *Ramraj, i.e., Sovereignty of the people based on pure moral authority.* (emphasis mine) The Congress Constitutions of Nagpur and Bombay for which I am mainly responsible are an attempt to achieve this type of *Swaraj*.

"Then take economic independence. It is not a product of industrialization of the modern or the Western type. Indian economic independence means to me the economic uplift of every individual, male and female, by his or her own conscious effort. Under that system all men and women will have enough clothing—not the mere loin cloth, but what we understand by the term necessary articles of clothing—and enough food including milk and butter which are today denied to millions.

"This brings me to socialism. Real socialism has been handed down to us by our ancestors who taught: "All land belongs to Gopal, where then is the boundary line? Man is the maker of that line and he can, therefore, unmake it."?[2]

Gopal literally means God. In modern language, it means the State i.e., the people. That land today does not belong to the people is too true. But the fault is not in the teaching. It is in us who have not lived upto it.

> "I have no doubt that we can make as good an approach to it as is possible for any nation, not excluding Russia, and that without violence. The most effective substitute for violent dispossession is the wheel with all its implications. Land and all property is his who will work it. Unfortunately the workers are or have been kept ignorant of this simple fact.
>
> "Let us now see how India came to be utterly impoverished. History tells us that the East India Company ruined the cotton manufacture and by all kinds of means made her dependent upon Lancashire for her cloth, the next great necessity of man. It is still the largest item of import. It thus created a huge army of practically unemployed men and women counted in millions and gave them no other employment in turn. With the destruction of hand-ginning, carding, spinning and weaving to a certain extent, perished the other industries of India's villages. Continuous unemployment has induced in the people a kind of laziness which is most depressing. Thus whilst the alien rule is undoubtedly responsible for the growing pauperism of the people, we are more responsible for it. If the middle class people, who betrayed their trust and bartered away the economic independence of India for a mess of cottage would now realise their error and take the message of the whole to the villagers and induce them to shed their laziness and work at the wheel, we can ameliorate the condition of the people to a great extent. It would be a terrible thing if laziness replaces industry and despair triumphs over hope.
>
> "The parliamentary programme is in the air. It has come to stay and rightly. But it cannot bring us independence. Its function is strictly limited though quite necessary. Its success will prevent the Government from claiming that ordinance rule or any measure restricting our progress to the goal was sanctioned by popular representatives. Hence the necessity for voters voting for the Congress candidates who dare not vote for unpopular measures without being liable to

Congress discipline. The success of that programme may also bring some relief in individual cases such as the release of Sri Subhas Chandra Bose or the detenues. But that is not independence, political or economic.

"Then look at it in another way. Only a limited number of men and women can become members of legislatures, say 1,500. How many from this audience can become legislators? And just now no more than 2½ crores can vote for these 1,500 members. What about the remaining 31½ crores? In our conception of *Swaraj* they are the real masters and 3½ crores are the farmer's servants who in their turn are masters of the 1,500. Thus the latter are doubly servants, if they will be true to their trust.

But the 31½ crores have also a trust to discharge towards themselves and the nation of which they as individuals are but tiny parts. And if they remain lazy, know nothing of *Swaraj* and how to win it, they will themselves become slaves of the 1,500 legislators. For my argument the 3½ crores of voters here belong to the same category as the 31½ crores. For if they do not become industrious and wise, they will be so many pawns in the hands of 1,500 players, it is of little consequence whether they are congressmen or otherwise. *If the voters wake up only to register their votes every three years or more, and then go off to sleep, their servants will become their masters.* (Emphasis mine)

"The only way I know to prevent such a catastrophe is for the 35 crores to be industrious and wise. This they can only be, if they take up the spinning wheel and the other village industries. They will not take to them unintelligently. I can tell you from experience that the effort means adult education of the correct type and requires possession of patience, moral fibre and a scientific and practical knowledge of the industry and worker seeks to introduce in the village of his choice.

".... Now perhaps you will understand the meaning of the message of the *charkha*. I said in 1920 that if the Congress truly and successfully worked the programme laid down in 1920, including the four-fold Constructive Programme of communal unity, prohibition of intoxicants, removal by the Hindus of untouchability and *khadi*, the attainment of

Swaraj within a year was a certainty. I am neither sorry for, nor ashamed of having made that declaration. I would like to repeat that declaration before you today. Whenever the four-fold programme is achieved in its fullness, you can have *swaraj* for the asking. For, you will then have attained the power to take it. . . . Is there communal unity today? Where is total prohibition? Have the Hindus rid themselves of untouchability root and branch? One swallow does not make a summer. Travancore's great procla-mation may be the beginning of the end, but it is not the end. If, we remove untouchability of *Harijans*, but treat Mussalmans or others as such, we have not removed the blot. 'All land belongs to God' has a deeper meaning. Like the earth, we of it, also belong to God, and hence we must all feel like one and not erect boundary walls and issue prohibition decrees against one another.

"This is the non-violent way in action. If we could fulfil this programme, there would be no need to offer civil disobedience, there would certainly be no need to do violence. Thirty-five crores of people conscious of their numerical strength as one man would be ashamed of doing violence to 70,000 white men in India, no matter how capable they are of dealing destruction and adminis-tering poison gas to millions in a moment. The *charkha* understood intelligently can spin not only economic slavation but can also revolutionize our minds and hearts any demonstrate to us that the non-violent approach to *Swaraj* is the safe and the easiest. Though the progress may seem slow, it will prove quickest in the long run."

We Need Not Despair

Listening to the original voice of Gandhi so far, I can understand that the situation is much the same today. My friends probably fear that it would worsen tomorrow. No doubt most of the good created by Gandhi's efforts have been ruined today. There has been a gradual decay. In 1935, after waiting for 15 years, Gandhiji says that *Swaraj* would have been achieved if the four-fold Constructive Programme had been honestly accepted and implemented. Today after 48 years of freedom we seem to be at the same situation. Some pertinent questions do rise, if we try to make an objective analysis of the situation today. Is there perfect harmony among all the communities and among all the peoples following different religions? Has not the caste-system become more virulent now than before? Is there a guarantee that equal respect is being given to the practice of all religions and that there is extreme tolerance in spite of our declaration of secularism? Has religion been separated from politics? Where is prohibition today? Has it not been sacrificed in the base-room of filthy lucre? Gandhiji declared that if he were made the dictator for three hours, the first thing he would do would be to close down all *arrack*, toddy and liquor shops without any compensation. But today in spite of the fundamental principles, India is floating on liquor. Take the case of untouchability. Is there any political party which has not the welfare of the '*harijans*' at its heart? What do we gain today by driving a wedge between Gandhi and Dr. Ambedkar—the two great personalities who worked for their emancipation. Can we suspect their motives or of their sincerity? Has injustice against those people stopped? In fact, both the sides are hardening their attitudes against each other. That is the situation today, and the popular apprehension is, and rightly too, that untouchability is on its way back! Then about *khadi*. Gandhiji has time-and-again said that *khadi* represents a spirit, which is more important than the product itself. He symbolised it to the wheel of rural progress. He likened it to the Sun in the solar system of the rural industrial pattern. But what is the position of *khadi* today? The less said about it, the better. It has become a commercial commodity, even as polyester cloth is a commercial commodity. Without the ideological background of *khadi* as a symbol of non-violent non-co-operation with the exploiter, the black-marketeer, the hoarder, and the usurer, can *khadi*, just as a commercial commodity make any impact, let alone revolutionize society? Perhaps *khadi* will also vanish in time and all glory will go to the present Governments. All these are true.

My intention in narrating this story of decay is not to ring the alarm bell. Change is the inevitable part of Nature, and as Acharya Kripalani said, this is the period of lull, a prolonged one at that. But this situation will not be long. While on the one side, we hear automation being brought in through the back-door, we also hear that we have to go back to our old ways, live close to nature, conserve ecology and protect our environment. Already

Agricultural scientists have begun to tell us not to use chemical fertilizers and insecticides indiscriminately. They will come back to farm-yard manure and green manure soon. So also will those people who repeatedly remind us of the age of machinery and the age of computers, one day recognise the importance of manual work and human intellect.

As I said earlier, we are going through a period of 'search for purpose'. When the purpose is understood, and realities surface, people will understand the worth of Gandhian Thought and methods only too well. We shall then understand the hollowness of our 'passion for mechanization and will then turn to Gandhi, as the saviour.

I predict that in another 30 years, that is, about 2025, there will be a total change in our attitudes and methods. Our job in the meanwhile, will be to train our young men to take charge of the situation then and build up a strong nation. These thirty years should earnestly be spent in giving a 'fuller understanding of Gandhi' to all youth and that will be our greatest task. The revolutionary movement of the Mahatma shall have to be kept alive at any cost.

REFERENCE

1. '*Harijan*', dated 2.1.1937.

24

GANDHI'S VIEWS ON VALUE EDUCATION

Their Relevance in Twenty-First Century

—SANDHYA CHAUDHRI

Gandhi, who has been compared with Gautam Buddha and Jesus Christ, was undoubtedly a great man who influenced not only the course of history but was also able to change the life of many persons who came in contact with him. He dominated the Indian political scene like a colossus for about a quarter of a century and helped India to get independence without bloodshed, with the help of non-violence.

His influence on history itself is unparalleled as he not only won freedom for India but was indirectly responsible for providing a fillip to many subjugated countries. Hence Mahatma will be remembered when of his contemporaries hardly a name will survive. Einstein the celebrated scientist, paid finest tribute to Mahatma Gandhi when he said, "generations to come will scarce believe that such a one as this ever in flesh and blood walked upon this earth".

Regarding Gandhian Political Thought in the 21st Century it seems most of his teachings are as relevant today as they wore 50 years ago when he was alive. The values upheld were not time-values and his outlook was not confined to his time alone. His social, economic and political ideas constitute a talisman beneficial for future-man as well as society. Many of his ideas like truth and non-violence were based on external human values being practised in society for times immemorial. His technique of conflict Resolution viz., *Satyagraha*, ideas on social justice upliftment of women and amelioration of the condition of *Dalits* have permanent value as far as the establishment of an egalitarian social order remains a cherished dream. Similarly, his views on education which play a pivotal part in the reconstruction of any society are as valid today as they were in his life time and will continue to be so in the Twenty-First Century.

In this paper I would like to elaborate his ideas on education and the need to impart value based education because of its significant role in nation building. Education has been defined as a technique of transmitting civilization. It is unfortunate that it has not been given that high a priority in India which it deserves. Lee Kuan Yew, when asked to elaborate the factor responsible for the phenomenal success of Singapore attributed it to education which was at the highest priority in his state. Similarly, President Mitterrand of France realising the role of education in nation building considered it "priority of priorities". He said, "in future nation's power will depend less on its financial wealth than on its grey matter".

Similarly, John Major, British Prime Minister, put education on the top of his personal agenda for the 1990s and said that education is the key to a mobile, dynamic and diverse society'. The United States Government's Commission in 1983 exhorted the Government to take firm and prompt measure to raise the level of education if the future of the country was not to be imperilled. If United States can be called "A nation at risk" India deserves to be called "A nation in dire peril" in the light of prevailing rate of illiteracy in the country.

Of all the problems that the country is facing today, none is so pressing and urgent as the problem of educational recons-truction. The system of education introduced by the British served their ends but is not relevant to the needs of the youths of free India. After independence, efforts have been made for evolving a new policy of education suiting to Indian genius and requirements, which may prove useful for national reconstruction.

Today even after about half a century of India's indepen-dence, the country finds itself faced with serious tensions and challenges of casteism, linguaism, provincialism, regionalism etc. Value oriented education can go a long way in curbing these fissiparous tendencies and inculcate the sentiments of unity and solidarity amongst various sections of the Indian society.

Etymology of Education

Etymologically education has been derived from Latin word.

Education, comprising two Latin words 'e' and 'duco' meaning 'out of' and 'to lead' respectively. Thus the word education means to bring out the inside to outside. Function of education is, hence, to draw out rather than to put in.

Some educationists also trace the root of education from 'educere' and 'educare'. The former meaning development or brining about and the latter meaning 'enhancement' or improvement and progress.

According to this root education means the art of developing and enhancing the cultivation of various physical, mental and moral powers of the learner. In this sense it is to be taken as a process, not as a product. Education is a continuous process or life-long process. It starts from birth and continues till death.

Types of Education

Education can be both formal as well as informal. Formal education is deliberately and consciously planned and its curricula are pre-designed and goals are pre-determined. It is imparted through educational institutions such as schools, colleges and universities. Informal education is generally received by living and communicating with others. It may or may not be provided consciously or deliberately. This can be or is generally offered at the convenient place, time or level of understanding. It does not have fixed course of study.

Aim of Education

The aims of education have been determined by philosophical, social, economic, political and cultural norms of society. According to Rig Veda. 'Education is something which makes one self-reliant and selfless. Ancient Indian concept of education laid emphasis on higher knowledge, freedom from ignorance, salvation and self-realization.

According to Vivekananda 'Education' is the manifestation of divine perfection already existing in man. To Swami Dayanand education is an instrument for character formation and righteous living. Tagore opined that education enables man to find out the ultimate truth which emancipates us from the bondage of the dust and paves way for universal brotherhood.

According to Gandhi, education is an all round drawing out of the best in child and man-body, mind and spirit. Gandhi's views on education were influenced by his general philosophy of life viz., belife in God, truth, *ahimsa*, dignity of labour, a new social order having justice and equality. According to him education should aim at developing an all-round vigorous personality. He laid equal stress on education of heart i.e., refinement of emotions and awakening of deepest feelings of love, sympathy, fellowship and right ordering of loyalties. It is a life long process and should help in cultivating the spirit of toleration, cooperation, public spirit and a sense of responsibility.

Gandhi was critical of the then existing system of education as he believed that to be wasteful and positively harmful. His ideas regarding education did not emerge all of a sudden, but were the outcome of long years of sustained thoughts and experiences in social economic and political fields. His views on education have made a revolutionary contribution to the educational thought and entitles him to be termed as a great educationalist. Being a man of action rather than a theorist, his theory of education is also by and large objective and experimental rather than subjective and speculative. In fact there is no divergence in theory and practice.

The evolution of his philosophy of education has been greatly influenced by three great personalities who left a deep impression on his life—Raychand Bhai by his living contact. Tolstoy and Ruskin by their books '*The Kingdom of God is Within You*' and '*Unto This Last*'. Teachings of Tolstoy and Ruskin made Gandhi perceive that education without the use of one's hand and feet would atrophy the brain.

Gandhi's value oriented education was based on the golden principle of simplicity. In fact, simplicity was not only the corner stone of his educational ideas but also of his life-style. He wanted students to lead a simple life and do all their work by themselves viz., washing their clothes, cooking their food etc. The thrust of his view's is simplicity in education by training the children in self-help and self-reliance. He considers the life of students to be akin to that of a *sanyasi* student, according to him, should follow the dictum of 'Simple living and high thinking'. He should derive pleasure from his studies. For Gandhi there could not be a greater pleasure for a student than to march from knowledge to more knowledge.

He made a distinction between literacy and education. He believed that literacy in itself was not education. It was neither the beginning nor the end of education. It is only one of the means whereby men and women can be educated. In fact, Gandhi wanted the literary education to follow the education of the hand. He did not consider reading and writing indispensable for man's moral, physical or material growth, though, he admitted, it added grace to life.

He believed that along with information emphasis should also be laid down upon values. Too much stress on the former has relegated to the background, the significant aspect of personality like physical, emotional, moral and spiritual. Consequently, it has obstructed the growth of right attitudes, habits, values, skills and interests among pupils.

Indian policy based on the principle of socialism, secularism, democracy, nationalism and internationalism requires an education based on the criterion of inculcating values in the youth for promoting equality, social justice, national cohesion and democratic citizenship.

For Gandhi, character building aspect of education was very important. He firmly believed that character of a person was bound to have a considerable impact on the masses. Therefore, he wanted students as well as teachers to give more importance to character building, moreover national progress was dependent on men of sterling character. This point is of utmost importance for a country like India, having groaned under the heels of colonialism for about two centuries. He considers schools and colleges as factories for making of character. That is why his educational curriculum has the attributes of character building.

Bertrand Russel, the famous writer has referred to four virtues essential for an ideal character viz. vitality, courage, sensitivity and intelligence. Gandhi also talked about these virtues in 1932 when he said, "I would try to develop courage, strength, virtue, the ability to forget oneself in working towards great aims. . . ." He believed that these virtues can be inculcated with the help of education.

He also laid stress on spiritual development of man through education. The ultimate goal of education, according to Gandhi is self-realisation of the ultimate reality, knowledge of truth or God. Self-realisation is the summon Bonus of life and education, but, for realising this objective, Gandhiji did not think of isolating education from life.

Though 'individual' was the centre for Gandhi yet he was not oblivious of the social goal of education as individual can develop to the fullest possible extent only in the society. He said in *Young India* dated march 26, 1931. "A nation cannot advance without the units of which it is composed advancing and conversely no individual can advance without the nation of which it is a part also advancing. He wanted education should aim at producing not only good individual but socially useful citizens who understand their social responsibilities as an integral element of society.

Basic Education

Gandhi's concept of Basic Education has got the maximum attention. It aims at all-round development of human personality. His primary emphasis is on the 3 H's. viz., head, heart and hand rather than on 3 R's. i.e., Reading, Writing and Arithmetic. For Gandhi the true development of head, heart and soul are necessary for a satisfactory system of education.

In his scheme vocational training or work experience occupied a central position as he wanted education to be responsive to socio-economic needs of the Indian Society. Perhaps this was one of the reasons for his aversion to book-centred education at the expense of education through crafts.

At primary level, the education was to be imparted through a useful handicraft in a scientific way so as to enable the child to start producing from the time he started his training. Moreover the vocation centred education could prove useful for saving a large amount of public money. It also emphasized the principle of dignity of manual labour among students from school stage to university resulting in the inculcation of work-ethics. The training of head, heart and hand brings about productive results. In fact, Gandhi wanted that theory and content of education should be linked with concrete life situation in social and physical environments.

But craft education was not to replace book education rather it was to be an adjunct to it. He knew systematic knowledge of skill could be acquired with the help of books. His emphasis on work experience was due to the fact that it stimulates individual mind for creative thinking. Basic education was further based on the principle of 'learning by doing'. Gandhi himself was an actionist first and theorist afterwards. In conformity with this view, the education system conceived by him also contained the practial aspect first. He believed in close interaction between the teacher and the taught laying emphasis on values such as cooperation, discipline, sacrifice, integrity and fearlessness.

To sum up it can be said that Basic education envisaged by Gandhi aimed at producing self reliant and good citizens. It was centred round craft activity and production work in order to be useful for individual and society. It also aimed at interlinking the physical environment, social environment and craft work with the individual. This was specially important for rural population of India as Gandhi rightly believed that in order to make education compulsory in village of India, it ought to be made self supporting. Moreover craft work and manual labour in basic education could also inculcate in youths appropriate work-culture.

It is student centred by training individuals in right direction from their formative years in order to make them meaningful and socially useful citizens. It is cooperative as it aims at integrating the individual with the society in a spirit of cooperation. The physical, mental and growth of individuals is sought to be achieved through non-violent means. Emphasis is laid on the full and free development of natural impulses of individuals.

Gandhi further lays great emphasis on Truth and non-violence in individuals life. Basic education also places truth on a high pedestal. It also aims at the establishment of an exploitation free society having a just social order where in individual can develop himself without any hindrance.

To sum up it can be said that education is the foundation stone on which depends India's political salvation. Our country should be built not on bricks, but on brains, not by cement, but by enlightenment.

In order to regain India's lost glory and prestige, Gandhi's education ideas based on value-orientation have to be reemphasized. The education curricula should be value laden as well as information oriented. Eradication of illiteracy and spread of education is the prime need of the hour so that the citizens of Twenty-first century can be alert and enlightened.

25

INSTITUTIONALIZING PANCHAYAT SYSTEM IN INDIA

—CHANDRA B.P. SINGH

Broadly speaking, the strength of a society to overcome crises, face challenges, and fight stagnation depends largely on the vitality and well-being of the institutions within its fold. Insti-tutions are instruments of society through which it fulfils its needs and aspirations. Society creates, restructures, modifies various political, social, economic and educational institution in accord with its changing requirements and growing constraints. In this regard, Panchayati Raj Institutions (PRIs) are far more crucial as their impact on the rural society is more pronounced than that of institutions of any other variety. But this holds good for only such PRIs which are healthy and effective. There are a number of them which are congenitally sick. There are still others which grow, reach a plateau, and keep stagnating or degenerating thereafter they cannot be vehicle for realising the dreams of a society.

This paper makes an attempt to identify the factors of institution-building for PRIs. The purpose is to maintain a diagnostic view throughout in order to suggest some remedies for avoiding institutional degeneration and accelerating the revival process.

Institution: Conceptual Inquiry

Human groups in all walks of life acquire or form organisations but not all of them turn into institutions. All institutions are organi-sations but not vice versa. Efficient and healthy organisations may be institutions provided they work much more and much beyond. The distinction covers a whole spectrum in terms of time, levels of activity, and levels of decision-making An organisation is relevant for a period of time during which a target has to be achieved through a set of relevant relationships and resources. When the target is achieved all these relationships and resources and even the organisation itself do not matter for the society. Institutionalisation, on the other hand, means infusion with value beyond the technical requirements of the task at hand. Once established an institution embodies, fosters, and protects normative relationships and action pattern and performs functions and services which are valued in the environment.[1] Whatever distinctions may be, conceptual overlap between an effective organisation seems unavoidable. Yet it is evident that when organisations become institution they tend to be ongoing and continuous entities rather than remain instruments for achieving a limited purpose or goal. The role relationships in the organisation go much beyond the technical requirements and mature into a source of immense personal pleasure and satisfaction for the members. It is still a debatable matter whether Panchayati Raj in India has received a status of institution. Granting legal status may be a good attempt for revival of an institution The more important thing is to see how members involved in institution building affair go beyond the role relationships and imbibe values that are necessary for an institution.

The conceptual clarity applies more to PRIs than institutions of any other variety This is precisely because public organisations have a natural tendency and essential elements for growing into Institutions. Even in common parlance the term `institution` is invariably used in public context rather than in many other spheres of our social life. In other words, institutionalisation is a natural corollary of the kind of activities that are expected to be practised in public organisations and hence the need for the same is felt more prominently than in any other variety of organisations. It is also true that an organisation in terms of structure, rule-bound orientation and quantitative target realisation cannot be a frame of reference of an institution. The principles of work organisations like contractuality, elaborate structural arrangement rule boundedness, and prescribed relationship may bot be adequate enough for the goal of PRIs. There are innumerable instances of Panchayat system in Vedic period which existed till long beyond structural support. The Panchayat system maintained its morphological characters even during the Mugal period. Soon after advent of the East India Company, the Panchayat started fading and the feudal system eclipsing the grassroot democracy. But the colonial rule failed to overthrow the Panchayat system. That is why at the call of Mahatma Gandhi a need was felt to revive the old Panchayat system in India: The idea of PRIs came into existence when Balwant Rai Mehta Committee in (1957) felt an urgency to grant constitutional status to the three-tier system for encouraging people's participation in socio-economic development at the village level. After that Ashok Mehta Committee in 1977 followed by G.V.K. Rao Committee (1985), L.M. Singhvi Committee (1986) and Sarkaria Commission (1988) have been constituted to make PRIs more functional and effective. Since 1989 there also have been three serious attempts to accord constitutional status to PRIs. Unfortunately 64th [1989] and 74th [1960] Constitution Amendment Bill could not be translated into Act, with the introduction of 73rd Amendment, Panchayats have come into a regular existence like any other institution in India. In short, Panchayats have not only survived for centuries but, in many instances, have resisted deterioration defying logic of organisational death. However, there should not be confusion that modern structured organisations can be oriented to become institutions and consequently, more useful to the society. This is more so because the need for institutions in the field of rural development is more demanding as compared to other areas. The state government may be an instrument but cannot be an institution of development. Ultimately people should take responsibility of institution-building affair.

Bipolar Model of Institution Building

Two salient issues have been engaging the attention of social scientists for quite some time: (a) Dose an institution naturally grow? And (b) Do individuals decide the institution-building process? The first issue adopts an evolutionary view and recognises slow and incremental changes and spontaneity in development of an institution. External instrumentation or elements of purposive induction of change does not matter to be of much importance. Like any other institution Panchayat is said to be a reservoir of social energy by which symbiotic pattern maintains its own rhythm. Social energy is nothing but a group effort with specific form and direction. Once social energy is channelised in the right direction, the institution starts taking a shape and members involved in it dissolve their individual interests. This new form of social arrangement takes more care of moral binding instead of legal binding. The second approach to institution-building focuses on crucial role of individuals in the entire process and refuses to import this idea that development of needs in a society will naturally lead towards crystallisation of an institution. In recent years the idea has gained impetus that development of a society demands a different kind of institutions which do not necessarily evolve through the process of natural selection and adaptation. Instead, they have to be purposively created: designed, and structured in order to mobilise human and material resources for the realisation of definite goals and objectives. J.B.P. Sinha appositely remarked that "institutions have to be built up rather than to be left to the evolutionary processes.[2] The latter model of institution building deals with social technologies by which members are trained to work within a system. Most of the well-established organisations of today are carefully designed to maintain synergetic system.

Panchayats as Institutions

Panchayati Raj Institutions (PRIs) in India popularly known as an agent of rural transformation are not merely a formal arrangement with specific form and function but have a certain legitimacy and meaning by which they are identified. After independence there have been several attempts to make panchayat a more viable institution and crystallize certain practices which are necessary for rural development. Unfortunately, Panchayat as an institution failed to make its own identity. A number of factors can be attributed to the failure of it. Taking into account all global as well as contextual factors, one point becomes more obvious that institutions have, in general, a longer life span than individuals or organisations. Sometimes they decay over time and become attenuated or even extinct. Very often they change or adopt themselves to the changes taking place in the wider society. By the same token it is argued that the Panchayat system has enormously changed over time but is still recognised as an institution today.

The new PRIs differ from the old ones not only in their morphological forms but also in the value that give them meaning and legitimacy.

The Constitution (73rd Amendment) Act, 1992 is definitely a welcome step to revive the old institution with a presumption that power to people can (a) lead to the third stratum of government: (b) help panchayat retain the image of institution and (c) translate the dream of grassroot democracy into reality. For this, not only decentralization of power has been rationalized by law but an opportunity is provided to people for participation in formulating plan, executing it, and monitoring the process of goal realization. A healthy institution has its own in-built system coordinating various activities for realising the target. Members perceive stake at any stage when the administrative loop impedes the process of coordination by which the goal is realized. An attempt to restore the health of a sick institution demands a close coordination among members, administrators and agencies involved in it. If sources of ailments are not treated properly, there is every possibility of relapsing the symptoms of sickness. Under the circumstances the immune system of the institution becomes feeble and additional care is required for its revival. Most of the well-established institutions of yester years are today a pale shadow of their glorious past. Consistent decline is palpable in every sphere of their existence. Endeavours to fight stagnation and arrest decline are seen only in bits and pieces. They are neither being regenerated nor being replaced by new institutions. On the other hand, a variety of NGOs claiming to offer a wide range of options are springing up in every nook and corner to cater to the needs of evergrowing population. Most of them are still born. Many are just money spinners. Some which initially show promise start declining after a while. Only a microscopic minority of them seem to be institutionalizing in the true sense of the term. Taking a lead from early experiences an attempt to identify factors accountable for institution building for Panchayati Raj appears to be the need of the hour.

Politicisation

The birth of an institution is not necessarily a crystallisation of needs of people of an area. It is more often an outcome of a fit between needs of people and political expediency of leaders. In many cases institutions are created to solve local problems with the help of governmental support as the state government gets no time to look into the local matter. Probably, a major part of institution-building process centres around the problem of autonomy granted to an institution. The powers, authority, and responsibilities of panchayats discussed in Article 243G of the Constitution [73rd Amendment] Act, 1992 reflects the amount of autonomy conferred on PRIs by the State Legislatures "Subject to the provision of the Constitution, the Legislature of a State may, by law endow the panchayats with such powers and authority as may be necessary to enable them to function as institution of self-government and such law may contain provisions for the devolution of powers and responsibilities upon panchayats at appropriate level, subject to such conditions as may be specified therein, with respect to (a) the preparation of plans for economic development and social justice; (b) the implementation of schemes for economic development and social justice as may be entrusted to them in relation to the matters listed in the Eleventh Schedule." Thus institutional arrangement for PRIs depends on the extent to which these bodies are allowed to function with least political and bureaucratic interferences.

Autonomy of PRIs is still a good measure of field reality by which political intention can be assessed. If politics is an instrument of power to achieve particular ends in accordance with certain accepted codes, it is difficult to see how public institutions can be wholly insulated from it. This is also applicable to PRIs. If panchayat is to be self-governing institution it must make room for some form of politics within its fold. When an institution becomes politicised beyond a point, every problem in it seem to a political problem and no problem appears solvable except in political terms. Politics cannot be expelled from any institution that values self-governance. The fact is that every living institution has to accommodate some corruption and some injustice as a part of its ordinary existence. The real challenge is to work within the existing set up and to evolve control mechanisms of self-governance that ultimately regulate in-built system of an institution.

Leadership

Leadership, however, alone cannot sustain the quality or

effectiveness of an institution. The leader will have to build a system by effecting systematic and behavioural changes through positive interventions. However, many chair persons of panchayats who succeed in managing their affairs, fail to negotiate with outside forces, particularly the centres of resources as it usually requires some manipulation deviation from standard procedures and lot of networking. Very strongly, rural leaders involved in panchayat activities take more personal interest in sharing resources with other officials not for development affairs but for widening their influence network. This explains why some mukhiyas are more powerful but have contributed nothing to their panchayat. The two spheres of institutional life, thus, place different and sometimes contradictory demands on leadership. Instances can be found where panchayat leaders have achieved spectacular results in adverse circumstances. If leaders with a sense of mission, a team building participative decision making orientation, and strong networking capabilities are put in charge, it is likely that institution-building values will set in panchayat system.[3]

Boundary Management

Institutions need to protect, maintain, and enlarge their boundaries over a fairly longer period of time. It is often known as boundary management affair. PRIs are open, flexible, and dynamic and hence, are likely to be affected by external forces. There can be two sets of forces which can pose a threat to institutional health. Firstly, there are forces emerging out of global decline of socio-political environment on which panchayats have no control. Such a decay process, sooner or later, engulfs the institution. Secondly, there are crisis situations, pressures which flow over if strongly resisted. Once rebuffed, the probability of recurrence of a similar situation goes down considerably. The process of regeneration sets in motion. The cohesiveness of group members resolve and commit-ment accelerates this process.

Environment

No institution can exist in isolation and maintain total immunity to restraining forces of environment. There may be two types of environment-receptive and rigid.[4] In the receptive environment, people become catalytic forces and start extending support the existence of institutions. Contrary to it, rigid environment promotes anabolic forces where institutions suffer from inherent disorder. Consequently, institutions even at the time of birth do not feel comfortable. This explains why panchayats, despite good intention, failed to work as self-regulatory system at the grassroot level. Instead it still survives under governmental care and coverage. In many instances decline in grassroot institution can be correlated with simultaneous decline of political and social institutions in the environment. For instances, the lack of political will and instability failed to hold panchayat election in Bihar since 1978. The unusual delay in execution of the Bihar Panchayat Raj Act, 1993 is another glaring example of restraining forces operating in institution-building process.

Ground Realities

It is often said that good people make good laws but good laws do not necessarily make good society. Prior to the birth of an institution, intention to run it for good purpose matters in many respects. Even the best of intentions can turn out to be a damp squib if it is not expressed in time. Although previous experiences of PRIs lend support to good intention of the Central Government as is evident from the constitutional status accorded to PRIs, the efforts of promoting healthy relationship between the elected members and government officials have not yielded desirable dividend.[5] As a result, PRIs could not evolve normative relationship which is necessary for coordination between ideas of authority and ideas of knowledge. For better result coordination is another term of an institution. In absence of mutual trust between the elected members and government officials, no coordination can be visualised. Generally; the mechanism for coordination, vertical as well as horizontal, suffers from lack of proper appreciation of authority of ideas. Today, the strategy for coordination, for instance, in rural development administration tends to over-emphasize authority of office. It is underpinned by too much scriptory assignment to the technical persons, too many meetings between bureaucrats and politicians, rigidity in technical, administrative and financial sanctions on the part of rural development programmes.[6] It has led to ineffective coordination, restricted operational freedom, and delayed action causing nonadherence to time schedule and nonfulfilment of task. Unfortunately; the development administration still holds some prominent features of traditional administration which demands high conformity to general standards, methods, and procedures. It is also argued that continuation of existence of an Institution depends on how well it is maintained. Although the leader is not a great system builder, he can fill the slot with the help of coordination and can run an institution even in the odd situation.

In its long span of existence the institution faces strong outside forces which must be taken care of as a preparation of future. However, total immunity to political degradation and social upheavals taking place in the environment is nearly impossible. It is worth referring to the observations of Ashok Mehta Committee (1977) : "It will be wrong to think that Panchayat Raj should be viewed as a God that has failed. It has many achievements to its credit, the more important of which may be identified here politically speaking, it became a process of democratic seed-drilling in the India soil, making an average citizen more conscious of his rights than before. Administratively speaking, it bridged the gulf between the bureaucratic elite and the people. Socio-culturally speaking, it generated a new leadership which was not merely relatively young in age but also modernistic and prosocial change in outlook Finally, looked at from the developmental angle, it helped rural people cultivate a developmental psyche.

REFERENCES

1. S.R. Ganesh, *Institution Building for Social and Organisational Change*, Organisation Studies, Vol.1 (3) 1980.
2. J.B.P. Sinha, Institution Building for Development: An Indian Perspective. Meeting of Experts on Exchange of Knowledge for Endogenous Development, Paris. UNESCO, October 3-7, 1983 p.3.
3. S.R. Ganesh and P. Joshi, Institution Building : Lessons from Vikram Sarabhai's Leadership. Vikalpa, Vol 10, 1985.

4. J. Moniha and C. Perrow, The Reluctant Organisation and the Aggressive Environment, Administrative Science Quarterly, Vol 10, 1965.
5. Iqbal Narayan, Panchayati Raj Administration in Maharashtra, Bombay, Popular Prakashan, 1974.
6. M.A. Muttalib, Democracy, Bureaucracy and Technocracy, New Delhi, Concept Publication, 1980.

26

GANDHIAN THOUGHT IN THE 21st CENTURY

—M. SREEDHARAN PILLAI

We, the Human Society, at present, bid almost good-bye to the 20th century and are welcoming to the 21st century 'child'. The World-Human society is facing many problems day by day. He is striving to come out this cage. Instead of coming out of it, he is caughthold of in new ones. Can these problems be solved? What is his new innovation in facing the problems of human society?

Did Gandhi give anything to solve human problems? Some people said that he dragged and raised many new problems to Indians; but no one is solved. Was his thought a success or a complete failure for giving solace to human society?

Gandhiji often said, "I shall not give any new system or any philosophy or isms, 'My life is my message'. In 'the vision of Nehru' Rajiv Gandhi, the former Prime Minister of India, stated, "The Past becomes something that leads up to the present, the moment of action, the future something that flows it and all three are intrinsically intertwined and inter-related."[1]

We should study Gandhi's contributions to the society, we have to study his past and contemporary circumstances, historical evidence, his speeches and writings.

Gandhi himself said, he was not a Gandhian he said, he felt he was far short of being a Gandhian of his conception. We cannot accuse Gandhi of false modesty though we can say that it was his great humility to say so.[2]

Nehru once remarked, those who can study Gandhi well should lead like the life of Gandhi. His public life and private life were the same and there is no secrecy. Gandhi is an encyclopedic subject; since its dimensions are as varied and vast as the beginnings of man on earth and his distant divine destiny here. Though his life on this earth was not very long he touched and experimented all the subjects under the sun.

For him, man-woman was the main and perhaps the only subject of greatest concern; man's horizontal as well as vertical evolution his living in peace, harmony, happiness and mutuality for rising level after level to perfection here on earth were what he aimed at. Gandhi dreamt always of human beings 'living together', a social living which would promote the all-round good and perfection of all; living was not merely to be good physically but also vitally, intellectually, morality aesthetically and spiritually.

It is no wonder that Gandhi who was spiritually inclined emphasised the importance of living together in harmony for mutual benefit and all-sided evolution. For him individual-in-society in nearer truth than an individual entity as such. This newly dawning sociality both scientifically and spiritually has to be the guide for life and living. To him, no other arts are not beautiful than human life.

We are all formally concede that the whole humanity is one family. Since Homo sapiens every where on earth belongs to one -----specie scientifically. But do we behave with each other as one family? The human psyche today is plagued by the superiority-inferiority complex based on blood and birth and there is no end to tensions and conflict resulting in violence, suffering and misery and what not.

Gandhi had a fresh thought at the whole thing and thought of equality of status for all who could be classed as human beings? There is no miracle mongering or anything of the kind in the whole of Gandhi story. He lived an open life of house-holder with wife and children and acted as on a public platform. Secrecy was sin in Gandhi eyes. Conspiracy or diplomacy if any it was open and public for all to see and know. Thought, word and deed were strung together. Body, mind and soul were in unison and harmony as in orchestral music. Seldom do we find so integrated a personality.

In his Autobiography, Gandhi reveals "I simply want to tell the story will take the shape of an Autobiography".[3]

After India became free, the government had not given due regard for Gandhian ideas. In his last days Gandhi was worried. He was weeping", Every one is eager to garland my pictures and to worship my idols; but none follows me. That is why I feel very sorry". Towards the end of Pandit Nehru, the Prime Minister of India understood that the Indian Government has realized. That the generation of employment can be brought only by having a decentralized economic system. That is one step of Gandhi's thought.

Then, we can see how the eminent personalities have evaluated Gandhiji. The famous Malayalam Poet Vallathol in his famous poem 'Entey Gurunathan' writes as this, "For Gandhi, the whole world is his *Tharavadu* (one family), in which the plants, insects, and grasses are the members of his family. Service for his fellowmen is the only end of his life and simplicity is the prime aim of his progress; The Seer of Yoga—My teacher—be live in Victory".[4]

Gandhi, was aware of all the problems that the world faced in several decades ago and tried to evolve alternatives. But unfortunately we failed to grasp the full meaning of Gandhi. This condition has net changed considerably even today. Here our task is to interpret Gandhi in the light of world developments and show the thoughts emerge as an alternative to the present and future crisis. For doing this, we have to understand the modern world with all its complexities and interpret Gandhi in a most creative manner.

Gandhi's Greatness

Dr. Martin Luther King, the Nobel peace laureate wrote, "The intellectual and moral satisfaction that I failed to gain from the Utilitarianism of Bentham and Mill, revolutionary method of Marx and Lenin, the Social Contracts theory of Hobbes, the 'back to nature optimism of Rousseau and the superman philosophy of Niezsche, I found in the non-violence resistance philosophy of Gandhi. I came to feel that this was the only morally and practically sound method open to oppressed people in their struggle for freedom".

Dr. Arnold J. Toynbee, the greatest historian of the century wrote: "On the eve of the of the advent of the Atomic Age, the Mahatma Gandhi had demonstrated that it is possible to make a revolutionary political change with recourse to violence that has customarily been used for making politically revolutionary changes in the past. If the human race refrains from committing mass suicide, it may come, in retrospect, to recognize in Gandhi, one of its historic saviours. He may be remembered as the timely prophet of his generation and the timing of the achievement has surely been providential".

Dr. Albert Einstein, the greatest scientist of this century said, "Generation to come, will scarcely believe that such a one as this, ever in flesh and blood walked upon this earth". Dr. Eric H. Erikson, the leading psycho-analyst says, "Gandhi turned into the father of his nation and he extended the paternal feelings to mankind. Obviously be acted for the species".

Some one asked Bernard Shaw, "What do you think of Gandhiji as a man?" He returned, "Gandhiji was not a man, he was a phenomenon.

Pandit Nehru cried on January 30th 1948: "The light has gone out of our lives". Then he corrected himself and said, "Yet, I am wrong for the light that shone in this country was no ordinary light and a thousand years later; that light will be seen in the country and the world will see it. . . . For the light represented the living truth".

Dr. Gene Sharp writes, "Mohandas K. Gandhi held office in no government and led no terrorist gang or rebel military army. Yet his intentions and actions aroused, the millions of Indians, shook the empire, and proved both ridicule and admiration among people through the world. This strange man for nearly fifty years challenged, first the European masters of S. Africa, then the British masters of India, and, finally even, the basic tenets of Orthodox Politics".

Though Gandhi lived in this earth only for 78 years and 4 months his Collected Works run to more than 80 thousand pages. He was one of the most learned men in the world. He touched all kinds of problems which others may not like to face. Above all, his thoughts are not only relevant to his times but also relevant and suitable for the welfare of all times. It may take centuries for us to fully understand and utilize the legacy of Mahatma Gandhi.

The Relevance of Gandhi

Dr. Ramjee Singh writes, "Indeed it is like a paradox that a man who was once regarded as an avowed critic of modern civilization is being acclaimed today as the saviour of the Modern World".[5]

Non-violence is the only Way

Today the choice before us is not between Non-violence and violence but between Non-violence and non-existence. Gandhi gave a new content to the concept of non-violence. And this is of the utmost importance today. The Gandhian theory and practice of non-violence as an alternative to all forms of violence and war has to be further developed and war strengthened. A few years ago about 60 Nobel Prize winners, in a joint statement, while expressing their concern and anxiety over the deepening of world-crisis, 'have looked towards Gandhi as the hope of humanity'.[6]

Gandhi, as the apostle of peace, had rendered the most remarkable service in the field of peace for humanity. I always doubted: Why did the Nobel Committee ignore his service? Has it any possibility that the committee would correct its shortcomings?

Gandhi as a great social scientist and practical idealist had his own clearly defined ideals and experimented them in his personal life and public relations before he exhorted them to others.

The basis of peace in social and political life is love. "I am fascinated by the law of love. It is the philosopher's stone for me".[7]

Acharya Vinoba Bhave says, "These days absence of war is regarded as peace. But peace really connotes absence of fear. There would be peace only when no part of the world is afraid of or exploited by any other part".[8]

Richard Gregg aptly states: "You cannot pursue peace but you pursue truth and non-violence and peace will be a by-product".[9]

Peace is not static but dynamic. It is an active force. According to Gandhi, peace does not mean the calmness of the graveyard. It has value only when it has the power to solve the problems which may arise on any occasion. Peace should permeate every walk of our life—social, political, economic and religious. This is possible only when we raise our society on the strong foundation of truth and non-violence.

Causes for Conflicts and Tension

It seems that humanity is always in tension and it is not possible to maintain peace and in the ever conflicting, warring and struggling society. But Gandhi believed that it is possible to establish peace permanently, if we work towards this end.

The caste system creates hatred in the minds of the people where love has to prevail. As Gandhi pointed out untouchability is the most ugly manifestation of violence in our social life. The essence of all the religions is the practice of love as a way to achieve God. But they differ widely in their practice and rituals which are the causes for religious conflicts.

Various Methods of Maintaining Peace

Gandhi approached the problem of maintaining peace from many sides—social, legal, political, economic, cultural, educational, religious and spiritual. He wanted to create a new man through his ethical principles such as the 'Seven Vows' and new society through his constructive programmes. If mutual trust is established among individual groups and nation's peace on earth can be maintained.

Education is one of the areas which demand our concentrated attention. True education should be a 'man-making' one. People should know how to live peacefully with their fellow being. The principle life, according to Gandhi should be mutual help and cooperation. He advised whenever there is dispute, people should be ready to settle it by peaceful methods such as discussion, persuasion and arbitration.

The lovers of peace need not surrender themselves meekly to injustice. Gandhi has evolved a more powerful method to fight against injustice is '*Satyagraha*'. Vinoba says, "Gandhiji taught us several things, but the most important of which is *satyagraha*. Faith in truth, in the whole conduct of life is *satyagraha*. Control of the body, speech and mind is also *satyagraha*".

The Government tries to maintain peace in day to day life by using its Police force. The Police force uses violence and threat to maintain peace. Gandhi envisaged a different type of police force which he described as, "The police of my conception will, however, be a wholly different pattern from the present day force. Its ranks will be composed of 'believers in non-violence'. They will be servant, not masters of the people. The people should be render them every help and through mutual co-operation they will easily deal with the growing disturbances. The Peace Brigade of his conception is called "Shanti-Dals" that would risk their lives in dealing with riots and work for the welfare of the people. Gandhi was both its commander and its first soldier. As a Commander he issued the order 'Do or die' and as a soldier he obeyed it. That is, his life and actions give us a complete picture of what the Shanti Sena is. No doubt, he also expounded his ideas freely in words, but it was through action, through life that his thought was most fully expressed.

Gandhi had suggested the following eleven vows to be adopted by the Indians for conducting a peaceful life. Non-violence, Truth, Non-stealing, Brahmacharya, Non-possession, Body-Labour, control of the palate, Fearlessness, Equal respect for all religions, *Swadeshi* and spirit of exclusive brotherhood.

Gandhi's Contribution to World Peace

According to Gandhi war on earth is the result of man's failure to realize his unity with God. As war is the result of the thoughts in the minds of the rulers, war could be eliminated by a change in men's thought.

To Gandhi, non-violence is a life force and not a policy. So he ceaselessly worked for internal and external peace and hence his methods are more spiritual in nature. "The discovery of *satyagraha* was the historic necessity of the 20th century if mankind was to survive at all. We must now admit the possibility of substituting non-violent collective action for militarism. Gandhi showed the way upto a point. We must now advance further from that point towards world-peace".[10]

"All men desire peace but very few desire those things which make for peace"[11] Huxley says.

Gandhi has deep belief in prayer. Prayer is the greatest binding force, making for the solidarity and oneness of the human family. If a person realizes his unity with God through prayer, he will look upon everybody as himself. There will be no individual distinction between a touchable and untouchable and Hindu with other faiths.[12]

Gandhi writes : "My religion teaches me that whenever there is distress what one cannot remove, one must fast and pray. 'Congregational prayer "said Gandhi, is a means of establishing the essential human unity through common worship.[13]

Gandhi as a Humanist

R. R. Divakar states, "Gandhi is a distinct landmark in the cultural history of mankind. His vision was not limited by narrow patriotism for a nation, but he was a patriot of Humanity. He envisaged a human family which would grow and prosper and live in harmony and happiness with the twin human social virtues of Truth and *Ahimsa*.[14]

Gandhi's humanism was the pivot of all the different aspects of his wonderful personality. According to Gandhi the highest service to man will be our sincere endeavour for drawing out the divine nature in man. To gain this end, we have to be in communion with God and to worship him as the source of all our noble virtues. By virtue of his humanism he attracted like a magnet the people of different races, religions and creeds unto him and his followers in large number clusters round him to form a happy family as it were. His humanity was undivided and he loved all men irrespective of caste, creed or colours.[15]

To him, all men are brothers and sisters in this world.

Unique features of Gandhian life style—Its relevance in today's and tomorrow's world

Gandhiji led a very simple life. This simplicity was born out of a belief and conviction that the earth's resources are limited and human beings also should limit their requirements. They should use only their biological needs. Gandhiji said himself, "I own no property and yet I feel that I am perhaps the richest man in the world. For I have been in want either for myself or for my public concerns".[16]

I understood the *Gita* teaching of non-possession to mean that those who desired salvation should act like the trustee who, though having control over great possessions regards not an iota of them as his own". Another feature of his life style was his identification with all the living beings Gandhiji believed in the unity of life. Another feature of his life style is that he never said a thing which he himself did not practise. By simple living and high thinking are his motto.

Abdul Quadir, who is a participant in the Round Table Conference, 1931, recorded: I saw him waring with half-naked dress mounting the carpeted stairs of Buckingham palace. None is attracted me except Gandhi:

What was the search of this power of Gandhi? He himself answered once:

> The secret?
> A clear heart,
> A clear conscience,
> A cool head
> Regular communion with God
> Abstention from carnal food and pleasure
> No alcohol, smoking and condiments;
> A strict vegetarian diet,
> And love for all my fellow men.

But not only in today's world, but also for ever Gandhian style of life and his approach are very relevant. 85 per cent of world's wealth is still held by 15 per cent of its population. Gandhi's belief that human wants should be kept at minimum and that a balance must be maintained between man and nature and that one should not act for the destruction of the other still holds good. Nay this is an eternal truth and this will hold good for the present and for the future. Alternative group that formed different parts of the world especially in the west (viz. The Limits to Growth by the Club of Rome, UNICEF's Green house effect etc.) began to practise the life style of Gandhi.[16] This is proof of the relevance of Gandhian life style for 'the now'.

Peace Education

Education for peace is more urgent than ever before. "Peace education is a life long learning process and it can succeed in an atmosphere of non-violence".[17] In sum, peace education will have to adopt a multiprolonged strategy embracing the whole gamut of social life and involving a variety of agencies, channels and levels. Peace education must have personal level as well as structural level components. The strength of Gandhian strategy lies precisely in its ability to bridge the two levels around the organising principles of training and non-violence.[18]

A vision of the future—The Gandhian outlook: Gandhi was

far ahead of his times and so many could not understand him then. But as days roll by, people realise his significance. His influence is bound to grow in the years to come. His clarion call of building from below at the village level should be remembered. He was definitely of the view that poverty in equality and exploitation could be ended only 'by a reorganization of society in which village life will predominate".

Scientific and technological advancement have proved themselves incapable of answering fundamental questions regarding the genuine developments of humanity. What man could be and should be in the 21st century?

This is where Gandhi comes in. He exhibits in his speeches and writings a depth of vision which have not been able to find in history. In the beginning of the 21st century the humanity will face different problems, viz. over population, unemployment, famine, energy crisis and pollution of air, water, soil etc. It is in this context that Gandhian thought comes to our help. He dedicated his life to a number of existential causes grounded on absolute convictions and all he has solved by practical experiences.

At the educational front: Gandhiji envisaged a system of execution that affected and changed the lives of the downtrodden millions of India rather than focus on a few who would take undue advantage at the cost of others. Education can have a hundred of definitions. But the class-room practices as going on today will be covered and justified by only a few of these. According to Gandhi, education should cater to the all-round development of the whole man body, mind and spirit. His basic educational system surpasses all other systems of education in the world. Education should prove to be the best vehicle for the upliftment of the masses of India. Unfortunately, India has not framed a suitable educational policy since India got freedom.

A Future Technology

All scientific and technological developments are meant to serve man's progress in desirable directions. It is envisaged to come down to the level of the poverty ridden common-man and lift him from his state of nostalgia.[19] His vision of future technology does not lead man from luxury and sophistication to a level of super sophistication. He emphasises a "need reduced life" within the framework of a cost reduced economy.

Sarvodaya: Voluntary limitations of wants, ending toward system and building up a new world order, unity of mankind and judicious sharing of the resources, bread labour, simplicity, recycling, living in tune with nature etc. are the basic features of such a life-style. Adoption of this at a mass scale will bring in welfare of all and liberation of the last man.

Dr. E. F. Schumacher says, "If India should be able to move along the path of equality through trusteeship she would be a name in the world".[20]

Man and Nature

Gandhi considered life is an art; at the same time it is a craft. Many people do not really enjoy living. The modern man is always living in a world of vanity. Greed should be controlled. After reading the book 'Return to Nature' Gandhi was convinced that he should share his life not only with people but also with animals, birds and trees and plants in the environment. Life is to be one of the mutual sharing and not of exploitation. He built his settlements and *ashrams* in waste lands adjacent to villages. Gandhi settled in Sevegram to live the life of sharing and mutual aid and thereby demonstrate to the world at large that the future lies in the human beings living in tune with eco-system in small communities.

Nature Cure

Gandhi knew that the Allopathic system was too costly to meet the requirements of everyone. So he recommended to the people that they should follow nature cure.

Gandhian approach to population control: He opined, "A large part of the miseries of today can be solved if we regard ourselves as trustees of today can be solved if we regard ourselves as trustees for the moral welfare of the future generation".[21]

"Self-indulgence leads to destruction and renunciation to immortality".[22] Population explosion in India like any other country is a 20th century phenomenon. Gandhi was deadly against the artificial forms of any methods. His married couples adopted practically *brahmacharya*. He agreed to say that from that period onwards his family life became more ideal and happy.

Erik Fromm, wrote Gandhi is truly a prophet of the 20th century world in that he was an uncompromising concrete symbol of the common man.

The world has a definite purpose and the purpose is manifested in all aspects of human life. This fundamental purpose of human existence on earth is employed by Gandhi as the principal parameter to judge all the affairs of life. All his writings and speeches bear testimony, that religion with God and religion with ethics are the part and parcel of every aspect of man's life. Joseph Mukalel says, "Our behaviouristic, structuralistic, psycho analystic and pragmatic perceptions of reality have darkened our eyes and blocked our vision of reality. Here comes the relevance of the Gandhian vision of the future."[23]

Gandhian future economic view: Gandhi said that the new economics that India needed must be based on self-reliance and self-respect. He wanted economics is to be spiritualised even as politics. J.J. Anjaria says, "Gandhian economics is a mixture, perhaps a queer mixture, of science and technology".[24]

Working for economic equality means abolishing the external conflicts between the capital and labour. Gandhi suggests the doctrine of Trusteeship as a way to establish 'equalitarian' society. The concept of Trusteeship implies spiritual attitude towards wealth.[25]

As Sir Geoffery Vickers said in a British Radio Broadcast: we are involved in an economic system in which multiplying goods, multiplying wants and multiplying populations endlessly excite one another. The economic problem of mankind is not whether we can continue to prosper but whether we can make the mutual relations of man and nature sufficiently stable to provide an acceptable basis for human life".

By concluding I say the greatest contribution of the charismatic leader given to the future world society is *sarvodaya* a new dimension of freedom. This objective can create a world of oneness, a big family of Man where the strings of identification are those of love and mutual understanding married to the idea of communal peace and harmony. Moreover he showed us that only by inner and well directed effort can a man rebuild himself.... Yes,

Gandhi's thought will become an eternal success and it gives solace, to all not only fit for 21st century but also for all the coming generations.

REFERENCES

1. Rajiv Gandhi, The vision of Nehru, *Gandhi Marg*, Nov.—Dec. 1988, p. 456.
2. Divakar R.R., *Trying to Understand*, Journal of Gandhian Studies, Institute of Gandhian Thought and Peace Studies, Gandhi Bhavan, University of Allahabad, p. 1.
3. Gandhi M.K., *An Autobiography*, Navajivan Publishing House, 3rd, 1982, Introduction, p. ix.
4. Vallathol, 'Eutey Guru Nathan', *National Book Stalls*, 11th ed., p. l.
5. Ramjee Singh, *The Gandhi and the Modern World*, Preface, p. 1.
6. *Ibid.*, p. 1.
7. Gandhi M.K., *Young India*, January 8, 1925.
8. Vinoba Bhave: *Harijan*, 1.1.1955.
9. Pichard Gregg: The Power of Non-violence, *Navajivans*.
10. Ramachandran, G., *Religion and Peace*, Seminars sub-committee for the Gandhi Century, New Delhi.
11. Aldus Huxley, *Ends and Means*.
12. Gandhi, M.K., *Young India*, 25.9.1924.
12. Gandhi, M.K., *Harijan*, March 3, 1946.
14. Divakar R.R., Souvenir of the Gandhi Bhavan, Allahabad University, 1985.
15. Gandhi, M.K., *Young India*, April 10, 1925.
16. Ananth, T.S., A Gandhian Approach to Technological Wonders, Delhi, *Gandhi Peace Foundation*, June 1987, p. 8.
17. John, M.S., *Gandhi Marg*, July 1990, p. 201.
18. *Ibid*.
19. Joseph Mukale: A Vision of the Future: The Gandhian Outlook, *Gandhi Marg* of Oct, 1980, p. 337.
20. Ramjee Singh: Quoted in the *Relevance of Gandhian Thought*, p. 242.
21. Gandhi, M.K., *Self Restraint Vs Self Indulgence*, p. 91.
22. Gandhi, M.K., *From Yervada Mandir*, p. 59.
23. Joseph Mukalel: *op. cit.*, p. 342.
24. Anjaria, J.J. *Gandhian Economics*, 1945, p. 10.
25. *Harijan*, 20.11.1935.

27

MAHATMA GANDHI'S ECONOMIC IDEAS AND ITS RELEVANCE IN TWENTY-FIRST CENTURY

—ANUBHA ROY

Independent India embarked on the path of planning to achieve growth with social justice, consistent with other socio-economic objectives. More than forty-five years have elapsed since then. Huge investments have been made, far reaching experiments and institutional changes have been attempted to gear up the growth rates of national product, per capita income, agricultural and industrial production.

History reveals that Lord Mountbatten referred to his first interview with Pandit Nehru on 24th March 1947, when he asked Panditjee what he thought was the greatest problem confronting India. Nehru replied, "the economic problem". This problem is still persisting when Indian Republic is very close to its middle-age.

Nobody can deny the fact that production of foodgrains in India increased from 52 million tons (1950-51) to 182 million tons in 1993-94. Public stocks of foodgrains with the central pool stood at 30 million tons on 1st Janaury, 1995. Although, the renowned scientist Dr. D.N. Rao expressed that "if poor people of India start eating more than one meal everyday, India would have shortage of food-stock". Since the First Five Year Plan, villages electrified increased from 346,000 to 487,000 in the Seventh Plan. Actual power generation increased from 1.10 MKW to 14.50 MKW during the corresponding period. National income stepped up from Rs. 8,979 crores to Rs. 1,73,207 crores during the same period. Our per capita income at 80-81 prices was Rs. 2,282 in 1993- 94 (Rs. 6,234 at current prices.)

It is remarkable to note that life-expectancy has touched the level of 61 years (1992). Infant mortality rate is 79 per thousand (1992) and the literacy rate in India is 52% (1990) and the participation of women in total employment is 25%.

But, there is also other side of the coin. We have achieved quantitative growth without qualitative development. Our gross national income has accelerated, but not gross national prosperity. Different sectors of our economy still living in different centuries, so far as basic necessities and cultural awareness are concerned.

Inspite of forty-five years of planning, the removal of poverty and unemployment—the two long term objectives, remained a mirage. The problem of unemployment is acute. The back-log of unemployment in India has estimated at 23 million persons (open unemployment) at the beginning of the Eighth Plan. The total number of persons requiring employment would be 95 million over the period of ten years, i.e., 1992 to 2002.

More than 350 million Indians (of whom 270 million in rural areas) are below the poverty line.[1] Today, India has as many persons below the poverty line as the entire population of the country at the time of independence in 1947.

The World Bank warned, "by the turn of this century, 54% of all illiterates will be in India".

In India, there is scarcity of 3,10,00,000 houses. The economic-survey of 1994-95 observed that debt-service payments on past-debt will continue to be high and may touch $ 13 billion in 1995-96. (The cost of serving old debt next year at Rs. 1,22,480 crores will be more than 120% of the centre's total revenue of Rs. 1,00,787 crores). Consequently, the Government has to borrow more and more to pay interest and repay instalments of loans. Thus, 'debt trap' is going to be a 'death trap' in near future.

Mahatma Gandhi observed, "The soul of India lies in its villages" and the foremost aim of the greatest Indian was to "Wipe out every tear from every eye". But the stark truth of today is that there is a vast chunk of his countrymen dwelling in slums and hovels, quite ignorant of their freedom. " They do not even feel its pulse, nor do they recognise any trace of it".

The spectacles of the present are too coloured to provide a dispassionate view and now it has been realised that political freedom, is undoubtedly incongruous and dangerously incomplete without socio-economic emancipation of the masses. Economic discontent is like dynamite; it may ignite at the mere touch of a spark and wreck the whole society. The painful gap caused by the inequality of economic status and the disparity of material possessions must be narrowed which will stabilise the material basis of the society.

It is unfortunate to express that several political ideologies have created conflicts both at the national and the international levels leading to war threats and sometimes to civil war in the country. In this background, solution lies in Gandhism.

Mahatma Gandhi did not compose voluminous treaties on economic ideology. In several lectures, in '*Young India*' and '*Harijan*', he made references to the kind of economic system, which according to him was 'ideal' for India.

Generally, ideas, of a man are the outcome of many external influences of one's own thinking and philosophy. He has perhaps drawn inspiration for his thesis of the universal obligation of 'manual labour for all human beings' from Tolstoy, Ruskin and the Russian writer Bondart. While writing in '*Harijan*' (1936) Gandhi observed that God created man to eat his bread by the swcat of his brow. It means, man must earn his bread by labouring with his own hand.

He was deeply influenced by Ruskin's '*Unto the Last*' and he was of the view that by nature all human beings were equal and there should not be any economic discrimination or disparity among different individuals in respect of income, consumption and other basic necessities of life.

The unbridgeable gulf-between the peasant and the landlord, the workers and mill-owners, the people of the states and the Indian princes, the classes and the masses deeply exercised Gandhi's mind. In his scheme of things, there is nothing unhealthy, inherently conflictual or contradictory in the interests of the capitalists and labourers. Unlike the Marxists, Gandhi believed that the labourers and the capitalists could work together in harmony like a great family, with each functioning for mutual advancement.[2] Gandhi, therefore, believed that the 'capitalists were to regard themselves as trustees for those on whom he depends for the making, the retention and increase in his capital".[3]

Gandhi's economic ideas were framed in such a manner which avoids exploitation of man by man. He was in favour of decentralisation of economic power. He frequently quoted, "If

India is to evolve along non-violent lines, it will have to decentralise many things.[4] He revealed that " capitalist class which was exploitative of the talent and resources available in the society". It does not require much argument to assert that concentration of economic power has created a gulf between the privileged few and the under-privileged majority. In an under-developed economy, concentration of economic power in the hands of the few has created more confusion. So, for him, decentralisation of economic power is the panacea for all evils.

Gandhi's movement was a "mass-movement". The basic philosophy of Gandhism is to change the society. Unlike the movement of renaissance and reform which were mainly the products of urban environment. In Jay Prakash Narayan's terminology "un-Indian and elitist".[5] Social reconstruction of Gandhi was mainly rural oriented. Gandhi's thinking was the manifestations of a wider movement aimed at transformation and revitalization of Indian values, norms and institutions, which was initiated in the beginning of the eighteenth century. His national movement aimed at 'total social revolution' with the help of '*Satyagrah*.

In the economic sphere, he believed that the economic salvation of India depended upon the economic regeneration of vast millions of Indians living in 5,90,000 villages. He believed in 'Gram Swaraj', which is synonymous to village self-sufficiency. Gandhi visualised—villages to be self-sufficient and autonomous, so that every village is capable of managing its affairs itself, even to the extent of defending itself against the onslaught of the environment. '*Swaraj*' is a comprehensive term and infinitely greater than the concept of independence.[6]

Gandhi opposed colonial imperialism of British Government, which aimed at utilization of raw materials in the villages of India and made it a 'dumping ground' of British manufactured goods. So, he aimed at developing village industries. The development of village industries will not only check the heavy exodus of rural population into urban areas this will also regenerate the entire nation from the grass-root level. This valuable ideology was adopted by the Government during the post-independence when the community development and Panchayati Raj was introduced for the development of Indian villages. His rural development emphasised on 'equity', 'dignity of labour' and participation of common masses.

He considered, Machine has its place; it has come to stay, but it must not be allowed to displace human labour. An improved plough is a good thing, but if by some chances, one man could plough up by some mechanical invention of his the whole of land of India, and control all the agricultural produce and if the million had no other occupation, they would starve and being idle, they would become dunces".[7] In another place; he wrote, "I consider it a sin and injustice to use machinery for the purpose of concentration of power and riches in the hands of the few. Today, the machine is used in this way.[8]

His economic thinking is very often mis-interpreted by social scientists. So, Mukherjee[9] in his writing has very aptly remarked, "it would be wrong to argue that Gandhi was against large scale or mass production. He was not against big machines, but he was against the use of machine to exploit individuals. He did not want the machine to cripple the life of man."[10]

In order to develop a harmonious relationship between labour and capital, his trusteeship principle emphasised on a balanced relationship between the rich and the poor. He opined, "the rich cannot accumulate wealth without the co-operation of the poor in the society.

'Trusteeship' principle of Mahatma Gandhi aimed at "transferring accumulated private wealth to community ownership, where labourer and peasants are co-partners with capitalists and landlords. Through trusteeship every individual would be able to get sufficient work to enable him to provide his daily requirements. Such an ideal could be universally realised if the means of production of basic necessities of life could remain under the control of the masses".[11]

The Gandhian ideology of 'socialism' placed more stress on the rural masses and the lovely simplicity of the village uplift. For him, "Democracy was the art and science of mobilising the entire physical, economic and spiritual resources of all the sections of the people in the service of the common good of all". The 'Economist' rightly, remarked that "socialism as practised in India has been a 'fraud'. Our brand of socialism did not result in transfer of wealth from the rich to the poor, but only from the honest rich to the dishonest rich".[12]

An important economic concept— "Wants are unlimited", which has been contradicted by Gandhi. He believed that they are limited and can be fulfilled without impeding development of socio-cultural and spiritual life. In this direction, the present era has posed a question "whether Gandhian ideology will survive or not?" People may apprehend a break-down of the normative socio-economic structure in the midst of a strong propaganda of 'consumerism'.

'Non-possession' and 'bread labour' are the two important concepts of Gandhi. Non-possession signifies not having food or anything beyond immediate need and 'bread labour' means that every man should labour with his body for his food and clothing. J.D. Sethi, a well known Gandhian Economist explains the principle of 'bread labour' in this line— "Bread-labour in simple terms implies that amount of physical labour, given the arts of production and the society determined necessities. That much labour time must be spent by everybody in physical labour. Any one who does not work with his hands or other limbs runs the risk of being a parasite. Even the greatest thinker, poet or philosopher is likely to be misled by his own ideas and plagues of sophistication, if he is not involved in some physical action".[13]

The twenty-first century, which is less than 1700 days away. So, the anxiety to move into this 'century' is very acute among the intellectuals and now it can be clearly stated that "there is no other visible alternative than the Gandhian model of economic development, given the compulsions of the contemporary world situation. The drive towards rapid industrialisation and urbanisation, the persisting tendency towards concentration of economic and political power, political and economic corruption, heavy exodus of rural population into cities, poverty, unemployment all have infused a sense of urgency and relevance to the Gandhian model. For the maladies of recent time, Gandhian idealism and moralism can provide effective solutions and results."[14]

In this context, the message of Mahatma Gandhi in his 125th birth anniversary year is more relevant, "build India by your own efforts, be a sovereign power, become self-respectable and never compromise in principles. West is bound to come to the east, for it is again a question of their survival, interest and self-interest. They also need us as much. as we need them". The relationship should be one of equality and not of 'slavery'.

The 21st century may be the generations of those who "will

scarcely believe that such a man as this ever lived in flesh and blood and walked upon the earth" (Einstein). But his economic ideas have got their philosophical background. No age or no society can fade its brightness and usefulness and these ideas are essentially a process, continuation and culmination of years old civilization.

REFERENCES

1. CMIE, *Basic Statistics*, August, 1994.
2. Nagvi, S., "Economic Thinking of Gandhi—The Theory of Trusteeship", in S.C. Biswas (ed), *Gandhi—Theory and Practice: Socio Impact and Contemporary Relevance*. Simla, Indian Institute of Advanced Studies, (1969), p. 212.
3. *Young India*, March 26, 1931, p. 49.
4. *Harijan*, December 30, 1939, p. 391.
5. Jay Prakash Narayan's forward to J.D. Sethi, *Gandhi Today*, Vikash Publishing House, New Delhi (1978), p. VIII.
6. *Young India*, Vol. III, p. 547.
7. *Young India*, 5.11.1925.
8. As cited in a J. Nehru, *The Discovery of India*, New York, 1960, p. 327.
9. Mukherjee Dhurjati, *The Towering Spirit*, Chetana Publication, New Delhi (1978).
10. Sharma, B.D., "Gandhi as a Political Thinker", Indian Press, Private Ltd., Allahabad, 1956, p. 138.
11. *Young India*, Vol. III, pp. 923-24.
12. Quoted by N. Palkivala in 'Forty-three Years of Independence' Forum of Free Enterprise, Bombay.
13. Aziz Abdul, "Gandhian Economic System: Its Relevance to Contemporary India" in *Studies on Gandhi* edited by V.T. Patil Sterling Publishers Private Ltd., New Delhi, p. 89.
14. Patil, V.T. and Anikivi, A.S., " An Enquiry into Gandhian Model of Democracy" in *Studies on Gandhi* edited by V.T. Patil, p. 33.

28

NON-VIOLENCE IN THE TEACHINGS OF MAHAVIRA AND MAHATMA GANDHI AND ITS RELEVANCE IN THE 21st CENTURY

—KOSHALYA WALLI

Time changes. With the change of time, human beings change but no change of time urges the change in humanism. Humanism distinguishes human beings from other species in creation. Humanism comprises: truth, non-violence, strength in character, non-stealing, non-possession, purity, devoid of jealousy, penance, self-study, surrender to God, taking senses from external sphere to inner sphere, concentration on a point of conviction, meditation on Cosmic Energy, absorption in the ultimate.

Gandhiji became Mahatma on account of following the above mentioned principles in letter and spirit not only in his own life and family but in his public life as well. Despite the fact that he wanted to have his own self-realization through the service of humanity and initially was not having any idea of becoming a politician, circumstances threw him in the fire of politics to free the Nation from the clutches of slavery. His service of humanity started in South Africa, where, he had bitter personal experiences as a traveller in train, as lawyer and as an Indian. He saw the ill treatment meted out to his fellow Indians who would work there as coolies. His sense of self-respect as a human being, as an Indian made him to work for the rights of resident Indians in Durban in South Africa. Therefrom the concept of *Satyagraha* originated in his mind. As a devotee of Truth, he insisted on owing the truth individually and collectively at the cost of his own comforts and convenience. He abstained from food to purify his own mind, intellect and heart to the extent that he could appeal to the conscience of his other fellow human beings to accept truth as that was the only way to live and let live. He did not believe in taking cudgels against anyone whatever the attitude of the other party. He primarily believed strongly that spirit was abiding everywhere. Spirit was one.

To appeal to the Spirit in others by not resorting to normal food and thereby purifying his inner self by purifying his mind and senses was his discovery rather research in the practical field that he named *Satya-agraha*—persistence to follow truth by him as well as by others. He believed in collective *Sadhana* in the public life. Thus started his sojourn to free his motherland from the clutches of the foreign reign by means of non-violence, fearlessness and right of self-determination. India ultimately won the freedom by means of non-violence without shedding blood and without resorting to war.

Free India was advised by Gandhi to bring forward those to run the government Who were not freedom fighters. Let them contribute their mite to the extent they can and wherever they needed the help, the required help and guidance would be provided there and then. Unfortunately, Gandhi's advice, fell on deaf ears. He found himself alone in this idea. So called followers of Gandhi proved to be ambitious and desirous to run the government of Free India and did not care for Gandhi's advice. Gandhi felt all alone and gave up the desire to live upto one hundred and twenty-five years.

The division of the country on the eve of independence was an intolerable shock to Gandhi. The communal frenzy cost Gandhi's life and he left us on 30th January, 1948.

Today, after forty-eight years of freedom, India finds herself in crisis. The leaders of Free India by their omissions and commissions gave birth to some problems that are staring at our face in 1995. Common innocent masses sacrifice our face in 1995. Common innocent masses sacrifice themselves for the sake of the nation. Soldiers die for the defence of the borders of the country. Innocent young wives of soldiers find themselves widows and children fatherless. Moral values of Indian cultural heritage are nowhere visible old values are gone. New values have not taken place. Physically we might be free but mentally we are slaves; for, we look to the West and are not receptive to the vibrations of our motherland. Our pattern of education still continues on Lord Macauley's line. Sanskrit—the backbone of Indian culture does not find any place in the national pattern of education of today. We forget that Gandhi desired the roots of valuable Indian culture to be planted in the minds of the youth. That Science and Sanskrit go together is not comprehended by the present day leadership. Gandhi is remembered on 15th August, 31st January, 26th January and on 2nd October as a ritual. We deceive ourselves before deceiving anybody else.

Women of today may be high degreeholders, I.A.S. Officers, Professors, Lawyers, Engineers, Doctors, Computer-scientists and the like, but basically they do not have the vitality to fight the dowry ridden customs, and, other social problems that stare at them. Gandhi's trained women were fearless, self-confident, simple yet high thinking with originality adhering to honesty, punctuality and dedication. It were women who at Gandhi's instance went for picketing at wine shops. Lord behold every one got astonished—Bapu sending sisters for picketing at wine shops! But Gandhi's originality in understanding the innate power of motherhood paid dividends and sisters became successful in the propagation of prohibition. Gandhi's faith in self-control should have solved the problem of population control but the so called associates of Gandhi did not have basically the innate faith in Gandhi's approach to Free India's way of development. Consequently, we find ourselves today attacked by terrorism, overpopulation, rights without performing duties, unemployment, violence, restlessness, lawlessness, corruption and the like.

Life has become a puzzle in today's Free India. Suicides, deceit, suspicion, burglary, rape, aggressive attitude, mistrust rule the day. Fearlessness is not known. The whole world is a fire, it seems, nationals of free India are found as refugees in their own country. With the passage of time, it seems the present leadership, it is observed, has developed an attitude of indifference towards these unfortunate refugees who know not whom to approach for redressal of their grievances. They have no systematic arrangement for the education of their children. Examinations are held at Jammu, the planning for the same is done in the Valley ruled at the moment by the militants. Results are delayed at the cost of the students' career. Under the given circumstances, we have no other alternative but to return to Gandhi.

To start with, a family of the 21st century has to have equal rights and responsibilities for man and women. Till date, women may have equal rights in the pages of the constitution but in practice, a so-called educated girl of today when gets married is not sure of her self-respect and suitable place in her in-law's house. Today also we find that after marriage mother-in-law venture to find spots in moon. The daughter-in-law is victimized by the whims of her in-laws in general and mother-in-law in particular. She (mother-in-law) dares the ousting of her newly wedded daughter-in-law from her home and boasts of getting her son married for the second time. This is not a myth, not a novel; but, a stern reality of 11th December, 1994. Only, if girls could be educated on the lines of Gandhi's definition and pattern of education. Only if boys would know their duties of married life and the place of wife in their life along with parents. Boy has not any grievance against the girl but does not find courage to face the mother who feels even in this last phase of 20th century that she can play with the life of the daughter-in-law, in any manner she likes.

Education to Gandhi meant drawing out the latent faculties in man, courage to resist the wrong and own the correct attitude, fearlessness, humility and the like.

Today we find the degreeholder youth piring for jobs. Gandhi's education aimed at job-oriented education, self-reliant education, self-dependent degree. Macaulay's system of education shall have to be said 'alien' in case we really desire to have education in tune with our rich cultural heritage.

In the field of economic development, multinational companies are to be discouraged. Import of grains already in stock with our farmers is to be done away with. The common man faces incessant hike in prices. This rise in prices is due to wrong economic policies. Corruption has eaten into the vitals of the nation. The present economic policy makes the poor poorer and the rich richer.

The villagers find themselves unemployed. Wasteful expenditure is encouraged. Natural resources are carelessly dealt with. Factories and industries produce articles that are not being consumed for having no purchasing power with the masses. The big economical organizations adopt the economic policies to serve their selfish ends. Common masses have virtually no voice. Consequently, black money is on increase. Villages are being uprooted. Today we find *juggis* in abundance. Disappointed common masses being below poverty line resort to violence.

Gandhi advocated the cause of villagers to encourage them to continue with their cottage industries. The need of the hour is to revive and revitalise handicrafts in our villages. Our traditional village art should find place in our day to day work with ultra modern industries. Increase in production, equality in distribution, control in consumption—These three formulas are to be owned and implemented by the consumer revolution. The poorest farmer finds it beyond his access to get the bank loan that is basically earmarked for him and people like him. Decentralization is the need of the hour. The dire need of the hour is the awakening of the masses.

Today, we have the valueless politics in practice, masses are in slumber, pinning away for both ends meet with respect and dignity. Democracy in reality means healthy formation of public opinion. Our so-called leaders are awakened on the day of election in five years. For the rest of their tenure, they are the slaves of their whims, unbridled desires, ambitions and satisfactions.

The election process is highly expensive. Leaders by and large cross the floor for the lure of power, post and so called position.

The political parties should be registered. The money donated by the companies to various parties to fight election should be necessarily included in the expenses of election. The accounts of the political parties should be audited. Voters should have identity cards at the time of casting their votes. Computer facility should be availed of to prepare the result of the candidate on the day of election itself. Gram Panchayat election and Municipal elections should take place.

Before the election, there should be President's rule and the party in power should resign. The Central leadership should continue to work till the election result is out. The adhoc Central Government should not start any new work, only carry on with normal routine work. The list of voters be prepared every year instead of once in five years. Formation of Gram Sabha is "A Must". The service class is victimized, so far as taxes are concerned. The middle class is the target for Tax department. Red tape is in increase. Without personal influence and without bribe, people complain, no work fructifies. Decentralization is the only answer to cure these political ailments.

Indian masses have to unite, think collectively. Pollution is to be checked. Gandhi fought with the weapons of Truth and Non-Violence. Today, Indian leadership is taken away by pomp and show of western way of administration.

The basis of Indian cultural heritage is 'Spiritualism'. The values are to be given place in our political set-up or else, we allow ourselves to be annihilated. We have invited the western civilization out of sheer ignorance. Gandhi said—"We have attained political freedom. From the viewpoint of villages and villagers, we have to attain social, economical and ethical freedom. Complete freedom (*Poorna Swarajya*) is yet to be completed. Voters need being awakened. Having said so, Gandhi left us after a very short span of time.

Gandhi's followers forgot Gandhi. Indian culture and civilization got forgotten by masses. Western approach was owned in economic and democratic arena. The result was centralization of the polity and economics. India of today has no self confidence. Masses are looking towards this government or that government the crisis of today is the crisis of confidence.

The whole power should be vested in the people. People should prove worthy of the same. They should be awake, alert and honest as also sincere. Eternal vigil is the price to be paid for the perfect attainment of social, economic, ethical freedom besides political independence that we got in 47 but is today in a chaotic condition.

National practice—Indian first and Indian last—should be the goal as also our day-to-day practice. Corruption is to be done away with. Every one of us has to change ourselves along with the circumstances around us.

Even now it is not late if we awaken ourselves from the slumber of selfishness, embrace selflessness, be fearless, have unity in our thought, word and deed, practice truth, honesty and ethics in our practical life. That was what the father of nation desired from us, that is what Mother India demands of us.

To sum up, Gandhi's relevance in 21st century is more than it ever was.

29

THE WAY THE WORLD IS MOVING AND THE INSIGHT AND FORESIGHT OF MAHATMA GANDHI

—SISIR K. DHAR

Life has a value when it has something valuable as its object

—Hegel

I

Is there anyone in this world, except insanes, who would note like to be happy in life? Mahatma Gandhi, to whom "The supreme consideration is man," holds "human happiness combined with full mental and moral development" as the goal of life. There can be not better goal for man than happiness and all-round development of the mind, that makes one 'a traveller in larger world'—and, that is the fulfilment of life. Verily, a developed mind is the greatest asset of man.

What do we mean by happiness and mental development? I have long felt—and this conviction is all the stronger at the age of 75 years, that the happiness or the sense of satisfaction of a mentally developed person is something richer—qualitatively different—than that of an under-developed person. The wise are happy, felt Plato. The sense of satisfaction of a Buddha deliberately giving up the kingdom and dear ones in search of the well-being of others in the world, is something different from that of a ruffian for success in his sphere, just as the taste of a ripe fruit and a rotten one differs. Buddha or Socrates' satisfaction to too deep for perception by the ruffian. It is not for nothing that 'Isopanishad' enjoins one to 'enjoy through sacrifice'. One in whom inner development has kindled an awareness of something or things great, might do away smilingly with things that ordinary minds crave for. By mental development we mean the blooming in a man of basic richer qualities of mind. To me, they are compassion or goodwill, moral sense, sense of beauty and truthfulness—a quest to reach the roots of questions, something not identical with scholarliness.

How far does the modern industrial civilization help or hinder attainment of this goal of happiness and mental development? This civilization is prominent most in the Western countries, while non-Western countries have since long accepted it as the model. (We may call this Western civilization for this reason, capitalist civilization as capitalism and industrialism grew as twins of a single process, and modern civilization as it grew during the modern period of history—since the Industrial Revolution in the West. We may also call it a materialist civilization, that it is basically, facilitating a sort of material abundance along with growth of materialists utilitarian values and having no avowed spiritual aim).

While considering the question raised above, we must recognize the contribution of this civilization, based on an immense growth of science and technology, to a vast advancement of the society in different directions and enrichment of the standard of living of the mankind as a whole. The distance between the condition of the early men—an insecured life in caves and jungles with little knowledge of things before them and with no worthwhile tools and instruments—and the condition of citizens in a modern society is immeasurable. Since the earliest days, after he had acquired language, or some rudiments to start with, and was thus capable of transmitting experience, mankind has moved ahead from commonsense to science, and the stride, gigantic in its totality, continues. We need not recount here in detail all the advances thus attained stage by stage and we may instead look at the condition in our own time to gauge the extent of this contribution.

Obviously, science and technology, as the foundation of this civilization, have carried the human society from a nadir of existence to a rather dazzling height—from a state of helplessness against the vagaries of Nature to one of great control over Nature and to a state of considerable security and plenty. In fact, science and industrial growth have acted beneficially in different spheres of human life. Thus, apart from a promise of eradication of poverty and hunger with an abundant production and actually with some remarkable success in the matter mainly in the countries of the West, there has been a great increase in the quantity of human knowledge and increase in the facilities for education and health, a noticeable growth of rationalism as compared with the blind superstitious faith of the primitive man. This increase of knowledge has led to less dependence on the mercy of a supernatural force on the one hand and to more desire for better social arrangements, institutions etc. on the other, to a greater scope for leisure owing to higher productivity and dirty work being done by machine, relative advance in women's position, greater facilities for communication and transport, entertainment and amusement etc.

II

One of the most obvious aspects of human frailty is too much concentration on the immediate, with too little care for future consequences, ...[1]

We have just indicated the beneficial side of the modern civilization, only very briefly, as people today are so conversant with the benefits of science and industry, when even an average school boy or girl can prepare a long essay on this subject. Rather, to have a balanced view, we should discuss at greater length the other side, not at all rosy, of the matter that generally gets much less attention in our academic or intellectual circles.

In striking contrast to the common notion, as early as in 1908, in *'Hind Swaraj'* Gandhi deprecates the modern industrial civilization in very strong terms: "drive out Western civilization. All else will follow." I consider the *'Hind Swaraj'*, in which he "pits soul force against brute force," the most basic of all that Gandhi has written. All that he has said afterwards are more or less the elaboration of the basic theme of the *'Hind Swaraj'* —the supremacy of 'soul force'.

A great spiritualist humanist, Gandhi's supreme concern has been the inner development of man that distinguishes man from all other animals. With this development, a man is, in Poet Shelley's words, "the king over himself; just, gentle, wise." In this inner development, Gandhi had no doubt, lies happiness and fulfilment of life. I admire and respect with all my heart this uncommon man, who wants "to wipe every tear from every eye" and dares to fight all evils and injustice with love and without arms. But our respect or admiration must not cloud our judgment. Right or wrong, I notice streaks of one-sidedness, extremism, exaggeration and over-simplification in not a few of his pronouncements made from time to time. (Looking at, what I feel, his excessive preoccupation with the evil of sex, I ask myself: Is not Gandhi a bit puritan?) The '*Hind Swaraj'* is a coherent thesis against industrial civilization. His mentor, Gokhale thinks it "so crude and hastily conceived." His disciple, Mahadev Desai, also feels the language about machinery "rather crude". But at least as late as 1938 Gandhi sticks to his views in *'Hind Swaraj'*. I believe, he sticks to them till the last, and I accept as invaluable the basic thrust of his thoughts and approach.

One may attribute the above-mentioned drawbacks in Gandhi's statements to the fact that, active in a tumultuous world of politics, he was a man in a hurry. By nature, he is however, strikingly calm and resolute. More plausible than this explanation is the possibility that, fighting single-handedly against prevalent ideas and approach, he is inclined to lay emphasis—and sometimes he lays over-emphasis—on his ideas. Also plausible is the possible idea that there are 'two Gandhis' in the same person. This fact is of utmost help in understanding him whom so many have found an enigma. On the 'two Gandhis', one is an 'idealist', who left to himself will strive unwaveringly to reach the farthest point of his ideal in its perfect form; and there is a 'practical idealist' who is convinced that much more important than presenting a 'blue-print' of a perfect utopia is leading the people themselves even one step towards the ideal. The 'practical idealist' never turns his face away from the ideal, but recognizes that our ideal is like a pole star—it cannot be reached, it should guide us; and he sometimes makes concession to the realities of the situation and to the imperfection of human nature, e.g. on the question of machine.

Gandhi recognizes the spiritual emptiness or rather the degrading materialist character of the industrial civilization. Essentially, his basic thoughts are not much new, which he claims are "as old as the Himalayas". The thoughts have roots in the '*Upanishads*', '*Gita*', Buddha, Mahavira, Jesus and such others, including Tolstoy and Ruskin. In his own land, and in his own time, Poet Tagore, whom Gandhi called 'Gurudeva', also had presented in his writings the concepts of inner-development *('Atma-shakti')*, *'satyagraha'* (*cf.* the drama *'Prayaschita'*— Atonement), a simple life, rural reconstruction, constructive activity etc. But not only thoughts, action was Gandhi's forte, that captured the imagination of the world.

In *'Hind Swaraj'*, Gandhi emphasises that the modern civilization is "a civilization only in name. Under it the nations of Europe are becoming degraded and ruined day by day." He says these even when he is conscious that the people in Europe, with bodily welfare as the object of life, are as a whole better off materially than earlier. He adds, "Formerly, men were made slaves under physical compulsion. Now they are enslaved by temptation of money and of the luxuries that money can buy." Again, "They keep up their energy by intoxication. They can hardly be happy in solitude." He does not ignore their good qualities: "They are enterprising and industrious, and their mode of thought is not inherently immoral. Neither are they bad at heart. I, therefore, respect them." Nonetheless, never does he like the life-style the materialist civilization creates.

Gandhi had witnessed closely the contributions of the modern civilization. But he was not enamoured, aware of its weak foundation: "This civilization takes note neither of morality nor of religion," he observed. He did not live to see the unimaginable advance of science during the post-World War II decades. But he was dismayed to see what havoc even a single atom bomb could cause. "There are now diseases of which people never dreamt of before," he said in *'Hind Swaraj'*. More diseases are emerging in the modern civilization. We indicate below, not only diseases that may afflict man individually, but also some deadly ailments and evils that this civilization produces darkening the future of mankind:

(1) The industrial civilization is over-exploiting, polluting and exhausting Nature and thus harming seriously the future of the inhabitants on the earth. The original object of science was: (i) to know the laws of Nature and to increase control over it, and (ii) to raise productivity especially through industrial growth to remove poverty and hunger. While the success in the first field has been conspicuously enough, very much remains undone in the second (as will be detailed later). However, a reckless pursuit for material abundance is threatening Nature and, if unchecked, cannot but

endanger the very human existence, when natural resources, mostly non-renewable and supplying raw materials for industry, are limited in supply. The over-exploitation of resources now going on as also technologies being developed for more production are harming the environment increasingly as production increases. As the authors of the valuable Report by the Council of the Club of Rome, Alexander King and Bertrand Schneider, observe, "the human race, in pursuit of material gain by the exploitation of nature, is racing towards the destruction of the planet and itself."[1]

There is, no doubt, a burning problem of a growing population with a rising impact on the demand for resources. Sir Julian Huxley described the exploding human population as "The cancer of the planet." Others also have spoken on the same lines. This growing population is encroaching menacingly forests and virgin lands. One shudders to think what will happen to the existing stock of natural resources if this growth continues or if this large, growing population, mostly in the Third World, happens to acquire the standard of living of its Western brethren. Yet, when we speak of the environment pollution, it will be erroneous to lay the entire or even the major blame, as several writers do, on this population growth, though the gravity of the matter is undeniable.

Let us look at the matter in the correct perspective. Thus, as Walden Bello writes for Third World Network Features, (i) 80 per cent of the current consumption of the earth's resources may be accounted for by the 20 per cent of the world's population residing in the North; (ii) the average Swiss, for instance, pours 2,000 times more toxic waste into the environment than the average Sahelian farmer; (iii) if the levels of consumption and waste do not change, 57 million Northerners who will be born in the 1990s will pollute the earth more than the extra 911 million Southerners, owing to the gross disparity in the rate of consumption; and (iv) in the light of these data, one cannot but agree with the Treaty on Consumption and Lifestyle at the Rio de Janeiro Global Forum during the June 1992 Earth Summit that "While overall population growth is a danger to the health of the planet, it must be recognized that population growth in the North, due to the extremely high levels of per capita consumption is a far greater threat than population growth in the South." Let us add here that more than 28 per cent of global emissions of 'greenhouse gases' originate in the USA, all developing countries causing just around 5 per cent.[2] Similarly,

Japan is stated to be the world's largest consumer of tropical forest products and its insatiable demand rather than local population growth has been the main cause of rapid deforestation of a large number of the South East Asian countries, causing in turn serious erosion of soil, when the rain washes away every year fertile top soil. For the same reason, this happens in other parts of the world.

Again, pollution of different types afflict the environment, besides what the population growth causes. There are diffusions of toxic substances into the environment, acidification of water and destruction of forests caused by effluents, macro-pollution in the upper atmosphere caused by chloro-fluro-hydrocarbons, the 'greenhouse effect' etc. The pollution grow mostly because of the high level of consumption and eco-unfriendly technologies used for production. Disposal of effluents and garbages are major inevitable problems in the system of industrialization. In future, not far off, we shall face a grave water scarcity problem. While the demand for water rises with economic growth, many technologies also enhance it.

(2) *The destructive potential of the modern civilization is too high.* The world has not been without battles and wars in the past. But wars today—even a local one that took place in Iraq—are unimaginably costlier and ruinous. Perhaps, the total volume of destruction during the five years of World War II far exceeds that of all previous wars since the dawn of human history. But the end of that war has not meant the end of wars.

Today, a huge portion of resources are being deployed for military purposes. Here, trading by industrially advanced countries plays a big role. This lure of profit through sales of arms and weapons attracts not the Western capitalist countries only. Before its fall, the USSR was the largest dealer in arms in the third world countries. Now, China is eager to trade in this field. Anyway, such a large-scale trade in arms and destruction of humans, animals and resources are an off-shoot of this industrial civilization. It is stated that there is a four-fold rise in expenditure on armaments since the end of the World War II. "Over US $1 trillion is now spent worldwide on armaments each year, including $ 200 billion spent by developing countries."[1] The military expenditure is rising in most major countries including those unable to feed their people properly. In this our civilization, the people remain under a constant threat of annihilation with nuclear wars, chemical wars, space wars and so on. Science is commanded to create a Frankenstein's monster and peace recedes more and more.

The industrial system is also fraught with risks of devastating accidents, besides more frequent smaller ones, with incalculable suffering and losses.

(3) *The industrially advanced countries (IACs) thrive on exploiting ruthlessly the less developed countries (LDCs).* That exploitation is bad is admitted universally. Yet in practice, it continues glaringly. The IACs, enjoying a commanding position on the economic plane, exploit LDCs, first, by securing much-needed raw materials from the latter with uneven terms of trade. In the matter of technology transfer, the IACs dictate terms.

There are other exploitations, more obnoxious. The IACs find it difficult to dispose of toxic wastes locally and a number of these countries export their 'cargoes of poison' to poor countries in Africa that are willing to sell discharge rights. This is not done by the Western IACs alone. It is stated that apart from devouring South-East Asia's forests, the Japanese export of industrial pollution is on a massive scale to this region. Highly polluting resource-processing plants like copper-smelters were re-located from Japan to the Philippines and Malaysia in 1970s.

(4) *The industrial civilization perpetuates a gross unequal distribution of riches and other benefits.* The progress of science and industry should have made, as promised, much easier an abundance for all. But only a small section of the world's population enjoys most of the benefits and a much larger section continues to suffer from pangs of poverty, starvation, malnutrition and lack of education. Arnold Toynbee was optimistic that "Our present industrial revolution is. . . . perhaps the first, since the invention of agriculture, that has been potent enough to provide appreciable social and cultural benefits for <u>all</u> members of a society that has made it."[3] (He had underlined the above world 'all'.) Ironically, the same Industrial Revolution has widened the gap between the Northern and Southern parts of the world blatantly. King and Schneider observe: "In Europe, before the Industrial Revolution, per capita consumption was little different from that of many of the less developed countries today. Now the average per

capita consumption of materials and energy is about forty times greater in the North than in the less developed countries of the South. At its extreme, this disparity may be more than 100:1."[1] An unfortunate exploiter-exploited relationship—international and intra-national, grotesque and unkind, remains a stark fact for the humanity mocking at all rhetorics.

Available statistics regarding gross disparity in levels of income, consumption, health and educational facilities, possession of wealth, investment, share of world trade etc. tell a story of men's mercilessness towards man. A large population in the under-developed part of the world do not have safe drinking water. According to the World Health Organization, already about 1.3 billion people, more than 20 per cent of the world population, are seriously sick or malnourished. An inescapable conclusion is that "Scientific and technological advance in the industrialised countries tend to increase the economic disparities between the rich and the poor countries and to inhibit the latter from undertaking technological innovation."[1]

And, the depletion of Nature become more reckless, when the resource position demands of us to be more thoughtful. As stated in a paper presented in the recent Science Congress of India, world oil reserves, as estimated by geologists, currently stand at 136 billion tons. At an annual production rate of 3.2 billion tons, the reserves are likely to last another 42 years. World-wide natural gas reserves now 138 trillion cubic metres, are expected to last 69 years, if the annual production rate of two trillion cubic metres continues. The disparity in the rate of consumption of resources between the IACs and the LDCs is too high. A German economist suggests that to save the environment from ruin the IACs must reduce their consumption of commodities by 90 per cent (!), while for the world as a whole the rate of reduction should be 50 per cent. Efforts are on to invent technologies for utilization of renewable resources, to recycle wastes and to invent pollution free technologies. But these are mostly birds in the bush, rather distant ones. Success in these spheres, if any, and yet far from adequate judging by the needs, may perhaps mitigate a fraction of the problem. And it is too much to expect that any possible success, at least in the foreseeable future, will ensure the Western level of consumption in the entire world.

(5) *The modern industrial civilization causes injury to health (physical and mental) and leads to cultural impoverishment and spiritual degradation.* The conclusion here regarding physical health may *prima facie* should preposterous after all the progress in curative and preventive measures. The costly services are often beyond the reach of the majority. And we have also referred to the WHO's findings regarding serious sickness of a large population. The increasing and menacing environment pollution, telling on health, is a harsh fact. In its 1993-94 report, the World Resources Institute warns us that by the turn of this century one out of every three persons will suffer from respiratory problems or impaired liver and kidney functions, cardio-vascular and other related disorders making the megacities in our country a sick place to live in. And pollution does not differentiate between West and East, rich and poor.

What about mental health? "We find. . . . that the countries in Europe which are among the most democratic, peaceful and prosperous ones, and the United States, the most prosperous country in the world, show most severe symptoms of mental disturbance," observes Eric Fromm.[4] "Denmark, Switzerland, Finland, Sweden and the United States are the countries with the highest suicide rate, and the highest combined suicide and homicide rate. . . . The figures for alcoholism show that the same countries—the United States, Switzerland, Sweden and Denmark—which have the highest suicide rate, have also the highest alcoholism rate, with the main difference that the United States are leading in this group. . . .", he adds. If I remember correctly, somewhere Prof. Galbraith said that he noticed some peacefulness in an Indian villager (or peasant), which he did not notice in New York (or America). With reference to the modern society, an earlier report of the UNESCO said that "The signs of very great individual happiness are legion. They range from complete breakdown—suicide or permanent mental illness through sickness with a large pyscho-somatic component—to the obsessive thinking and morbid states of dejection. . . . Divorce, delinquency, and the myriad examples of anti-social behaviour not classified as crime are the repercussions in intimate social relations."

The trend appears to get stronger. According to a recent report, of every three Americans today, one is mentally ill and half of the population has sometimes or other been afflicted with such illness. Also mental fatigue, addiction to drinks and an inclination to avoid company of others are spreading in America like infectious diseases and the America tops the list in the matter of rapes, murders, drug addiction, accidents and military expenditure. The drug trade has become so well-organized in different countries. Surprisingly, "the total earnings from the drug trade exceed even that of the oil industry."[1]

The trends that we notice at the cultural level is hardly elating. So common is the vulgar ostentation by the rich of his richness, pomp, luxury and 'status symbols'. How much can a person use really? Things are purchased much beyond needs for displaying avidly. A venomous demonstration effect pollutes the cultural life. The atmosphere is growingly such that those too, not as rich, like to ape the rich even by borrowing. Corruption, that almost everyone condemns, thrives. So often today, one will notice a senseless demonstration of vulgarity and obscenity in the name of art and culture, a display of gaudiness and garishness in the name of beauty, of raucousness aided with numberless musical instruments in the name of song and music, of idiotic and ugly postures in the name of dance and so on. "Rock music, gadgets and cola drinks have forged a new, parallel and temporary (as long as youth lasts) society and created what the African historian Joseph Ki-Zerbo calls 'homo coca-colens'," say King and Schneider.[1] It is not that there are no things of beauty in the land of culture. But a 'Gresham's law' operates here forcefully: it leads to a parade of shallowness and pretension, when opiating raucousness and vulgarity thrive in the name of art, entertainment and culture.

Now, things of this sort providing excitement for a while, like that comes with intoxicating drinks, cannot ensure an enduring sense of satisfaction—drunkards seem to be so morose after the intoxication is over. And, things like drug-addiction, turning into Hippies and so on manifest an urge, though misguided, for distraction, and for escape through suicide, when the existing abundance, false glory and glamour fail to sustain the heart.

Cinema, TV, newspapers etc. are the most important mass media with a strong impact on the cultural life. But while possessing a valuable potential for mass education, they tend to acquire a potential for ill education—extremely pernicious, with a pronounced commercial bias—and, this is the stronger trend today.

Today, technological advance offers a variety of entertainments. Very many of them, however, appear trash qualitatively, utterly lacking in depth of thinking or feeling. Hardly do they serve to enrich the aesthetic sense of viewers. Rather, they harm an impressionable mind. Our child-psychologists are worried with the TV-addiction of our children who are so prone to imitate. The injurious things of this addiction are an aggressiveness in behaviour, confusing fantasies as realities and acquiring a distorted notion of the reality, harm to studies, wasting of time. Most or many of the films screened are loaded with vulgarities of sex, crime and violence, clearly with a commercial intent, when money is God. All these, repeated day in and day out, serve to fortify a conviction that crime and violence rule the world. They overshadow good things, erode faith on perennial values and create a belief that in a world where villainy pays and villains are heroes, honesty is foolish. Of course, there are other forces—most of all, unscrupulousness and hypocrisy of political leadership and ostentation of the rich—also working in the same direction: but others' sins does not make me a saint. One of our front-ranking film directors pointed out a year ago that nowadays gay and lesbian films are getting more and more place in film festivals. It seems, culture is decaying qualitatively but flourishing quantitatively: we have more films, more entertainments, even more books and so on but not many good ones. One will notice, even in big cities and towns while there are numberless shops offering an infinite variety of fashionable goods, drinks and so on, good bookstalls are few.

A large part of the mass-circulation of papers and journals are replete with advertisements, mostly to allure the gullibles. There is intrusion of more and more such advertisements into TV—run by the Government of India. Viewing such advertisements one feels that all the problems of the country except that of cosmetics and fashionable goods have been solved. The reports and discussions in the remaining pages of the papers pander most to the tastes of the elitist section; and problems and agonies of the masses, particularly in villages where the majority lives, rather trite to the elites, get a grudging accommodation. Thus, the mind of the people, it seems, is transported by our cultural media to a world of fantasy and indifference to others.

In short, judging by the most important test of cost-benefit ratio, I am constrained to conclude that this materialist industrial civilization is more costly than beneficial—all that glitters is not gold. One may ask, are all the evils mentioned above really products of this civilization? Many of them are so, as can be proved definitively. And those which cannot be so proved are found to be associated invariably with this civilization, and this suggestive enough.

III

The world is mad with violence; and cruel strifes continue.

—Tagore

The above words, from a song in Bengali of Poet Tagore (translated by me), describe aptly the world today. Rather, violence is more instant and deadlier and strifes more widespread and recurrent today. Very recently, Pope, John Paul II, expressed his anguish thus: "As I look at families in the light of Christmas, I turn my thoughts to the greater human family, unfortunately torn apart by selfishness and violence."

On the wings of science, modern civilization has conquered Nature, has brought the humans from jungles and caves to towns and cities, has ensured security as against a precarious existence, and it promises abundance and amenities, mass education, better socio-political institutions, law etc. Apparently, it has paved the path to progress and welfare of man.

Yet, ours is a society of crime, violence and strife, producing tension and lack of peace. The primitive society, marked with lack of education, had strife and other frailties of man, but not so ruinous and so regular as today. The modern society, boasting of prosperity, education and cultural flourishes, seems unable to banish cruelty, strife and other frailties and rather witnesses them almost helplessly. The modern civilization has made the world 'a global village', only technologically and not psychologically. It has enough of elating rhetorics, more than any in the past, that often overshadow the realities, not so elating.

"What shall it avail a man if he gains the whole world and lose the soul?" This is a question as old as the Christian religion and valid for ever. But our civilization fails as yet to offer a convincing answer, notwithstanding all its spectacular achievements. The failure lies in the fact that this materialist civilization, with all its achievements, is not in reality much worried with the question of the soul of man or his spiritual development. Ultimately, this is the most important thing in life to which everything else is subservient. But, there are scientists who would like to explain soul or mental qualities as epiphenomenon of matter.

As Whitehead points out, "The materialistic basis of science had directed attention to things as opposed to values." But with all its phenomenal growth, science tends to create an illusion of its omnipotence, that science will turn the entire world into a prosperous Europe and America, that it will solve, today or tomorrow, all human problems by making known all that is unknown. In the realm of knowledge on the material plane, mankind's progress has been one of from commonsense to science. Science has an immense potential and is very valuable for man on this plane, of course, depending on how it is used. But beyond a range, science has a limitation. Thus, Bertrand Russell, a philosopher and scientist himself, says plainly: "Science, by itself, cannot supply us an ethic." Tolstoy's emphatic comment is: "Science is meaningless because it gives no answer to our question, the only question important for us, 'What shall we do and how shall we live'." "Modern science has force, speed and action, but no direction," comments Acharya Vinoba Bhave. Then, let us listen to the great scientist, Einstein, himself: "The clearing away of obstacles does not by itself lead to an ennoblement of social and individual life. For along with this negative result, a positive aspiration and effort for an ethical-moral configuration of our common life is of overriding importance. Here no science can save us. I believe, indeed, that overemphasis on the purely intellectual attitude, often directed solely to the practical and factual, in our education, has led directly to the impairment of ethical values. . . . Without 'ethical culture' there is no salvation for humanity." Obviously, the world will gain if both the potential and limitation of science are appreciated rightly along with an appreciation of the supremacy of human spirit, yearning for, as Einstein says, "an ethical-moral configuration" in life.

Commencing with a promise to create a better life, this civilization has done much in several fields. But because of its essential materialist character, indifferent to spiritual values, it has entered into a blind alley. Where everyone wants more and more and seeks to elbow out everyone else, the much needed fellow-feeling, which is the basic sustainer of the society and which, more than laws, restrains from recourse to the law of the jungle, suffers and we cannot but have an environment of greed and selfishness, envy and intolerance, violence, cruelty and strife. This is happening more and more beneath all the glitters of the civilization. We have before us now a world where, not to speak of animal life, even the human life itself is becoming the cheapest commodity, where ghastly crimes and brutal murders do not shake the human heart—as if they are normal things—when peace and spiritual development become matters of another planet.

Most people today admire this materialist civilization and its materialist values. Not to speak of the average people, not even many of our so-called educated persons seem to realize that this civilization converts life into a sort of profligacy in different spheres. "The goal of material influence seems to generate greed and selfishness. Not that these features have ever been absent in individuals and societies, but they appear to be magnified by the shrinking of non-materialist values," observe King and Schneider, two writers with an intimate knowledge of affairs in the West and with a strong perception of the things in the rest of the world. Thus, a pursuit of materialist gratification as the sole object, unmindful of the fundamental questions of life that Tolstoy had raised, leading to a state of spiritual emptiness is the greatest failure of this civilization.

Science has conferred prosperity and power. But how many persons in the world—even in the prosperous countries, can claim that they are satisfied with life? We have referred to the wide-spread prevalence of psycho-neurotic disorders and resultant tragedies making the life "a tale told by an idiot, full of sound and fury, signifying nothing." What is very striking here is that even in a country like Sweden, where the Social Democrats have ensured a high degree of equality, liberty and security—some laudable social objectives, along with prosperity, the suicide rate is the highest and juvenile delinquency, various crimes and violence are on the rise (when the criminals are reported to resort to murder pedes-trians for no ostensible reason with modern weapons.) Here, Eric Fromm asks: "Could it be that the middle-class life of prosperity, while satisfying our material needs leaves us with a feeling of intense boredom, and that suicide and alcoholism are the patho-logical ways of escape from this boredom? Could it be that.... modern civilization fails to satisfy profound needs in man?"[4]

We have indicated with relevant details five major evils that this industrial civilization produces, the harmfulness of which will only cumulate if not arrested early: (i) over-exploitation and exhaustion of Nature and pollution of environment, (ii) its destructive potential, (iii) ruthless exploitation by the IACs of the LDCs, (iv) perpetuation of a gross inequality between the two, and (v) injury to physical and mental health, and cultural impoverishment and spiritual degradation of man. Can the civilization overcome these evils without a substantial rectification of itself?

The civilization has not a few of its dazzles. But they allure men along a downward path. What else does generation of greed, ambition and selfishness, cruelty and unending widespread conflicts, along with production of lethal weapons and their unhesitant use signify? It is difficult to say if since the dawn of human history to this day the basic nature of man has changed at all or much, for good or bad. May be, the mental traits as greed, ambition etc. and also love and generosity are inherent in human nature—in the same man simultaneously and some are awake and others dormant in a given situation. According to *'Gita'*, every human possesses three qualities—spiritual (*'swatwik'*), lordly (*'rajasik'*) and vulgar or depraved (*'tamasik'*) simultaneously. While one such quality is awake in him at one time, the two others are dormant. This implies that we should cultivate and attain the best quality. But the unprecedented violence, strifes, murder etc. and the striking insensitiveness to others' woe and agony, seem to suggest that there must be factors in this materialist civilization that blind the mind and fuel baser instincts in man. Perhaps, this civilization with all its shallow lures, shallow consumerism and foppishness—the 'Macbeth's Witches'—will prove ruinous in the long run not only to the blocking of man's mind but it will also take men back to a life that is 'nasty, brutish and short' after Nature has been ruined.

Mass production, the fruit of technological revolution, occupies a pride of place in the industrial civilization with a promise of plenty. But if the promise remains unfulfilled for the huge millions in a larger part of the world so long after the Industrial Revolution, that has enhanced the disparity, it will remain so for at least the insurmountable resource and environmental constraints. The problem of ensuring the LDCs the standard of living as obtains in the IACs is too big to be solved with any likely technological miracle, however one may welcome that. It is questionable how long even the IACs can carry on the present rate of plunder of the limited resources, mostly non-renewable. As E.F. Schumacher says, "the modern industrial system, with all its intellectual sophistication, consumes the very basis on which it has been erected."[5] On the other hand sophisticated labour-replacing technologies create an acute unemployment problem in the LDCs (and also in the IACs). According to the International Labour Organization, 30 per cent, i.e. 82 crores, of the total number of workers in the world are unemployed now. The number is rising. And, as the ILO reports, in the very IACs of America and Europe, the army of unemployed is now as large as thirty-five millions. We are not against technological innovation. It should be related to the welfare of man. The concept of an alternative technology, propounded by humanists from Gandhi to Schumacher, augmenting production without inviting the vices of the modern sophisticated technologies, makes much sense in this context and researches in this field is a paramount need. Our economists also must get rid of such commonly held fallacies as (a) technological progress is the production of bigger and better machines, (b) labour-intensive production is backward and capital-intensive one is progressive, (c) small-scale is backward and large-scale is modern, and so on.

Eulogies are showered on the benefits of science and modern technology like mass production. But any benefit must be judged in terms of costs. Here, significant is Edward Carpenter's affirmation that the ever-increasing powers of production engendered by modern science and technology alienated man: (1) from Nature, (2) from his true self, (3) from his fellows and it worked "in every way to disintegrate and corrupt man. . . . to break up the unity of his nature."[6] And so says Bertrand Russell: "Modern industry, in fact, is a kind of rape." He points out, "Everyday many square miles of forest are turned into newspaper, but there is no known process by which newspaper can be turned into forest." He adds: "All industry depends upon such irreversible processes; it all uses up the earth's capital. Modern industry is, in fact, a spendthrift, and sooner or later must suffer the penalty of spendthrifts."[7]

But has been the impact of mass production at the

psychological level? Scientific and technological growth is helping production of an almost infinite number of consumables. Whether serving real needs or not, they create a 'Niagara of wants' in the people. Even those living in shanties or footpaths are infected with a consumerist culture today. A pronounced trait of this culture is that the people tend to hanker more and more after luxuries, paradoxically, with an indifference even to basic needs—a hankering, for instance, for a bottle of highly advertised soft-drink, unmindful of the need for a little milk.

Those championing the industrial civilization may perhaps argue that an increase in luxuries, beyond the bare needs for physical existence, is a sign of advancement of civilization. We do not suggest that men may remain in jungles instead of in houses or may keep contented wearing barks of trees for cloths. But there must be a limiting principle on multiplication of wants and that principle is man's spiritual development. It is also asked by the champions, where do we draw a dividing line between necessaries and luxuries, when today's luxuries are tomorrow's necessaries? True, we cannot draw a clear dividing line on many matters. But we can distinguish between the concepts of 'necessity' and 'luxury' and that is sufficient to guide us in the practical field if we like to be so guided. It is also true that even luxuries that one gets habituated to using turn into unavoidable needs if we carry on the process of conversion of luxuries without restraint or discrimination. Thus, smokes, drugs, drinks and so many things become essential to the patrons, often more essential than food. Unrestrained, the hunger of power, wealth and ostentation also becomes the master. The senselessness of this unrestrained conversion of luxuries or addiction to things, that one can easily do without or which is even injurious, points the need for some restraint in every walk of life. Actually, one with a developed mind, refusing to be indiscriminate, can live a joyful and creative civilized life without multiplying luxuries. Like Gandhi, Tagore also felt that "Man's real needs are not many." He always kept the question of creative development to the fore. He too noticed the developed capitalist countries' tendency to convert unnecessaries into necessaries and called it "a dangerous outrage by a greedy civilization." I call it a greed-producing civilization.

When I first came to know of the 'Say's Law' in the economics class that 'supply always creates its demands', I was a bit sceptic about its soundness as being contrary to the commonsense notion that demand creates supply—'necessity is the mother of invention'. Today, the 'Say's Law', named after the French economist, J.B. Say, operates vigorously. In the IACs, a torrent of new and newer items, beautified with nice packing and made highly attractive with the eloquence and ingenuity of advertisers, whet relentlessly the hunger of the people—'commodity fetishism', as Marx called it—whether or not they had earlier even imagined the need for any of these items. And the LDCs think that being modern means imitating the IACs.

In the past, besides agriculture, manufacturing industry and service were the two major sectors in the economy. Now, advertisement has become another major sector, helping creation of an environment with consumption as a dominant passion in life. And, 'created needs' outstrip 'felt needs'. Billions are spent on advertisement to rouse demands—to hypnotise and to dictate the people—for a ever-widening range of luxuries and labour saving gadgets. (Their utility is questionable at least in over-populated countries, where also there are incessant efforts to create demands.) The unfortunate result is that when the GNP grows, say, by five per cent, the aspirations grow at a higher rate, and discontent for many at a still higher rate.

One concrete result of such consumerism is that it raises a larger trade deficit even in a country like the USA. Relevant to our present discussion is the fact these advertisements do not help consumers much. Rather, the huge amounts spent on advertisements and propaganda enter into prices of commodities. They can also be misleading and even harmful. To take a major example, a persistent propaganda is on for long to make the people beliefs that a little wine is good for health. Recently, this idea has been scotched by the World Health Organization whose experts affirm that propaganda of this sort is actuated more with a commercial intent and that drinks may cause liver troubles, cancer etc.

This trend has a noticeable fall-out even in the poorer countries where a large section fails to secure even two square meals. Now, in this acquisitive or 'the more the merrier society', producers and traders are in league to flood consumers with more and more supplies, regardless of their real needs or buying capacity, for needs also will be produced now. If the buyers cannot pay readily, the sellers will offer credit facilities. Payments with interest are to be made afterwards. In this civilization, you earn more and more, honestly or otherwise, or you will perish.

"The materialistic technology-based approach to development has penetrated into societies and cultures of all types, and even the most rigid fundamentalist culture find it impossible to resist the promise of power and affluence which it appears to offer," points out King and Schneider.[1] China is a state founded on an avowed ideology. But China is brushing aside rapidly different canons of Mao, just as many Indians opine that the ideas of the 'father of the nation' are back-dated. There, the modernizing supremo, Deng Xiaoping, pronounced a decade ago that "To be rich is glorious" and moved ahead to modernize the country and its economy fairly on the Western pattern. China is moving along the charted path. At the same time, as a recent report says, corruption, smuggling etc. are on the rise in China and high officials are involved in them. As another reporter observes, "Money has replaced Marxism as China's God." And she adds: "As society loosens up, so does its morals. Lawlessness, highway robbery, drugs and prostitution are all on the rise. Young women from all over China are drawn to Shanghai, Shenzhen and other cities. The unlucky are reduced to letting truck drivers grope them for 50P a time, and do not even earn enough money to return to their home villages. The successful ones end up with beautiful clothes, a flat of their own and a mobile phone to talk to their clients many of whom are overseas Chinese who pay hundreds of pounds for a night. Some of these women have become local heroes, returning to their home towns with a fortune to start up a factory."[8]

What else can be the eventual outcome in a civilization in which "To be rich is glorious"? May be, it is not as crude for all as is the case with these girls, but substantially not much different. Consumerism, a major contribution of this civilization, polluting man's mind, is a deadlier monster than environment pollution, another contribution of the civilization. A gluttonous urge, the craze for more and more and new and newer things infinitely that the industrial civilization fuels, is surely injurious to man's mental health. The shower of things, mostly afar from basic needs, enslave mentally both rich and poor. An individual is surrounded with dazzling showrooms of fancy goods and their advertisements at home in the TV and journals repeatedly, and he so often hears discussions among friends and relatives so much on them and little on noble thoughts and witnesses in the daily life acts hardly ennobling. This is the common picture for most people today. The brainwashing of them and particularly of the youth, to be at the helm of affairs tomorrow, is thus complete. In an atmosphere like this, all the beautiful, serious and valuable things become something distant, hazy and unimpressive. Now, a person rich or wielding power, whatever his personal integrity, will be more honoured than one possessing rich human qualities, if without power and wealth. A profligate life-style, that it is, paves the path that is shallow and tainted with vices. "One specific aspect of modern life (is) the repression of the awareness of the basic problems of human existence," observes Eric Fromm.[4]

A humanist thinker of renown in India, V.M. Tarkunde, describes thus the present situation: "There appears to be a sharp fall in moral standards in both developed and developing countries of the contemporary world. . . . The fall of moral standards is indicated by the enormous rise of corruption in political administration, by the adoption of increasingly unscrupulous methods in business enterprises and by the growing rate of crime in all parts of the world."[9] Plainly, if the socio-economic arrangement be such that man is induced to disdain all restraints of mind, things cannot be any better. And also if the arrangement be such as to create 'a Niagara of Wants' with man constantly running after them, so many of the wants will remain unfulfilled and discontent will be the constant companion. "The mind is a restless bird: the more it gets the more it wants, and still remain unsatisfied," said Gandhi. An individual, himself discontented, cannot be generous or sympathetic towards others, but is rather envious, intolerant and aggressive. As Bertrand Russell, not a mystic himself, would say, "the soul which is not at peace with itself cannot be at peace with the world, and external wars have to continue in order to hide from individual men that the real war is within." And he adds: "For these reasons the war of man with himself is that which at the end of human evolution assumes supreme importance."[7]

There is a noticeable 'commercialization of atmosphere' in this civilization, expanding in all directions, which, in the words of Karl Marx, "left no other nexus between man and man than naked self-interest, than callous cash payment." In this atmosphere, people 'purchase beauty' from beauty parlours, buy costliest cosmetics and so on, realising hardly that good health is the best beautifier. Instead of moving the limbs by way of physical exercise or labour, valuable for good health, they prefer in their mental sloth short-cuts that shops offer. Then, there are patrons of 'fast foods', multiplying in number, when the traders know the 'art' of making money. Now, do these patrons ever think that normally one can prepare delicious foods at home with less cost, which is tastier as one's own knowledge and labour have made them? Do they realize that the delight of enjoying the beauty of flowers in one's own garden or even a small courtyard, that bloom with one's love's labour, is something richer than that obtainable from flowers in the market? Unfortunate is one who is ignorant of the joy of creativity, obtainable from things large and small. The modern civilization induces people to become more a buyer than a producer—a creator. Commenting on "modern man's relationship to his fellow man" Eric Fromm says: "Everybody is to everybody else a commodity. . . . Even love and the relationship between sexes have assumed this character."[4]

It is true that industrial workers have today greater leisure hours when mechanized production demands less labour. Some dirty work is also done by machine. Good, as far as they go. But the leisure they enjoy is hardly creative and means practically more lazing with boredom or seeking excitement: as Herbert Read says, it is "a pervasive emptiness. . . . A vacuum, a desperate state of vacancy." Their recreation is not re-creation. John W. Gardner, a former U.S. Secretary of Health, Education and Welfare, comments: "We have to face the fact that most people out there in the world of work are more stale than they know and more bored than they would care to admit." The prevalence of mental ailments, already referred to, does not speak well of this leisure. Of course, not to be compared with the poverty-stricken life in the LDCs, it however, means dull and boring hours, barring the hours of excitement.

Then, scientific and technological advance can claim to have helped much the spread of education. But the spread has been grossly uneven owing to the uneven distribution of the benefits of science. That civilization is not very civilized where a very large section of the population remains hungry and uneducated. And not only the quantitative aspect, we must consider qualitative aspect of education also: ill-education should worry us no less than uneducation, if not more. We shall consider later this qualitative aspect. We may state here only that the modern education, for all its worth, is an education more of the brain than of the heart. With little social and ethical orientation, it makes man intelligent and knowledgeable but not as much wise or virtuous. Half a century ago, G.M. Trevelyan stated in the 'English Social History' that rapid spread of education had created a large mass who knows to read but not what is or is not readable. True to the philosophy of life behind the modern civilization, the education is more for earning than learning, worshipping the maxim "To be rich is glorious."

Commenting on the views in the *Hind Swaraj*, among several other thinkers, G.D.H. Cole contended that "I do not believe that it (the Western civilization) rests upon a sheer denial of what is necessary to the human soul." *Prima facie*, this is an acceptable contention. The Western civilization does not explicitly deny the importance of the human soul. Not a few Western thinker would readily recognize the importance, while an average Westerner, I believe, is not much interested in the question itself. Perhaps, this shows how the spirit or atmosphere of a civilization acts on the common men, who are more moulded with the atmosphere than a learned man with an independence of thinking. Should we not judge the character of a civilization by its impact on the millions? Also, what is important here is that the path actually followed by this civilization with above all a materialist goal impoverishes the human soul.

Unlike Cole, another Western writer says that "Since the birth of Christ, the West has produced no great apostle of non-violence equivalent to Mahatma Gandhi. Our civilization has spawned crusaders, inquisitors, conquerors, and tyrants—Torquemadas, Napoleons, Hitlers and Stalins—but not a single prophet of brotherhood and peace. The Western world, which we like to think of as 'the cradle of civilization' has been the breeding ground of most of the fratricidal conflicts with which the human race has been afflicted for the past two thousand years. The fatal weakness of Western Man has been the insatiable acquisitiveness and his inability to live at peace with himself. Both are the products of a materialism insufficiently restrained by humanitarianism and moral sensibility."[10]

Another important question before us is: are the evils we have noted in the industrial civilization attributes really of capitalism? Gandhi condemns the industrial civilization, while socialists blame capitalism. R.H. Tawney holds that the principle on which the capitalistic society is based, is domination of man by things. To escape the trap of the "demoralizing industrialism" and true to his philosophy of life, Gandhi urges on a conscious limitation of wants by man. Of course, this does not mean a life of poverty. He fought all his life against the poverty of his countrymen, though with a simultaneous solicitude for their spiritual growth. Karl Marx envisaged a condition of abundance in the socialist society, even though he too condemned "commodity fetishism". But though strongly against poverty and squalor, he did not look at consumption from a moral stand-point and did not think of any conscious limitation of wants. In the 'Communist Manifesto', he eulogizes repeatedly the "capitalist engine of production" and advanced technology raising productivity. He was for a better, humanist distribution of the abundance of industrialism, not available in capitalism, and was not against industrialism. The general run of socialists accept Marx's view on this subject.

Socialists must ponder over the matter. Some of the evils we have mentioned, like environment pollution, depletion of Nature, their impact on health, growth of high destructive potential, strenuous condition of modern life with resultant maladies, disparity between different parts of the world are related to the industrial civilization. Obviously, industrial growth, eating up the limited resources of the earth, cannot expand itself as much to create the same abundance to all in the world. The option of an unlimited growth is not available hence for the socialists. They must also recognize that just distribution, equality etc. are not materialist but humanist-ethical goals. Gandhi's humanist-moral sense makes him feel "What cannot be had for the millions is taboo to me" and to live a life as he says. If the members of the socialist society lack in fellow feeling and morality and are guided with selfishness can the supposed humanist-ethical character of the socialist society be retained? As Jayaprakash Narayan says, "If the poor tried to establish equality merely by distributing the wealth of the wealthy among themselves, without accepting the philosophy behind it, they would soon recreate different forms of inequality amongst themselves."[11] Mere removal of capitalism is not socialism. It must be built on the foundation of an alternative appropriate technology, culture and philosophy of life. Socialism can be spiritualist as also materialist or acquisitive, democratic or totalitarian, and a noble society must have a corresponding foundation.

IV

> *Without a global revolution in the sphere of human consciousness, nothing will change for the better. . . . and the catastrophe towards which are our world is heading will be unavoidable.*
>
> —Victor Havel, President, Czech Republic

We have indicated so far the way the world is moving today. Our analysis of and criticism against the present industrial civilization have suggested at least implicitly the way it should move. We must now consider, as specifically as possible, what is to be done keeping ever in view the *summum bonum* of happiness and mental development of man.

We must admit at the outset that this civilization is so established that it cannot be ended completely and it is to be mended as substantially as possible. "It is no easy task to do away with a thing that is established," recognizes Gandhi. Also, a civilization, unlike erecting a building on a clean plot with a blue-print, is not imposed from above. It is a long-term evolution with an interaction between the existing condition and an awareness of new values, major innovation etc. and acculturation may play a role. Basing idealism on realism and not being just utopian, our aim shall be to create the ground for a more compassionate civilization that also helps growth of constructive creativity in man. To the extent the endeavour succeeds, the wealth and power grabbing character of this civilization will weaken and hence the ground for conflict among men.

This civilization cannot be rejected wholesale today as it is deeply entrenched and the society also will not give up the good things it has given unless they are too costly in terms of benefits or constraints of resource and ecology intervene. With a strong condemnation of this civilization, Gandhi is against so many things in it but he accepts some of them as a "necessary evil".

Despite his criticism against machine, he recognizes that destroying all machinery and mills "requires a higher simplicity and renunciation than the people are today prepared to pay for." Also, "machines will remain because, like the body, they are inevitable". So he suggests how best those machinery which are needed may be handled to serve the people. He also urges our being guided not with a craze for machinery as such. Clearly, our approach should be of a reform and not a revolution. But then, sustained meaningful reforms over a long period, gaining a momentum of its own, may in the long run signify revolutionary changes minus the sound and fury.

True to the goal, we should think of a positive approach with an understanding of what is achievable at the most. The Report of the Club of Rome, indicating, it seems, a fairly comprehensive approach suggests that "We must be more explicit about the importance of values and ethics in the different areas. . . . Our efforts must be directed towards the creation of a sustainable world society, and caution dictates that the profligate life-style in the industrialized countries should be curbed through a slow-down of consumption—which may, in any case, be forced on us by environmental constraints. It is also imperative that renewed efforts be made to eliminate poverty throughout the world."[1] The approach does not smack of any utopian idealism nor also of any unidealized pragmatism. Its two concrete aspects are: (i) curbing the profligate life-styles through a slow-down of consumption, and (ii) elimination of poverty throughout the world. And, our action, unless guided with an appropriate philosophy life, may follow a wrong direction. Hence the essentiality of an explicit recognition of the "importance of values and ethics", the corner-stone of all endeavour for a better society. In Einstein's words, "The most important human endeavour is the striving for morality in our actions. Our inner balance and even our very existence depend on it. Only morality in our actions can give beauty and dignity to life." The creation of a sustainable society, that meets the needs of both the present and future generations, we hope, will flow the curbing of profligate life-styles. Such life-styles should not infect the LDCs where we are to eliminate poverty.

We have referred to some major evils in the modern civilization. In it, the people are by and large in a state tension, when peace and content, as distinct from transient pleasure and excitement, elude them. Clearly, this civilization has shown what it can and cannot do. It has reached the end of its path and cannot offer anything new qualitatively. The materialist path does not lead to spiritual development. It keeps man opiated with small things and keeps life arrested at a shallow level. Science may still help even larger exploitation of resources, some, but not enough, substitution of scarce resources etc., but resource constraints put a severe limit to enhancement of mass production. Also, maximization of production is not maximization of happiness. Science, ill-directed, may be the grave-digger of the human society.

"It is high time that civilized man turned his mind to fundamental things," urged the famous psychologist, C.G. Jung. He reflected the profound feeling of great prophets and humanist thinkers, who have urged invariably that the way to happiness and self-development lies in freedom from the bondage of greed, ambition and selfishness—that Spinoza called "forms of insanity", and in man's striving to be "the king over himself." (Shalley). "Man's happiness", Gandhi affirms, "really lies in contentment. He who is discontented, however, much he possesses, becomes a slave of desires. And there is no slavery equal to that of his desires." "Civilization, in the real sense of the term", he holds, "consists not in the multiplication, but in the deliberate and voluntary reduction of wants. This alone promotes real happiness and contentment, and increase the capacity for service."

The concept of a 'simple life', often mentioned by Gandhi, has not originated with him—he attributes this to the sages of the old. But he lives a life that he preaches for. The idea of a simple life has found an echo in the sensible minds of all times. If Zarathushtra says, "Practice simplicity in habits, simplicity of heart, and simplicity of character," Jesus feels that "a man's life consisteth not in the abundance of things which he possesseth." Long ago, the stoic emperor, Mercus Aurelius said, "Remember, very little is required to make a happy life." Writing about England in 1802, Poet Wordsworth felt sorry that people adored "the idolatory of rapine, avarice and expense," and "plain living and high thinking are no more."[12] Romain Rolland's terse comment is: "the more I have, the less I am."[12] A great historian of science, George Sarton, asserts: "There is infinitely more virtue and glory in creating beauty, justice, happiness than in creating wealth."[13]

What do we really mean by a 'simple life'? Gandhi gives a list of great men, "who deliberately embraced poverty as their lot." But his prescription of simple life for the common men does not mean a strict regimen, that he prescribes for those who join his *ashram* voluntarily. It is related to the level of mental growth different individuals. He does not urge for a life of sack cloth and ashes for the average people. Of course, 'awakened souls' from Buddha to Francis of Assisi do not wait to be ordained for the path of utmost simplicity of their own choice. Gandhi implores all for a conscious limitation of wants. Like Gandhi, Tagore also feels that "Man's real needs are not many". What Gandhi likes everyone to do is to strive earnestly to the best of one's ability for simplicity. He hopes that a man's earnestness will lead him ahead. (Actually, if we have any single lesson from the life of Gandhi, who happened to be a rather mediocre person, it is that earnestness carries a man ahead.) In the simple life that he visualizes, he is particular about man's health as also the basic needs—plenty of fresh, wholesome balanced diet; simple but artistic, durable cloths; sunny, airy, cozy dwellings amid agreeable surroundings. And the 'father of the nation' does not ignore the need for proper sanitation and clean hygienic latrines too—matters trifling to most leaders. (His economic system is capable of meeting these needs. We may add here that he envisioned self-sufficient villages. Even if a village cannot become completely self-sufficient, the more self-sufficient it becomes is better for all.) With a spirit of understanding, he concedes the use of electricity for the masses though not for his *ashram*. Perhaps, the 'Practical idealist' would not oppose man's ordinary fancies and hobbies, that might give one some innocent satisfaction, if they were not in bad taste.

Whether I am correct or not in my understanding of Gandhi on this point. I think ours should be a decent life, enriched with simplicity. One can cultivate simplicity without being a puritan. And morality is a mind's inward growth and not something imposed. Gandhi's simple life (rather extraordinary) and such qualities in him as cleanliness, dislike for gaudiness, orderliness and sense of discipline, punctuality, tolerance along with a firmness of conviction, placidity of mind and, above all, his compassion and a never-failing sense of humour—all these reflect a simple decent mind. Overall, his life itself is an art in a simple setting. With a spirit of understanding, he would not demand the same simplicity from all. Following Cardinal Newman, Gandhi recognizes "one step enough for me." More important than how much one has moved is the direction in which one moves—one step in the right direction paves the way for the next.

The simple life does not mean a complete rejection of matter—an absurdity. But for one aiming at elevation of the mind, commodities are essentially for meeting needs. They shall not dominate the mind, and shallow consumerism, different from rational decent use, is not in tune this aim. As Eric Fromm puts it, "After he (man) has satisfied his animal needs, he is driven by human needs. While his body tells him what to eat and what to avoid—his conscience ought to tell him which needs to cultivate and satisfy, and which need to let wither and starve out."[4]

Clearly, the question of self-restraint, so prominent in the thoughts of saints, Gandhi included, comes in as a vital element in human life. A man should exercise restraint when facing scarcity as also plenty. The acme of this self-restraint is 'non-attachment' (*'anasakti'* as stated in *'Gita'*), on which Gandhi is so emphatic. This precious quality of mind prepares a man to face sorrow and happiness stoically. "What chiefly distinguishes man from the beast is," says Gandhi, "that man from the age of his discretion begins to practice a life of continual self-restraint."

"Self-control, though I will not for a moment deny its necessity on occasion," contends Bertrand Russell, "is not the best way of getting people to behave well. It has the drawback of diminishing energy and creativeness. It is like wearing heavy armour, ... Those who rely wholly upon self-control become stiff and timorous through fear of themselves. But the impulses to which they allow no outlet continue to exist and, like rivers that are dammed; they must overflow sooner or later."[7] While accepting Russell's argument, we may point out that his criticism is not basically against self-control but against its possible misuse through excesses.

No doubt, some amount of self-restraint is needed by man. But to be fruitful, this must not be an imposition. It must be cultivated with an awareness of its value. To recognize and feel its value, as that of all important things, is the first thing. A car must have a brake and the driver must know its use or the care will meet an accident. So also, a man must know what to have and what not to have, how far to move and where to stop, and he must act according to the knowledge. Self-control in man is just like the brake in a car.

A word on science. Science can help and harm man—"a double-edged weapon", says Gandhi. So also technology—"With the help of new technology a resource-poor country can overcome its natural handicaps", says Stanislaw H. Wellisz.[14] We cannot oppose them in principle, but we guard against their misuse. Today, science gives man an unprecedented power. And as Shakespeare said, it is good to have the power of a giant but not to use it like a giant. Hence spiritual growth, meaning transcending the self and in the process overcoming one's frailties, and self-control—actually two aspects of the same process—are all the more needed today. As Russell also points out, "To stop war, we must not only work on Governments; we must cleanse our own hearts of the poisons that make war seem inevitable: pride, fear, greed, envy and contempt."[7] Gandhian wisdom emphasises on the same point rather in a perennial context, knowing that even if atomic weapons are abolished men may still hate and fight, if they remain slaves of passions and baser instincts.

Will not a simple life with unhurried contentment and peace become a dull, boring life? "A quiet life will be a boring life", Russell feels.[15] I would submit that both joy and boredom are related much to the development or its absence of man's creative faculties, where the environment plays an auxiliary role, good or bad. We have noted that the industrial workers' life is commonly dull, despite better material conditions. A man whom compassion relates to others, one actuated with a sense of beauty or one in quest of truth, is likely to create things good and beautiful and to enjoy the life. An artist like Abanindranath Tagore found satisfaction by creating excellent things with dry, discarded twigs, overlooked by others. To persons, devoid of such qualities of mind and doing just some compulsory work, the life cannot but be dull and tiresome. Such a person does not live but only exist. The best life is one that is intensive and extensive in its creative endeavour. "Everything truly valuable in this human universe of which man can be proud has been brought into being and developed by his constructive creativity. . . . For these reasons maximum cultivation and development of this creative grace is man's paramount task of the present and the future," asserts Pitirim A. Sorokin.[16] The lives of great men from Buddha to Gandhi, Tagore and Vivekananda, and those before and after them—lives of dedicated humanists, thinkers and artists—exemplify how active and creative—and so joyful, a simple life can be. This is true of also a lesser man having a degree of creativity.

In short, a simple life society must be much less haunted with greed and selfishness and resultant evils, notably the conflict between man and man. In it, the conflict between man and Nature also will be less and the future generation will have a safer world. One will find immense meaning in Edward Carpenter's argument, already stated, that Gandhi valued much, in the context of a simple life society. Naturally, it will be more non-violent and more decent a society, cherishing more the richer values. "Simple living is a revolution by itself, for it goes against the prevailing taste and economy," says Dr. Lohia.[17] We may add here that some grave evils like various forms of environmental pollution can be arrested only with a simple life and not by the industrial civilization with its natural propensity.

But, how much simple can a simple life be today? For instance, we cannot give up electricity, railways and the like, not thought of in pre-modern simplicity. As stated, a simple life for the average people will not be one of 'saffron robes'. "It will not necessarily be a return to the old absolute simplicity," says Gandhi. It shall be a decent life. Yet, our attitude counts much. If one is earnest, one can discard a lot of things, without much strain. Not only itemwise, even quantitywise one can reduce consumption by refusing to have anything beyond one's real using capacity. Even such a reduction will mean a relatively simple life. And when one begins to realize the benefits of a simple life, one can move still ahead. Of course, those below the poverty line will have to rather 'un-simple' the life a bit, but not as much as to try to imitate the West. Actually, a 'simple life' is not only an idealist's yearning, it is a 'pragmatic must' today.

The elimination of poverty throughout the world is an urgent matter for reducing suffering, animosity and injustice. It is not a civilized world so long as it continues to be rent with cries of poverty and hunger and the sighs of the unemployed. Both poverty and profusion depress the soul. Thus, while Gandhi recounts that "In South Africa. . . . I observed almost invariably that the greater the possession of riches, the greater was the moral turpitude," he is as aware that "grinding pauperism" cannot but lead to "moral degradation". But the removal of poverty must honour the principle of simple life. Also sanity demands that the IACs should curb consumption to save resources and environment as also to remove gross inequality. This inequality also strengthens racial animosity that must go. An "economics of justice", as Gandhi calls it, must replace the predatory economics.

In our discussion we have related various evils and strifes in the world today to the modern civilization. I am not sure, how far an evil like male domination is related to it. However, let all of us realize that where women advance, the society advances. There is another virulent disturber of peace in the world today, that rouse the beast in man—a sectarian or herd mentality, expressing itself through bitter hostility along racial, communal or similar sectarian lines. "The instinctive root of race hatred is fear of what is strange," feels Bertrand Russell. It seems to me that the herd mentality and sectarian hostility are also a product of an irrational refusal by an illiberal mind to adjust to pluralities of customs, mores, rituals etc. Thus, both fear and intolerance are springs of this malady. Independent of the modern civilization in its origin, it is also influenced by this civilization when contestants fight with modern weapons for more power and wealth more fanatically. As in the case of various irrationalities, the herd mentality depends ultimately for its cure on more and better education of the misguided masses—while it afflicts modern countries also, and on firm action against ring leaders. Besides, where this mentality grows with a grievance of injustice, it demands removal of the same, if real, and greater clarification of the matter to all if it is not so.

How do we move ahead towards a society enshrining richer values? The society does not change itself. Man, the active force, is the builder. "It is man's privilege to overcome adverse circumstances," asserts Gandhi. True, none can live outside an environment that has its weight on man. But living within an environment, it is man who decides what to do or not to do and charts his path. The more developed a man is the more he moulds the environment and the *vice versa*. In reality, it is the quality or character of man that is the basic determinant of the human life. We must have desirable institutions, laws, programmes etc. But all these become as good or as bad as the human quality behind them. This human quality is shaped, most of all, by man's consciousness—his thinking and feeling. Thus any social change must mean basically a change in the quality of man's consciousness. There is no change if man remains unchanged. Side by side, the environment also should be reformed.

This means that we depend the most on education—on persuasion and moral appeal—in rousing the consciousness of a man. Values cannot be imposed by force. It is often said cynically that great, very great men have appealed to others from ages to be good and loving but with little impact. It is difficult to prove definitively the success or failure of great men in this sphere. Yet, it is reasonable to suppose that their contribution must have some impact on man's consciousness and culture and that our world might have been a poorer one without them. In our own time, we have seen how an unarmed Gandhi had roused a nation from its age-long slumber and had kindled a spirit of sacrifice even in ordinary, illiterate masses. But the fight begun by great men is not over. This is not always followed worthily. If the influence of good parents is undeniable, the role of 'the guardians of mankind' on our larger family cannot be denied.

Further, if incorruptible saints are not many in our world, incorrigible villains also are not many. The overwhelming majority of the population belongs to a third group of the average people. They are mostly aimless, confused and ill-directed today. Much more than the other two groups, they are amenable to education as also to environment. So, it is to be expected that honest, persistent and well-planned educational approach, side by side with efforts for reform of the environment, will not be in vain, though the change of mind is the slowest of all changes. We believe, as Gandhi did, in the basic goodness of these people despite their frailties and must look at them with sympathy and understanding. Selfishness, we may add, is a state of mental weakness, quite wide-spread, coveting more than what rational self-interest demands. It may be over-optimistic to banish it from the human society soon or entirely. Yet, a combination of good education, good environment and the basic goodness of man may have an impact for the better on this evil trait.

Compassionate minds have held education in the true sense as the foundation of a good life. In Buddha's words, "ignorance is the darkest night." No doubt, most of the problems in the world today are made by humans, greedy, ignorant, biased or prejudiced. The modern civilization has offered facilities for universal education and the benefit is spread unevenly. With all its worth, this education is imbalanced. Our literary education gives primacy to the education of the brain and is not value-oriented. Gandhi's conception of the education, aiming at an all-round development of the child, is based on his formula of 3-H: education of the heart, hand and head. As he wrote: "I did not believe in the existing system of education.... I regarded character-building as the proper foundation of their (children's) education and, if the foundation was firmly laid, I am sure that the children could learn all other things themselves or with assistance of friends." While he "fully appreciated the necessity of a literary training in education," he was convinced that "mere knowledge of letters" was not enough. Far-sighted thinkers like Swami Vivekananda and Tagore also accord primary to the character-building education. Bertrand Russell also warns that "Unless men increase in wisdom as much as in knowledge, increase in knowledge will increase sorrow." A gem of his idea is that "the good life is one inspired by love and guided by wisdom."

Without denying at all the need for brain education, we must recognize that the human heart offers the deepest spring of man's consciousness—of his feeling, and even thinking and willing. With good brain education, but without the deeper feeling, one can be a scholar. But as Poet Kazi Nazrul Islam, not a scholarly person, wrote in one of his poems: "All the prophets were shepherds and ploughmen, and they brought imperishable messages which are there and will remain for ever." (Translation mine). Also, as Amartya Sen says, it is to be admitted that so often Shakespeare or Tolstoy have seen and expressed social truths more clearly than social scientists. This does not mean that what the heart says is always free from errors. But the 'imperishable messages', elevating the mind, appear to originate with a deep feeling. We do not know how much academic education Gautama has received, but we honour Buddha as an 'awakened soul', whose heart became restless and then wise with the sorrow of man. The same thing can be said of many others, e.g. Ramakrishna Paramhansa, an almost illiterate person. Gandhi also was not a great scholar, who became a path-finder with qualities of the heart-truthfulness and earnestness: "I am not built for academic writings. Action is my domain," he says with characteristic humbleness.

Therefore, following the Gandhian spirit and with loyalty to the goal of loftiness of mind, we emphasise that the 'education of the heart', illumining the vision, is the most basic of all education. Large number of universities and colleges bring out a larger number of degree holders. But not many of them retain any serious connection with their study after leaving the institutions, and not many of them are keen on larger questions of life or have any concern about the larger society. In India, it seems, very few even touch any serious books after having obtained a degree, while learning is a life-long process. Commonly deemed educated, most of them are rather 'degree holders'. The knowledge they get, serving some practical needs, hardly develops a serious philosophy of life. With the education they get, they sever the connection at ease after the practical need has been served.

This education does hardly awaken the heart and our 'degree holders' are mostly 'sleep walkers'. "Ultimately, we are guided not so much by the intellect as by the heart," felt Gandhi. Reason is an extremely valuable faculty in man and when one is guided by heart one need not be indifferent to reason though one is at liberty, with caution, to transcend reason when one finds something too deep for reason. Extremely significant is a pronouncement by Bertrand Russell that "Instinct, intuition or insight is what leads to the beliefs which subsequent reason confirms or confutes; . . . . Reason is a harmonizing, controlling force rather than a creative one. Even in the most purely logical realm, it is insight that first arrives at what is new."[18]

A valuable observation by M.N. Roy is that the present crisis in the world arises from man's failure to distinguish between what possesses lasting, perennial value and what have only ephemeral value. This failure to distinguish between what is healthy and what is alluring is too common. And this pin-points the need, most of all, for a value-oriented education or education of the heart. This education, more a communication from heart to heart for imprinting of values more than imparting of knowledge of theories and laws, does not promise any instant success. "Value education is not simply a matter of precept or curriculum construction and classroom-teaching. It is more practice than precept," says Ishwarbhai Patel.[19] "It is possible for a teacher situated miles away to affect the spirit of the pupils by his way of living." (Gandhi). Even if many have forgotten him today, and many more know little about him, Gandhi is one of the greatest teachers that India has ever produced, beaming a moral appeal. In a family, affectionate and wise parents are the finest teachers. Even when the child is unable to fathom their wisdom, he feels the touch of the heart that, as Pascal said, has a language of its own. Actually, most persons are what they become in the early life. The teachers at institutions can influence, though having much less time at their disposal. Companions also influence. Unlucky is a child, influenced with heartless or wicked parents, companions, teachers and social leaders. On the impersonal plane, the wider society or the socio-cultural milieu moulds the child highly. Its influence is rather negative today and hence there is a crying need for reformative action here. The social and political leadership is rather poor not only in India but, it seems, in the world as a whole today in a context of humanist-ethical deficiency. The cultural and communication media, having a great moral responsibility, must be attuned to a constructive creative role, that is much lacking.

The need for sound curricula, even though subsidiary, must be considered seriously by those earnest about blooming of decent qualities in man. We may only stress here that learning virtues begins the best in childhood. The child must be acquainted both at home and school with accounts of inspiring lives and humanities cultural achievements through ages. The history of wars, cruelties etc., though taught, must not cloud a child's mind. He must know more of good things of life and must begin his onward journey with a robust optimist outlook and not with cynicism. Pessimism, fear etc., shaking confidence, and of course, ignorance, are the greatest enemies of progress. To a child, we must hold out alternative healthy models, ideas and programmes—things that deepens and broadens the mind, facing caterers of, as Tolstoy said, "growing insane luxury of the rich" and such other vulgarities and cupidities.

The influence of the materialist civilization is so wide-spread that we may appear to be swimming against currents today. It is rather late today as it is strong enough, and yet it is never late as it is harmful enough. And, as Einstein points out, "His (Gandhi's) work on behalf of India's liberation is a living testimony to the fact that man's will, sustained by indomitable conviction, is more powerful than material forces and that seems insurmountable." And, as Gandhi himself says: "Those who tread the path of virtue should not be disheartened by the thought that virtue is so rare in the world, and that they are in a minority. Their duty is simply to do the right, and leave the rest to God. They should never think of the result of their action; for the only reward of a thing well done is to have done it."

We have advantage also. It is not that only parents and teachers at school teach. Highly important, borrowing a famous idea of Hegel, the thesis of this civilization is producing its anti-thesis, telling on the life of the people. Man's own condition, his bitter experience, is a great teacher, creating a new awareness. It may act slowly but it acts. When, for instance, Stalin was consolidating his tyranny and basking in the glory of power, he was also helping weakening its hold on the heart of the people. Thus, people who groan under the heels of a tyrant, comes to realize the value of freedom. The discovery of nuclear weapons and the consequent horrors create a new awareness of the value of non-violence. So also the people may come to learn that acquisitiveness or an urge to dominate can make one rich and powerful but does not give peace and joy, rather destroy them. In varying degrees, the need to tame the demoniac in man will be felt. The saints and thinkers warn against this demoniac. They articulate what is inarticulate in the rest.

The unhappy results of man's shortsightedness are being felt more and more as the civilization shows its cruel teeth more and more. Never before have so many seminars, conferences, discussions etc. been held on the problems and maladies that this civilization is creating. Very many of them are being organized in the West by thinkers and activists who know the affairs of this Western civilization intimately along with a sound perception of the world as a whole. Although independent of Gandhi, their thoughts and reactions are so strikingly similar on major aspects to that of Gandhi. Thus, Gandhi's basic thoughts have a universality and they do not appeal only to a handful of romantic idealists. Today, far-sighted thinkers in the West also feel that material affluence generate greed and selfishness and erode spiritual values; profligate life-styles should be curbed; that poverty should be eliminated throughout the world; and the society must be explicit about the importance of values and ethics. These are the thoughts for man's healthy body and healthy mind and will surface more and more with the passage of time. Those who envision a better society cherishing these thoughts are not swimming against currents. '*Satyameva Jayate*'—truth shall prevail.

REFERENCES

1. Alexander King & Bertrand Schneider, 'The First Global Revolution' (A Report by the Council of the Club of Rome), Orient Longman Ltd. (1993).
2. *The Statesman*, Calcutta, 31.5.92.
3. Arnold Toynbee, *Faith of a Historian*, Bharatiya Vidya Bhavan, Bombay.
4. Eric Fromm, *The Sane Society*, Routledge & Kegan Paul, London.
5. E.F. Schumacher, *Small is Beautiful*, (Indian Reprint by Radha Krishna, New Delhi).
6. Edward Carpenter, *Civilization, Its Cause and Cure.*
7. Bertrand Russell, *New Hopes for a Changing World*, George Allen & Unwin Ltd., London.
8. Elizabeth Wright, "Capitalising on Communism", *The Statesman*, Calcutta, 3.4.94.
9. V.M. Tarkunde, "Morality in Modern Society", *The Radical Humanist*, New Delhi, (February, 1994).
10. James P. Warburg, *The West in Crisis*, Doubleday & Co., Inc.
11. *A Revolutionary's Quest* (Selected Writings of Jayaprakash Narayan), Ed. Bimal Prasad; Oxford University Press.
12. Quoted in Shriman Narayan, *Mahatma Gandhi* (Somaiya Publications Ltd., Bombay).
13. George Sarton, *The Association of Ancient and Medieval Science during the Renaissance (1450-1600)*, University of Pennsylvania Press.
14. Stanislaw H. Wellisz, "Modernization of Technology", in Ed. Myron Weiner, *Modernization: The Dynamics of Growth.*
15. Bertrand Russell, *Authority and the Individual*, George Allen & Unwin Ltd., London.
16. Pitirim A. Sorokin, "The Factor of Creativity in Human History", in Ed. T.K.N. Unnithan & others, *Towards a Sociology of Culture in India* (Essays in Honour of Prof. D.P. Mukherji) Prentice-Hall of India (Private) Ltd., New Delhi.
17. Rammanohar Lohia, *Marx, Gandhi and Sociolism*, (Rammanohar Lohia Samata Vidyalaya Nyasa, Hyderabad, India).
18. Bertrand Russell, *Mysticism and Logic*, (Penguin Books).
19. Ishwarbhai Patel, "Value Education Through Life Situations", in T.K.N. Unnithan, Ed., *Human Values through Education*, Gujarat Vidyapith, Ahmedabad.

INDEX